Great Inn

GETAWAYS FROM
CLEVELAND

Great Inn

GETAWAYS FROM
CLEVELAND

Doris Larson

GRAY & COMPANY, PUBLISHERS
Cleveland

This book is dedicated to my mother, Mary Weiland Teagle.

Gray & Company, Publishers
1588 E. 40th Street
Cleveland, Ohio 44103
216-431-2665
www.grayco.com

This guide was prepared on the basis of the author's best knowledge at the time of publication. However, because of constantly changing conditions beyond the author's control, the author disclaims any responsibility for the accuracy and completeness of the information in this guide. Users of this guide are cautioned not to place undue reliance upon the validity of the information contained herein and to use this guide at their own risk.

Maps by Rustbelt Cartography.

Library of Congress Cataloging-in-Publication Data
Larson, Doris.
Great Inn Getaways from Cleveland : 58 charming small inns perfect for a weekend or evening away from home / by Doris Larson.
1. Hotels—Ohio—Cleveland—Guidebooks. 2. Restaurants—Ohio—Cleveland—Guidebooks. I. Title.
TX907.3.032C5865 2004   917.71'306144—DC22

ISBN 1-886228-75-2

Printed in the United States of America
First Printing

Contents

*"All saints can do miracles, but
few of them can keep a hotel"*
— MARK TWAIN

Preface

I traveled 18,073 miles and spent 128 days on the road during the 18 months I researched and wrote *Great Inn Getaways from Cleveland*. I crisscrossed state lines—Ohio, Pennsylvania, New York, Indiana, Michigan, and West Virginia—and hopped over the border to Ontario. I stayed at each inn to be able to give you precise descriptions of the inn, to try out the beds and sample those sometimes decadent breakfasts. During my inn visits, I also checked out the best things to do and places to dine in that particular location.

Some of the joys of my journey were watching the sun set on Lake Erie from Pelee Island and the sunrise from the eastern shore of Kelleys Island. While staying at Niagara-on-the-Lake, Ontario, I watched the golden orb slide into Lake Ontario during dinner and on my return trip I awoke to a brilliant pink dawn over Chautauqua Lake in western New York. Other moments of beauty were caught in the silhouette of a black Amish buggy against a backdrop of snow-covered hills in Holmes County, Ohio, and the gardens of a Pennsylvania inn at their peak on a late July day.

I had a few exciting and frightening moments when I raced a tornadic sky to reach an inn deep in Ohio's Hocking Hills before dark. On another uncertain trip, I struggled to stay ahead of a heavy snowstorm pushing me back home from western Ohio.

Each time I set off to visit a new place, there was the anticipation of what I would find—the inn, the history, the architecture, and the people I would meet. Delightful surprises continually nourished me. I found a trio of young butlers at a chic city boutique in western New York and a warm welcome when I wandered into the midst of a reunion of the class of 1953 at an Amish inn in Indiana. I experienced solemn, awe-inspiring moments as I stepped over a stone threshold worn smooth by over two hundred years of use in a historic country inn in Pennsylvania and stayed in a room where a U.S. president had slept. I met innkeepers who looked like they belonged on Wall Street and innkeepers who came in from picking fresh flowers or herbs from their gardens to welcome me to their home.

Come along with me as an "armchair traveler" as you read about 58 inns and find a favorite accommodation not too far from Cleveland.

How to Use This Book

TYPE OF ACCOMMODATIONS

I considered a wide range of accommodations for this guide. A glance at the table of contents lets you know that you can look forward to a stay in a castle or a cottage, a grand old hotel from an earlier century, a contemporary inn by the lake, a city boutique hotel, a secluded spa inn, a historic village inn, or a bed and breakfast in the country.

I first looked for full-service inns of 20 to 150 rooms with a restaurant on site. If inns of this size were not available, I included larger bed and breakfast inns (B&Bs) which serve breakfast but not lunch or dinner.

I'm often asked how I select the inns for my books. I am always looking, even if the purpose of my trip is business or family-related and not part of my planned tour of accommodations. My family is used to the idea that when I spot a possible property, I say, "Let's pull over and have a look at this one." If it looks promising, I'll come back to stay overnight. As a member of the Midwest Travel Writers Association, I am in touch with other travel writers and value their recommendations. Travel reviews and travel literature are my favorite kind of reading—books, magazines, newspapers, brochures, web sites. Personal stays are critical to my reviews and I insist on staying at each inn. I look for properties that complement their setting and during a visit I get a feel for the innkeeper's style. I especially like to find menus that reflect the region's cuisine. None of the lodgings listed paid to be included in this book. Use this book as a research tool to find an accommodation that suits your style and pocketbook.

I've noted the inns and B&Bs in this book that are members of the Select Registry Distinguished Inns of North America (www.Select Registry.com, 800-544-5244) and those that are listed as members of the National Trust Historic Hotels of America (www.historichotels.org 202-588-6295).

TRENDS

A definite trend are the boutique inns, those chic smaller city inns that provide a getaway that's hip and appeals to both the corporate and leisure traveler. Fans of the boutique group of hostelries love the beds dressed with high-count linens, minimalist decor, and attention to detail and service. I found that Jacuzzi tubs and garden tubs are being given some competition by multi-head jetted showers. Purists looking forward to a stay in a traditional bed-and-breakfast in a quiet setting can continue to find their favorite kind of getaway. I discovered landmark hotels and inns that showcase the dedication of preservationists who turn shuttered-up buildings into sparkling gems. Inn-goers seeking a retreat from their workaday world find refuge in spa inns. Some of the most recently built inns feature atriums that fill their lobbies and common rooms with light. A final trend was the number of kid-friendly accommodations available today. At the full-service inns, I appreciated finding healthy lighter fare options and menus to tempt the younger set.

LOCATION

Two- or three-day getaways are gaining in popularity. You can find an inn within an hour's drive of Cleveland or look forward to a longer trip for a weekend stay. Many inns are located in Ohio while others will take you to Indiana, Michigan, Pennsylvania, New York, and that favored destination for Clevelanders: Niagara-on-the-Lake, Ontario. Are you looking for an inn with a spa, a city hotel, or a country location to just kick back for a few days? The inns are grouped into chapters to help you decide the kind of accommodation that fits your interest and time schedule—stays in Amish Country, City Inns, College Towns, Family Inns, Grand Old Hotels, Historic Inns, Lake Erie Stays, Spa Inns, and Castles and Villages.

THE IDEA INDEX

In addition to standard name and geographical indexes, I've included an idea index at the back of the book to help you find the inn that suits your leisure-time pursuits. Check this index, which lists the kind of experience you'll find at a specific destination. Maybe it's golf, antiquing, theater, hiking, museums, shopping, or historic sites that piques your interest.

DETAILS, DETAILS, DETAILS—THE GRAY BOX

I've gathered all the information you'll need to know—rates and payment, types of meals served, and special considerations such as if the inn is wheelchair accessible and if pets are allowed. You'll find this information in the gray boxes at the beginning of each inn's description.

The rates for the inns are listed in ranges to give you a general idea of what you can expect to pay for an overnight accommodation.

WHAT TO EXPECT

Many inns and hotels offer special packages. Check to see if there is a themed weekend or a special rate that appeals to you. Senior travelers find the shoulder seasons less crowded and a good buy for an inn stay.

Ask the innkeeper for suggestions for dining or exploring the area. I often find a basket with sample menus and brochures for golf, shopping, and museums in the reception area or the parlor.

Although there is a chapter devoted to family stays, look over the idea index for accommodations in other chapters that also welcome children.

If historic sites are on your agenda, check the hours and admission fees, as both can change. While pet-friendly inns are becoming more common, check on restrictions before booking your stay. Many of the inns listed have wheelchair-accessible rooms, which you'll find noted in the gray box of information in each review.

Great Inn

GETAWAYS FROM CLEVELAND

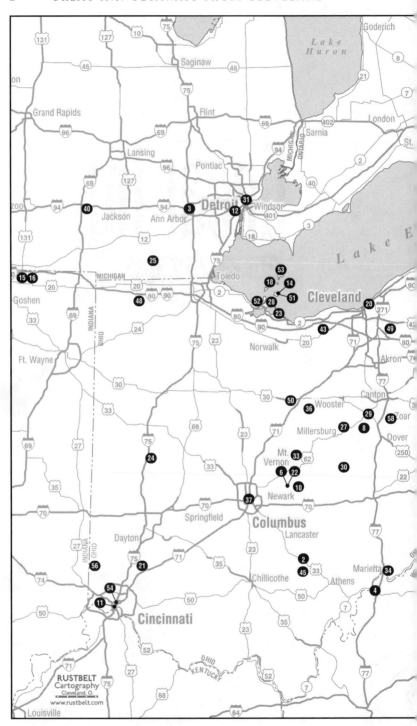

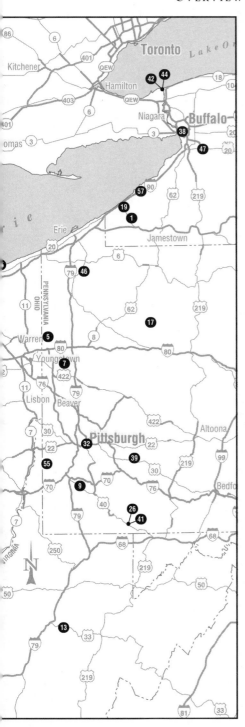

GRAND OLD HOTELS AND INNS

My search for the grand old hotels in this chapter was a nostalgic one taking me back to the days of summer resort and luxury city hotels from the 19th and early 20th centuries. These aging beauties survived hard times and economic ills and continue to welcome guests in the 21st century.

Trademarks of the American Victorian Summer Hotel style—spacious verandas lined with rocking chairs and wicker-filled parlors—are found in the Athenaeum Hotel on the shores of Chautauqua Lake and the Hotel Lakeside on Lake Erie. Two grand hotels—the Cincinnatian Hotel and the Historic Blennerhassett Hotel—remain as landmark urban properties. The Riverside Inn, an early health spa, attracted folks to the healing waters of Cambridge Springs, Pennsylvania. The Lafayette Hotel's riverboat-era decor reflects its location on the Ohio River. The newest accommodation in this chapter, the Summit Inn in Farmington, Pennsylvania, started drawing guests looking for a summer getaway in the mountains in 1907.

Each of the inns listed offers a myriad of things to do. Stay at the Athenaeum, located on the grounds of the Chautauqua Institution, and on summer evenings sample the cultural riches of theater, opera, ballet, and symphony concerts. Lakeside, known as the "Chautauqua on Lake Erie," was patterned after the Chautauqua Institution and offers classes and lectures. Make the Hotel Lakeside your base and walk to concerts by the resident symphony orchestra or enjoy the many recreational activities. The Cincinnatian, located in the heart of downtown, allows easy access to Cincinnati's shopping and museums. When you stay at the Historic Blennerhassett Hotel, you can walk to theaters or tour Parkersburg's historic Julia-Ann Square. It's a short drive from the Blennerhassett to the Fenton Art Glass Factory. Travel to Niagara-on-the-Lake, Ontario, and make the charming Oban Inn your base for the Shaw theater productions. Book a stay at the grand riverboat-era hotel, the Lafayette in Marietta, and have a front row seat for the Ohio Stern-wheeler Festival in September or the jazz and blues festivals in March. Using the Historic Summit Inn in southwestern Pennsylvania as a base, explore nearby historic sites from the French and Indian War or get in some whitewater rafting on the Youghioleny River.

Look forward to fine dining at the full-service inns included in this round-up of classic American inns and hotels. I found fare reflective of each accommodation's region in some of my stays and an ever evolving menu at others. You'll find crisp white-linen-tablecloth dining and award-winning wine cellars as well as casual meals.

6

Hotel Lakeside

*Lakeside . . . The Chautauqua
on Lake Erie*

Summer visitors have been
finding their way to the
Hotel Lakeside, a grand old
hotel situated on the Marblehead
Peninsula, since 1875. Built to accommodate those who came to
the early Methodist camp meetings at Lakeside, the hotel offers a
wraparound screened porch with
a spectacular view of Lake Erie.
The porch, lined with rocking
chairs and baskets of ferns, is the
perfect place to read on a sultry
summer afternoon or to linger in
the evening to watch the sunset on
the lake.

Filled with antiques and groupings of white wicker, the hotel's
lobby introduces the authentic
lodging experience that awaits.
Victorian gems like a walnut hall
tree, a Victrola, marble-top tables,
and a parlor organ are some of the
items given by the Friends of the
Hotel Lakeside. Lace curtains at
the windows, hanging flower bas-

Lakeside, OH
236 Walnut Dr.
866-952-5374 ext. 230
419-798-4461
www.lakesideohio.com

RATES & RESERVATIONS:
Hours: 24 hours/day
Season: Memorial Day–Labor Day
Rates: $90–$125
Reservations recommended
Check, Visa, MC, Disc accepted

ACCOMMODATIONS: 130 rooms,
127 with bath

AMENITIES: Cable TV, phone in
room, air cond.

MEALS: Breakfast, dinner

OTHER:
Not fully wheelchair accessible
Parking: Lot and on-street

kets, and carpet in a fruit motif with a burgundy and green background
continue the Victorian ambience. I learned as I was registering that the
marble counter and the office desk are original to the hotel.

Guest rooms with a lake view are the first to be taken, so reservations are a good idea. A spacious corner room on the third floor
looks out to Lake Erie. Furnished with two walnut double beds and
matching chest, the room is papered in an exotic bird pattern with a
floral background and a border of anaglypta lincrusta. The Friends of

the Hotel Lakeside also provided an eye-catching item in this room: a glass-fronted curio cabinet housing a collection of decorative elephants. Another oft-requested room features a burl walnut bedroom set with a beautifully detailed headboard, two marble-top chests, and a pier mirror. Recently renovated rooms boast Laura Ashley wallpaper, pristine white woodwork, and private baths. Ceiling fans and high windows with original wood shutters at the top and sheers at the bottom are staples throughout the guest rooms. It may confuse first-time guests to be given a key for a room on the third floor numbered in the 600s. The clerk explained that the other Lakeside Association hotel, the Fountain Inn, uses the 100 to 300 numbering system; thus the historic accommodation gets the 300 to 600 numbers.

A continental breakfast is available Monday through Saturday in the lobby for hotel guests. If your visit includes a Sunday, don't miss the brunch served in the historic Marine Dining Room. You're treated to yet another view of Lake Erie, perhaps seated on a cane-bottom chair at one of the long tables for eight that have been part of the hotel furnishings since it opened in 1875. Dinner buffets are available on Friday and Saturday evenings.

THINGS TO DO:

Lakeside, established in 1873 by the Lakeside Company and Methodist Church Camp leaders, continues in the Chautauquan tradition of providing lectures, concerts, religious programs, classes, and a variety of recreational activities. Today it's known as the Chautauqua on Lake Erie, and you realize upon entering the grounds that it's a multigenera-

tional place. Young families with strollers are joined by walkers and jog-gers traversing the historic pathways past Lakeside's cottages. A parade of cyclists of all ages bring their own bikes or rent them from Sypherd Cycles on the grounds. On an exploratory walk, I came upon tennis courts, playgrounds, and a miniature golf course set under sheltering trees by the lake. Shuffleboard courts are a popular venue in this retreat community, which is home to the Ohio Shuffleboard Hall of Fame and host of the National Shuffleboard Tournament. There's swimming by the dock, where the younger set find their own pool. The pavilion, with open porches on either side of the tower, offers another spot to relax in Adirondack chairs.

In the heart of Lakeside, Green Gables, a charming Gothic dwell-ing, is home to the Lakeside Women's Club. Weekly programs, book reviews, children's story hour, and bridge are a few of the activities of-fered.

In this village of Victorian cottages it's no surprise to find a long-time favorite dining spot, the Abigail Tea Room, made up of two cot-tages. You can dine on the screened porch sheltered by wild grapevines or in one of the dining rooms with geranium wallpaper, wood floors, and paprika red tables. Photos of luminaries who have taken a meal at the Abigail include Glenn Miller, Bill Monroe, and the Kingston Trio. The meals are home-cooked, the prices reasonable, and the wait staff made up of college girls, which seems to be a tradition at Lakeside. Menus change daily, with entrees like ham loaf, Lake Erie perch, and Swiss steak appearing on weeknights, while the Sunday menu brings in folks from outside the gate as well as Lakesiders for leg of lamb and

fried chicken. Hostess Elva Thomas comes in early to bake the pies and will know your name after you stop for a few meals. All the fruit pies are popular, but rhubarb may top the list, as it was sold out by the time we ordered our evening meal.

Stop at the Heritage Hall Museum for a look at Lakeside's history. The Lakeside Heritage Society offers walking tours of the town's central area during the summer season. Every summer resort seems to be known for a special food item, and at Lakeside it's freshly baked donuts, which folks line up for early in the morning at the Patio Restaurant. In the evening, they stop for ice cream cones after a film or concert. Shopping runs the gamut from balloons at the Silly Goose to Joseph Wise Fine Clocks with a master clockmaker on staff. Women love to stop at Miss Mercedes, a small space crammed with colorful garments. The kids have a favorite store—Marilyn's, where they find their favorite candy and are trusted to make their own change.

DIRECTIONS: I-80/90 to SR 2 West; right on SR 269; right on SR 163 for 3 miles; left on North Shore Blvd. to entrance for Lakeside.

NEARBY ATTRACTIONS: Cedar Point, Put-In-Bay, Kelleys Island, Marblehead Lighthouse

The Lafayette

A grand riverboat-era hotel

Marietta, OH
101 Front St.
800-331-9336
740-373-5522
www.lafayettehotel.com

When you stay at the Lafayette Hotel, you may be lulled to sleep by barge horns from the Ohio River and the next morning watch a sternwheeler like the *Delta Queen* come into port. A historic riverboat-era hotel in a unique triangular design, the Lafayette stands at the corner of Front and Greene Streets in Marietta. A plaque near the hotel marks the spot where the Marquis de Lafayette landed in 1825. A member of the Historic Hotels of America, the Lafayette is an official stop for the Delta Queen Steamboat Company's grand ladies—*American Queen*, *Delta Queen*, and *Mississippi Queen*.

Reminders of the Lafayette's location on the Ohio River are found in the hotel lobby. An 11-foot pilot wheel from the steamboat *J. D. Ayres* is suspended from the ceiling, and you'll find benchmarks indicating the flood levels of the Ohio and Muskingum Rivers in 1936 and 1937 beside the lobby elevator. Original riverboat paintings and model replicas of paddleboats are decorative accents in the Riverview Lounge, where you can catch views of the Ohio. Settle at the Amish-made hardwood bar or snag a table for a drink, snacks, or casual dining.

RATES & RESERVATIONS:
Hours: 24 hours/day
Season: Year round
Rates: $65–$175
Specials: Senior, AAA, frequent-stay special
Minimum stay required most weekends
Reservations recommended
Check, Visa, MC, Disc, Amex accepted

ACCOMMODATIONS: 77 rooms w/bath

AMENITIES: Cable TV, phone in room, Internet, air cond., Jacuzzis

MEALS: Breakfast, lunch, dinner, brunch, snacks; Beer, wine, liquor served

OTHER:
Parking: Lot

The 19th-century riverboat decor extends to the 77 guest rooms, parlor rooms, and suites, including four Jacuzzi rooms and two VIP suites. Hand-carved mahogany furnishings, Evans & Brown-designed RJF wallpapers, Fenton glass lamps, and a rich color palette of golds and greens with touches of deep red reflect the era. Some rooms have views of the Ohio and Muskingum Rivers, while three rooms access balconies facing the Ohio. One VIP suite comprises a living room with wet bar that can be used for meetings, a bathroom with Jacuzzi, and access to an additional king room. I found pencil drawings of area landmarks by local artists in the hallways and lobby. The Lafayette offers Captain's Club and Esprit de Corps frequent-stay executive programs. Children under 18 can stay free in their parents' room.

An outstanding collection of long rifles displayed in the Gun Room Restaurant includes one made by J. J. Henry & Sons that accompanied the Benedict Arnold expedition to Quebec in 1775. Check out a brief history of this handcrafted collection posted outside the restaurant. There's a New Orleans flair to the dining room, with another nod to the riverboat era in the colorful paddle-wheel design carpeting.

Traditional American cuisine is featured on the Gun Room menu along with daily specials. Dinner selections include starters of oysters Bienville or Savannah crabcake, followed by entree choices of chicken Wellington, Provimi veal liver, seafood supreme, or any of the house specials of certified Angus beef like the filet au poivre or Willie Carpet-bagger, a tenderloin of beef stuffed with crabmeat dressing served over a peppercorn and burgundy wine sauce. Specialties of the pastry chef are flourless chocolate torte and crème brûlée. Ice cream is made in

house. Weekend guests enjoy a grand breakfast buffet on Sundays.

Accommodation packages provide an incentive to come to the Lafayette for a themed weekend. Book early for these weekends, which often sell out. Marietta's Blues, Jazz & Folk Music Society stages a yearly competition, with the winners featured in the River City Blues Festival at the Lafayette in March. A jazz concert—The Red, White & Blues—happens in July. The Lafayette is the place to stay if you come down for one of Marietta's annual heritage events like the Ohio River Sternwheel Festival the weekend after Labor Day. Hard-fought sternwheel races are part of the celebration, and there's a big party on the Ohio Levee with food vendors, the sounds of a calliope filling the air, free live entertainment on a barge stage, and a fireworks show. It's a particularly beautiful sight at night when all the sternwheelers and pleasure craft are outlined in lights. A classic and antique car show is the culminating festival activity on Sunday. In December, the Lafayette is the venue for a popular community event, the annual gingerbread-house display.

THINGS TO DO:

The first settlement in the Northwest Territory, Marietta is steeped in history and makes an ideal getaway for history buffs. Members of the Ohio Company, under the leadership of Rufus Putnam, arrived in 1788. This river city has five museums, including the Campus Martius Museum, site of a walled fortification that encloses the original Putnam home and houses unique artifacts relating to the founding of Marietta. For an overview of the steamboat era and to learn about life on the river, allow time to stop at the Ohio River Museum at Washington and Front Streets. The *W. O. Snyder*, America's only surviving steam-powered sternwheeler towboat, is moored alongside the museum. The *Valley Gem* sternwheeler offers hourly sightseeing cruises, dinner cruises on Saturday evenings from mid-June to October, and fall foliage tours. You're invited to sing along, sob, and cheer at the melodramatic performances on the Showboat Becky Thatcher.

The Ohio Company's planning of Marietta was foresighted, resulting in today's wide boulevards, beautiful old trees, and public green spaces. Walk to see the 19th-century homes or leave the driving to Trolley Tours of Marietta, which offer a narrated tour of the city. Shop in the restored Riverfront District, filled with boutique shops. A great stop for lunch is the Levee House Cafe with yet another view of the Ohio River. Take home some pasta and sauces from Rossi Pasta's factory outlet store.

Doll aficionados delight in finding the Children's Toy and Doll Museum, featuring dolls and dollhouses from the late 19th and early 20th centuries. On Marietta's Front Street, a retail shop called the Doll Showcase is filled with a large selection of collectible dolls, bears, and doll accessories. Take a short drive to nearby Belpre, Ohio, to Lee Middleton Original Dolls, the nation's largest doll factory. You can adopt a doll baby from the "Newborn Nursery," where you find newborn dolls propped up in little Isolettes just as you would find in a hospital nursery.

DIRECTIONS: I-77 South to Exit 1 for Marietta; one mile to downtown Marietta on SR 7 (Pike St.)

NEARBY ATTRACTIONS: Fenton Art Glass, Middletown Dolls, Rossi Pasta, Ohio River Museum

The Cincinnatian Hotel

Cincinnati's luxury small hotel

Hitching posts lined the front of the Palace Hotel when it opened in 1882 in Cincinnati. Defined by its French Second Empire style, this grand hotel offered innovations like elevators and incandescent lighting. Guests found 300 rooms with a shared bathroom at either end of the corridor. Renamed the Cincinnatian in the early 1950s, the property deteriorated over the next 30 years and was set for the wrecking ball to make way for a parking garage. A four-year, $25 million renovation resulted in the reopening of the Cincinnatian in 1987. Three hundred rooms became 146 guestrooms, including seven suites. To appreciate some of the renovations, stand at the base of the marble and walnut grand staircase and look up eight floors to the skylight-topped atrium.

The traditional feel of the hotel was maintained in the renovation, and contemporary influences added in room decor give a fresh look to the classic interior. Color flow is a consistent use of soothing shades of blue, green, and beige with contrasts of brass, stainless, and chrome. The inn hallways house an extensive art collection that invites browsing as you walk from the elevator to your room. Suites have separate par-

Cincinnati, OH
601 Vine St.
800-942-9000
513-381-3000
www.cincinnatianhotel.com

RATES & RESERVATIONS:
Hours: 24 hours/day
Season: Year round
Rates: $125 +
Specials: Children, seniors, singles, AAA
Reservations recommended
Check, Visa, MC, Disc, Amex accepted

ACCOMMODATIONS: 146 rooms w/bath; 7 suites w/bath

AMENITIES: Sauna, cable TV, phone in room, air cond., Internet

MEALS: Breakfast, lunch, dinner, brunch, snacks; Beer, wine, liquor served

OTHER:
Parking: Valet ($25/night)

lors, sleeping rooms, baths, and generous entryways. Guest rooms have elegant Italian granite baths with oversized Roman bathtubs or dual-head marble showers. Some rooms have atrium balconies, whirlpool tubs, or electric fireplaces. You'll find luxurious extras like silk hangers and velour bathrobes in the closet.

Amenities for business travelers include multi-line phones, spacious desks, data ports, voice mail in four languages, high-speed Internet access, newspapers, a fitness center, and European mini-bars. The Cincinnatian offers six meeting rooms and state-of-the-art audiovisual equipment for corporate and social gatherings.

The Cincinnatian is known for its warm hospitality, which is evident from the first contact at registration. I returned to my room in the evening to find that the turndown service included the next day's weather forecast and two chocolate chip cookies on the bedside table. A full-time concierge stands ready to help with any questions or plans for a stay in Cincinnati.

For fine dining at the Cincinnatian, plan to have a leisurely meal in the Palace, the restaurant that carries the hotel's original name. It's an intimate dining experience with the room seating just 80. Paintings by Frederic Bonin Pissarro, great-grandson of Impressionist master Camille Pissarro, line the mahogany paneled walls. Fresh flowers, silver, and carefully paced service help make dining at the Palace an extraordinary experience.

The chef shifts the menus, featuring American cuisine with a French twist, to the seasons. Each course is so beautifully presented you want to take a lingering approach and feast first with your eyes. A sorbet refresher comes to the table in a frosted crystal lily that at first

glance appears to be a small ice sculpture. Entree selections include pan-seared Atlantic salmon on walnut thyme crust with chestnut puree and juniper berry infusion, and braised beef shortribs and crusted beef tenderloin with horseradish whipped potatoes and Cabernet reduction. You can't go wrong with the suggested wine pairings on the menu. A tempting tray of petits fours accompanied our after-dinner coffee. We soon learned that this plate of sweets was the precursor to the Palace dessert menu with choices like warm milk chocolate claufouti and apple tarte tatin cheesecake served with green apple sorbet and warm apple butter.

Tall ferns, a multicolored neon sculpture, and colors from the Art Deco era set the tone for the Cricket Lounge, where the hotel's original safe has a place of honor in a corner. The Cricket was the premier restaurant when the hotel opened in 1882. In later years, when the offices of the *Cincinnati Enquirer* were located next to the hotel, the Cricket became known as the local hangout for journalists from the newspaper. Stop in for light fare for lunch. In the evening you can expect live entertainment. While a guest at the hotel, Billy Joel took a turn at the piano in the Cricket Lounge.

It's a different atmosphere and crowd in the afternoon when a traditional English tea is served seasonally in the Cricket Lounge. Named by *USA Today* as one of the "Ten Great Places to Have Tea with Your Mum," afternoon tea at the Cincinnatian includes specialty teas, housemade tea breads, fresh baked scones, miniature tarts, and pastries elegantly served to the accompaniment of harp music. Reservations are advised.

Weekend packages are available for Friday, Saturday, and Sunday nights with extras like vouchers towards breakfast or dinner in the Palace Restaurant and valet parking. If you're spending the day touring the area or heading home, call ahead and order the Cincinnatian box lunch.

Along with a Four Star Rating from Mobil Travel Guide, and a Four Diamond Rating from AAA, accolades for the Cincinnatian include listing as one of *Travel & Leisure*'s top 500 Hotels of the World in 2003. In 2002, the hotel was included on *Travel & Leisure*'s list of the "World's Best Business Hotels." The Cincinnatian is a member of Historic Hotels of America and Preferred Hotels and Resorts Worldwide.

THINGS TO DO:

Located at Sixth and Vine, the Cincinnatian is in the heart of downtown, with boutiques, restaurants, and several large anchor retailers like Saks Fifth Avenue, Tiffany & Co., and Brooks Brothers within easy walking distance. Tower Place at the Carew Tower, a three-level shopping mall, offers over 75 shops and restaurants. Find a bench at Fountain Square, the center of downtown Cincinnati, and you have a prime people-watching spot. You'll find the new Lois & Richard Rosenthal Center for Contemporary Art a block from the hotel. The Convention Center and the Aronoff Center for the Arts are also nearby. Take time to visit the Taft Museum of Art, the former home of Charles and Ann Taft, filled with a collection of European and Asian fine and decorative art.

DIRECTIONS: I-71 South to Exit 2 for Reading Rd.; left on Sycamore St.; right on Sixth St.; on corner of Sixth and Vine St.

NEARBY ATTRACTIONS: Downtown Cincinnati, Kings Island

Riverside Inn

A gem from the
Mineral Waters era

The birds were singing when I arrived at the Riverside Inn, and their song continued throughout my mid-July visit. The inn's location on the banks of historic French Creek, with expanses of manicured lawns and luxuriant flower beds, is perhaps the attraction for these songsters.

This historic inn also brings folks of all ages to Cambridge Springs. During my stay, I talked to a group of five couples who travel together to country inns, golfers who arrived on Sunday evening to be ready for an early Monday-morning tee time, and several young families. As twilight fell, we lingered on the long porch that extends in two directions from the wide front doors. It's the kind of porch you expect to find at a summer resort hotel, with conversational groupings of wicker furniture and hanging baskets of flowers and ferns.

The Riverside Inn is on the National Register of Historic Places. It is thought to have been the first

Cambridge Springs, PA
One Fountain Ave.
800-964-5173
814-398-4645
www.theriversideinn.com

RATES & RESERVATIONS:
Hours: 7 a.m.–11 p.m.
Season: Mid-Apr–Christmas
Rates: $65–$125
Specials: Children, seniors, singles, AAA
Reservations recommended
Check, Visa, MC, Disc, Amex accepted

ACCOMMODATIONS: 74 rooms w/bath; 4 suites w/bath

AMENITIES: Pool, air cond.

MEALS: Lunch, dinner, brunch (Sunday); Beer, wine, liquor served

OTHER:
Guest pets allowed
Parking: Lot

health spa in the French Creek Valley. The discovery of the healing powers of springwater on the property by Dr. John H. Gray in the 1860s resulted in the building in 1884 of the Riverside Hotel, as it was known at the time. Guests came to Cambridge Springs for therapeutic treatments, including baths of all varieties—Russian, Turkish, cabinet, electric, sea salt, mineral, and needle baths. Supervised by licensed physicians, a Vibratory for electrical treatments and x-ray machines were added to the treatment regimen. The Mineral Waters era peaked by the early 1900s, and by 1905 the Riverside Inn was the only one of some 40 hotels and rooming houses remaining in business.

The inn was purchased by the William Baird family the year after it was built and remained in the Baird family for 50 years. After the inn stood empty for some time in the 1960s, a group of entrepreneurs took it over and began the long restoration process. Current owners Michael and Marie Halliday purchased the inn in 1985. One of their first challenges was to heat the place by installing 13 furnaces. History buffs and antique collectors, the Hallidays next took on the task of furnishing the inn's guest and public rooms.

In the lobby, a caged cashier's window of frosted glass, the original marble counter, and the bellman's bench remain from the hotel's early days. A long hallway serves as a gallery for photographs and documents that help tell the story of the inn. Glass cases line one wall, filled with china and silver from the first dining room and the Hotel Riverside trademark jugs used for the inn's special springwater.

My room reminded me of childhood visits to my grandmother's house. Everything was neat as a pin, with a stack of white towels at the end of the antique bedstead, an oak chest protected by a glass top, and white sheers at the window. A peek into other rooms down the hall revealed an overall decorating pattern using wallpaper designs ranging from crewel to frothy light flowered and striped papers.

Pets and children are welcome at the Riverside Inn. Note that while the inn does not have an elevator, six guest rooms are available on the main floor. One is wheelchair accessible.

A bay window with 11 panes topped by leaded glass centers the Concord Dining Room. A sign outside the dining room suggests proper dress for dinner and Sunday brunch. And it's a white-linen kind of place, with dark flowered wallpaper offset by white wainscoting. Burgundy table toppers are set with china in the American Rose pattern, a replica of the original china used at the inn. Some of the Hallidays' collectibles on display in the dining room include oil paintings, paintings on glass, and a collection of Anderson bird prints.

Lunch offerings include salads, pastas, and a wide selection of sandwiches. Beef holds a prominent place on the dinner menu, which lists prime rib, filet mignon, and strip steaks. Chicken, seafood, veal, and hearty healthy options round out the menu. All breads and desserts are prepared from scratch on site. Dinner buffets are featured on Friday and Saturday evenings. Brunches are popular, as are special holiday dinners, with more than 1,000 guests served at a recent Mother's Day dinner. Overnight guests come down to a full hot breakfast buffet of pancakes, sausage, bacon, an egg casserole, fresh fruit, and homemade biscuits and gravy.

Inn golf packages use several nearby courses, including Riverside Golf Course. One group of golfers has been coming back to the inn for 40 years. On-site watercolor workshops are offered throughout the year. Fans of Nelson Eddy and Jeanette MacDonald come yearly for a week filled with discussions and films.

THINGS TO DO:

Many come to the Riverside Inn for the dinner theater connected to the inn. Productions include mysteries, musicals, and comedies, along with the Medieval Feast at Riverside, which runs from mid-August through mid-November. Guests get into the spirit of medieval times with a feast served without utensils. Next on the yearly calendar is a Riverside Christmas. The holidays are an especially lovely time to stay, when you'll find seven themed Christmas trees throughout the inn.

Take time to stop at the Campbell Pottery Store and Gallery, showcasing Bill Campbell's pottery along with works by other artisans in a century-old dairy barn just outside Cambridge Springs.

In keeping with the history of the place, gentler pastimes—shuffleboard, croquet, badminton—can be found on the inn grounds. There's also an outdoor swimming pool, tennis, a putting green, and canoeing on French Creek.

DIRECTIONS: I-90 East to exit for Meadville (SR 19); south on SR 19; on left

NEARBY ATTRACTIONS: Dinner Theater at the Riverside Inn, Presque Isle

The Historic Summit Inn

*A grand porch hotel
on top of the world*

Farmington, PA
101 Skyline Dr.
800-433-8594
724-438-8594
www.summitinnresort.com

W
hen the Historic Sum-
mit Inn opened in
1907 along the old Na-
tional Pike (now U.S. Route 40), it
was called "a grand porch hotel on
top of the world." The description
holds true today when you make
the gradual climb up the mountain and find the inn, a red-roofed
structure with twin square towers,
perched on the crest of Chestnut
Ridge.

Wooden deck chairs and
wicker pieces line the porch, with a
view of the valley 2,300 feet below.
They say that on a clear day you
can see five counties. In the late afternoon of my August visit, a large
punch bowl of lemonade was set
out for those of us lounging or
reading. Other guests enjoyed the
sunporch, a few steps up from the
main veranda, which later became
the setting for cocktail time.

The Summit Inn lobby, filled
with original Stickley-designed
furniture, is a treasure trove for
enthusiasts of the Arts and Crafts

RATES & RESERVATIONS:
Hours: 24 hours/day
Season: Apr–Nov
Rates: $125 +
Specials: Children, seniors, singles,
AAA
Reservations recommended
Visa, MC, Disc, Amex, traveler's
checks accepted

ACCOMMODATIONS: 87 rooms w/
bath; 7 suites w/bath

AMENITIES: Hot tub, cable TV, pool,
phone in room, air cond.

MEALS: Breakfast, lunch, dinner;
Beer, wine, liquor served

OTHER:
Guest pets allowed
Parking: Lot

era. Other furnishings remaining from earlier times include the registration desk, key slots, a Black Forest coat rack, and a Bavarian cuckoo
clock. A grand staircase centers the lobby and branches off to east and
west wings. Note the pair of stained-glass windows as you ascend the

stairs. Take a minute to pause on the landing for a view of the room below. It's a period snapshot of Stickley furnishings set against walls of grained cypresswood stained a forest brown. The room is brightened by Arts and Crafts lighting fixtures and lamps. Guests of the Summit Inn tend to gather in front of the lobby's native stone fireplace where a fire is kept going on chilly spring and fall days. Historic documents and early photographs are nicely displayed in the lobby and a back hallway. The hotel register, with Henry Ford and Thomas Edison's signatures, dates back to 1917, when Ford and Edison brought a group of American "science wizards" to the Summit Inn to race motorcars up and down the mountain. While registering upon arrival, I noticed a weather-beaten sign behind the desk that was in use from 1907–1912: "Ask about our $4.55 daily economy rate."

The Don Shoemaker family purchased the inn in 1963 and continues to make improvements. General manager Karen Harris, Don Shoemaker's daughter, oversees operations. On a tour of the guest rooms, Karen pointed out that while this early 1900s structure does not have an elevator, you can request one of the 17 rooms on the lobby floor. Six are wheelchair accessible. If stairs are not a problem, some of the upper-level rooms—with panoramic views of the valley—make the upward trek worthwhile. A variety of decorating styles have been used in the 94 guest rooms, done in light, pleasing colors and fabrics. I found Queen Anne reproduction furnishings in my first-floor room, a modified sleigh bed in a smaller room, contemporary in another. King, queen, and double-bedded rooms are available. Spacious family-size rooms with sitting areas and adjoining rooms are popular. Redecorating and updating guest rooms is an ongoing process at the Summit.

You'll find traditional menu offerings for lunch and dinner at this full-service inn, with expected listings like chicken potpie for lunch and dinner choices that include prime rib and steaks, chicken Cordon Bleu, seafood dishes, chicken quesadillas, and Thai spring rolls. The kids' breakfast menu reflects area history, with French & Indian toast and Fort Necessity pancakes.

Dine in the Summit Room, centered by another of the inn's massive stone fireplaces, in the spring and fall. In warmer weather move to the windowed Edison Room or dine on the porch. Linger over drinks in the Wunder Bar, with live music on weekend evenings.

Families find plenty to do within the resort. During the high season I noticed a lobby bulletin board with times listed for special activities for children, cartoon showings, and movies. A choice of pools includes an Olympic outdoor pool, one of the first steel pools, dating from 1932, and a heated indoor pool. Take the family on a mile-long wooded nature walk that starts at the back of the inn. The nine-hole Summit Inn Golf Course offers spectacular mountaintop views.

THINGS TO DO:

History buffs find this area of southwestern Pennsylvania rich in the lore of the French and Indian War. A ten-minute drive from the inn takes you to Fort Necessity National Battlefield, site of George Washington's defeat on the great meadow by French and Indian forces on July 3, 1754. Another site related to the battle, Jumonville Glen, is nearby. Take time to tour the Mount Washington Tavern, one of the stagecoach stops on the National Road that is typical of the era's taverns.

Take off for the Youghiogheny Bike/Hike Trail or arrange a guided white-water raft trip on the Youghiogheny River. Sign up for a historic float trip on the Youghiogheny with a guide in 1750s period garb who narrates the river's history. Visit the Christian W. Klay Winery in an 1880s bank barn in nearby Chalk Hill. Spend an evening at the winery's Murder Mystery Dinner Theater with wine tasting and a buffet dinner as part of the package.

Travel 25 minutes from the inn to visit Frank Lloyd Wright's famous Fallingwater house, and then drive seven miles for a tour of Wright's Kentuck Knob.

DIRECTIONS: I-80/90 East to exit for New Stanton; south on SR 119; east on US 40

NEARBY ATTRACTIONS: Laurel Caverns, Ft. Necessity, Kentuck Knob, Fallingwater, Christian Klay Winery, Ohiopyle State Park, white-water rafting

Athenaeum Hotel

A grand old hotel set on the shores of Chautauqua Lake

The Athenaeum Hotel, often referred to as the La Grande Dame of Chautauqua, is set on the shores of Chautauqua Lake. And grand it is, this Second Empire building topped with a broad cupola. Painted in colors close to the hotel's original Victorian hues, the exterior is covered with a pale parchment highlighted by mulberry and mauve scroll-saw trim. Built on the grounds of the world-renowned Chautauqua Institution in 1881, just seven years after its founding as a summer training camp for Protestant Sunday-school teachers, the Athenaeum was recognized as one of the finest resort hotels of the time. With a columned veranda that wraps around the historic hostelry, the Athenaeum is often compared to hotels built in the American-Victorian Summer Hotel style, like those in Saratoga Springs and Mackinac Island. Ladder-back rockers line the veranda, where guests catch the breeze from the lake and from the maple-treed lawn. The Athenaeum is listed on the National Registry of Historic Places and designated a National Historic Landmark.

In the wide entry hallway, flanked by ferns and rocking chairs, original furnishings remain, including long wooden writing desks attached to the wall. Shelves with cubicles used for men's top hats in the hotel's

Chautauqua, NY
South Lake Dr.
800-821-1881
716-357-4444
www.athenaeum-hotel.com

RATES & RESERVATIONS:
Hours: 24 hours/day
Season: Year round
Rates: $175 +
Reservations required
Check, Visa, MC, Amex accepted

ACCOMMODATIONS: 156 rooms w/bath; 7 suites w/bath

AMENITIES: Cable TV, phone in room, air cond.

MEALS: Breakfast, lunch, dinner

OTHER:
Not fully wheelchair accessible
Parking: Lot ($5/day)

early days are utilized by today's guests to store those seat cushions Chautauquans tote to the Amphitheater to soften the wooden pew-like benches. To the side of the hallway, a high-ceilinged parlor furnished with wicker is variously used for late-afternoon recitals or set up for bridge games. It's a link to gentler times when you take the Otis elevator installed in 1924. The doors open, the highly polished grillwork is pulled back, then you step on and announce your floor to the young man at the controls.

Renovation and restoration efforts remain an ongoing project at the Athenaeum. In 1924, a four-story annex was built. The passageway that connects the original hotel to the annex serves as a sun parlor and is comfortably furnished with Arts and Crafts-style oak furniture. During an extensive renovation in 1983, all 160 guest rooms were painted and papered using 80 different wallpaper patterns. A grand double staircase was added on the lake side of the veranda, centered by a Victorian cast-iron three-tiered fountain. The most recent work completed in 2003 updated the dining room, including the addition of air-conditioning.

Plan to dine in the Athenaeum's formal dining room with its polished hardwood floors, flower-sprigged wallpaper, and paddle fans, or move out to the veranda in pleasant weather. Meals are on the American plan at the Athenaeum, with three meals a day included in the room rate. You're asked to dress for dinner, while casual attire is fine for breakfast and lunch. The breakfast menu includes old favorites like creamed dried beef on toast points and corned beef hash along with blueberry pancakes and eggs Benedict. Lunch buffets are bountiful spreads and on Fridays are themed, like the red, white, and blue presen-

tation I found on the Fourth of July or a Western buffet the following week. Think gracious dining for dinner at the Athenaeum, which can be a leisurely four-course affair if you book early enough to get to the evening concert on time. On my August visit, menu choices included appetizers of clams casino, sesame duck tenderloins, or southwestern black bean soup, followed by the Athenaeum mesclun salad and entree choices of baked fillet of sea bass, chicken breast Française with sweet pepper pesto cream, and seared pork tenderloin with apples and plum chutney. And then there's dessert. It's tradition at the Athenaeum to offer guests two desserts. For those visiting Chautauqua on their own, the Athenaeum has set up a table for singles.

Stories and anecdotes from Chautauqua's long history abound. Ask your server about Thomas Alva Edison's table in the dining room. Edison and his wife, Mina, daughter of one of Chautauqua's founders, Lewis Miller, dined at Table Number One next to a tall hinged window. To avoid autograph seekers, Edison could slip out the window onto the hotel veranda. Due to Edison's connection with Chautauqua, the Athenaeum was one of the first buildings anywhere to be lighted by electricity.

THINGS TO DO:

Chautauqua is a timeless, nostalgic place where visitors are asked to drive at no more than 12 miles per hour on the narrow village streets. Most park their cars across from the gated community and walk or bike the institution grounds. And a walk can be an architectural tour of early Chautauqua cottages as you come upon a variety of styles: Victorian,

Greek Revival, Gothic Revival, Italianate, Eastlake, and Stick Style. Front porches are graced with tall vases of gladiolus, one of Chautauqua's endearing traditions. As you stroll the grounds, you'll find classical architecture in buildings like the Hall of Philosophy, styled after the Parthenon. An open-air venue, the Hall of Philosophy is situated in a beautiful natural setting. Bells peal out from the Italianate-design Miller Bell Tower built in 1922, which helps keep busy Chautauquans on schedule for the myriad classes and lectures offered.

The Athenaeum is located steps away from the Amphitheater, site of thrice-weekly evening concerts by the Chautauqua Symphony. The resident ballet company takes the stage four times during the nine-week season, which runs from late June to the end of August. Theater and opera performances round out the cultural offerings. Part of the Chautauqua experience is learning. At 10:45 each morning, a guest speaker takes the podium to address topics relating to politics, international concerns, ethics, economics, or the environment. It was in this open-air forum that Franklin Roosevelt delivered his "I Hate War" speech in 1936. Other famous visitors include George Gershwin, who composed "Concerto in F" while a guest at Chautauqua in 1925. Four years later, Amelia Earhart landed her plane on Chautauqua's golf course.

If you'd like to have a look at the Chautauqua Institution grounds from the lake, book a tour on the *Chautauqua Belle*, an authentic stern-wheel steamboat, which departs from Lakeside Park in Mayville. Golfers enjoy taking on the challenge of the Chautauqua Golf Club's 36-hole championship course.

DIRECTIONS: I-90 East to Exit 60; left on NY-394 (North Portage St.) to Chautauqua

NEARBY ATTRACTIONS: Lily Dale, Panama Rocks, wine trail

The Blennerhassett

A beautifully renovated landmark hotel

A cornerstone of downtown Parkersburg since 1889, the historic Blennerhassett anchors the corner of Fourth and Market Streets. Renovation of most of the red brick hotel—a member of the National Trust Historic Hotels of America and listed on the National Register of Historic Places—was completed in 2003 to the tune of $3 million. I first stayed at the Blennerhassett in September 2000, and upon a return visit in November 2003 found that this landmark property had undergone a grand transformation.

The library, reminiscent of a clubby English gentlemen's lounge, served originally as a bank. One of the turret rooms on the hotel's main floor, the library has game tables for backgammon, chess, and checkers. It's next to the Blennerhassett Coffee Bar (featuring Starbucks coffee), so you can grab a cup 'o joe before settling down in a wing chair by the fireplace to relax or read.

Parkersburg, WV
320 Market St.
800-262-2536
304-422-3131
www.theblennerhassett.com

RATES & RESERVATIONS:
Hours: 24 hours/day
Season: Year round
Rates: $65–$90 Specials: Children, seniors, AAA Reservations required
Check, Visa, MC, Disc, Amex accepted

ACCOMMODATIONS: 91 rooms and suites w/bath

AMENITIES: Cable TV, phone in room, Internet, air cond., turndown service, ice delivery, and other personal services available

MEALS: Lunch, dinner, snacks; Beer, wine, liquor served

OTHER:
Guest pets allowed ($50 fee)
Parking: Lot

During the 2002-03 renovation, the walls on the fourth and fifth floors were gutted down to the studs and floors were stripped to cement surfaces. The existing 104 rooms became 91 rooms and suites. There's an understated elegance to the interior of the new classically designed

European-style rooms. Sherry Mitchell, IIDA, directed the interior renovation using furnishings, wallcoverings, textiles, art, and tapestries inspired by William Morris, the 19th-century English designer. The furniture is English-country style, the art specific to individual rooms, and the carpet custom designed. You'll find granite vanities and Italian tile floors in the bathrooms. High standards for guests' comfort mean triple sheeting and a choice of down or synthetic pillows. Motion sensors control the heating and air-conditioning as well as the lights in the closet, where you find wooden hangers for your suit jacket and lingerie hangers for your knits. In the luxurious bathrooms, rain-barrel showerheads are standard and Gilchrist & Soames toiletries are stored in brushed nickel and glass containers. Wheelchair-accessible rooms can be found on the fourth and fifth floors.

At the Blennerhassett, a range of room sizes appeal to both the business and leisure traveler. On the renovated floors, the Junior Suites offer a king leather sleigh bed, executive desk, sitting area with queen sofa bed, and twin-vanity bath. Superior Rooms welcome with a cozy reading nook and a spacious guest room. Antiques like the 1782 armoire from a French chateau I found in one of the Executive Suites are part of the furnishings mix. Business professionals find the one- and two-story Executive Suites with a food and bar area, desk with leather or suede chairs, and a table that can seat up to 10, ideal for small meetings and dinners. There's a powder room for guests and an adjacent conference center. High-speed wireless Internet is available in the guest rooms as well as in the library, the restaurant, and meeting rooms. Standard rooms and suites on the second and third floors in the original hotel

retain the historic ambience of the Blennerhassett, with high ceilings and Chippendale-inspired furnishings.

Three signature rooms at the Blennerhassett reflect the renovation planner's attention to history, honoring William Morris, William Chancellor, and Marie Antoinette. The Marie Antoinette-inspired accommodation occupies one of the turret rooms and showcases the French Provincial style. A portrait of the French queen hangs in the entry hall, gilt edges the picture frames and tables, and a king brass bed with a crown of luxurious fabric centers the room. In all my inn travels, I have never found a shower like the one in this Signature Room—an oversize marble spa shower with seven showerheads encased in glass inscribed with the Blennerhassett logo, a stylized fleur-de-lis. Amenities include plush robes, a box of Holl's Swiss chocolates, ice delivered to the rooms, and a daily newspaper. Ask about the Romantic Weekend package and the Blennerhassett Theater package offered in conjunction with the Actors Guild of Parkersburg.

There's fine dining in the hotel restaurant, Spats. Stop for a drink in the comfy lounge or plan a leisurely meal in the dining room. The original crown molding was retained and rich walnut wainscoting added by local master craftsman Tim Wiseman. Executive chef Kevin M. Cronin offers innovative menu choices based on TaBella cuisine, featuring dishes of Northern Italy. He brings the freshest seasonal ingredients from local purveyors to the table. Autumn menu samplings on my visit included a starter of butternut squash soup with candied beet and bay leaf, a salad of fresh mozzarella and heirloom tomatoes over baby greens, and a main course of grilled Lake Victorian perch with Israeli couscous; for dessert, a Spanish-style flan, Crema Catalan with Chantilly cream and fresh berries. Pasta choices of pumpkin ravioli and goat-cheese tortellini vie with entrees of grilled veal rib chop and Tuscan stuffed chicken breast on the TaBella menu. Spats offers an extensive wine list.

Fifty decorated Christmas trees are showcased in the front lobby and the promenade of the Blennerhassett for the Festival of Trees, an annual holiday event benefiting Easter Seals.

THINGS TO DO:

Take time during your stay to explore this historic river city. Pick up a brochure for a walking tour of Parkersburg's historic district, Julia-Ann Square. Stop at the Smoot Theatre, a 1926 vaudeville house saved by local preservationists and restored to its earlier grandeur with a hand-cut crystal chandelier and beveled mirrors in the lobby. Today's audiences come for musicals, plays, and children's theater. Trans Allegheny Books, situated in a former Carnegie Library building built in 1905, is worth a visit. Browse the largest stock of used books in West

Virginia, along with new West Virginia titles in the old library that features a wrought iron and brass spiral staircase, vintage wooden cases, and stained-glass windows.

Fenton Art Glass in nearby Williamstown, West Virginia, offers a factory tour that is ranked as one of the top 10 such tours in the United States. Watch skilled glassmakers create beautiful art glass and browse the gift shop to find a piece to take home.

Take a ride on an authentic sternwheeler to Blennerhassett Island, where you can tour the Blennerhassett mansion and learn the story of Harman and Margaret Blennerhassett.

DIRECTIONS: I-77 to Exit 173 for Camden Ave.; west on SR 95 to SR 14 North; left on Market St.; on left.

NEARBY ATTRACTIONS: Smoot Theater, Actors Guild Playhouse, Cultural Arts Center of Parkersburg, Blennerhassett Island, Blennerhassett Museum

Oban Inn

An old English resort hotel in a picture-postcard setting

The Oban Inn's magnificent setting in Niagara-on-the-Lake appeals to first-time guests as well as theater buffs who return to stay each season for the productions staged at the renowned Shaw Festival. Surrounded by English gardens and manicured lawns, the view from the inn takes in the historic Niagara-on-the-Lake Golf Course across the way and Lake Ontario beyond.

The history of the Oban Inn is a rather remarkable one. Built at 160 Front Street in 1824 as a home for sea captain Duncan Milloy from Oban, Scotland, the property became a hotel in the late 1800s. Destroyed by a fire on Christmas night in 1992, the inn was rebuilt to original specifications. A touching story related to the tragedy tells that guests routed from dinner on that frigid Christmas evening were invited back to finish their interrupted meal when the inn reopened the following November. I first visited the Oban Inn in the late 1980s and was saddened to learn of the loss of this Niagara-on-the-Lake landmark. However, when I returned in 1996, there it stood—the same white stucco building with green shutters and glassed-in porch dining room that I remembered.

Niagara-on-the-Lake, Canada
160 Front St.
888-669-5566
905-468-2165
www.vintageinns.com/properties/oban/

RATES & RESERVATIONS:
Hours: 3 p.m. check in; 11 a.m. check out
Season: Year round
Rates: $125 +
Specials: AAA
Reservations required
Visa, MC, Disc, Amex accepted

ACCOMMODATIONS: 26 rooms w/ bath; 3 suites w/bath

AMENITIES: Cable TV, phone in room, Internet, air cond.

MEALS: Breakfast, lunch, dinner, brunch, snacks; Beer, wine, liquor served

OTHER:
Parking: Lot

You'll find a cozy pub at the Oban, Shaw's Corner. Photos of the great playwright and memorabilia from more than 40 festival seasons line the walls. Red predominates in the pub's tartan carpet and walls. Comfy conversational seating groupings make Shaw's Corner a prime spot to have a Scotch, beer, or lager, and sample the menu. Choices include traditional English pub food and East Indian cuisine.

For a quieter space, make your way to the library, a welcoming room with a fireplace, tall windows, and floor-to-ceiling bookcases. I found guests relaxing with wine and cheese in the late afternoon and early the next day coming back to read the morning newspapers.

The Oban Inn, reminiscent of an old English resort hotel, is a comfortably sized hostelry with 26 rooms and suites. Wheelchair-accessible rooms as well as pet rooms are available. Room decor is the expected traditional English style, with a variety of floral wallpaper, antiques, and reproduction furnishings. The spacious premium rooms have a fireplace, Jacuzzi, and the best views overlooking Lake Ontario. The traditional rooms offer another pleasant view out to the gardens and well-preserved homes of this charming neighborhood. Book the suite next door at the Oban House and you find a separate living room with gas fireplace, a desk, wet bar, and hardwood floors. Fresh floral arrangements brighten the suite and there's a TV in both the living room and bedroom, a luxurious space with dark wood furnishings against burgundy walls. At turndown, I found a rose on the pillow of the king bed and a card with the weather forecast for the next morning—an example of the exemplary personal service at this member inn of the Vintage Inns. Complimentary in-town transportation is provided.

Check the inn specials for romantic getaways like the "Days of Wine & Roses" February package and theater packages that offer accommodation, meals, and a Shaw Festival performance.

Dining at the Oban can be an elegant candlelight dinner in the formal dining room or a casual lunch on the porch. While traditional entrees remain—slow-roasted rib-eye of beef with sour cream and chive mash, and Yorkshire pudding—the menu's contemporary offerings include items like appetizers of garlic-steamed blue mussels with roasted tomato and parsley cream sauce and, with a nod to regional cuisine, warm Ontario goat cheese on house-baked grape focaccia bread served with sweet garlic jelly. The poached Atlantic salmon entree arrives with a side of green cardamom cabbage and potato stew, the grilled venison T-bone with soya roasted mushrooms and five-spice potato ragout. There's traditional English fare on the inn's pastry menu: sticky toffee pudding, warm rice pudding, and the Oban trifle with cognac-soaked berries and iced custard. The timing and presentation of meals make for leisurely dining, with time to enjoy the English garden setting. You might spot one of the kitchen staff picking herbs for your luncheon salad.

THINGS TO DO:

In this most English of Canadian towns, take time to stroll the neighborhood near the inn. Immaculately kept gardens and beautifully restored homes offer a visual delight no matter the direction you take. Browse Niagara-on-the Lake's charming shops on Queen Street and adjoining side streets. In this rich viticultural region, wineries await exploration and some offer fine dining as well as wine tastings. But for many of us, including this writer, the play's the thing. It's the Shaw Festival that brings us to town.

The Shaw Festival is the only theater program in the world that specializes in the works of George Bernard Shaw and his contemporaries. The plays run in repertory from Tuesday through Sunday in three theaters during a season that starts in early April and runs through the

first week of December. Catch a performance at the Festival Theatre, the flagship theater used for large-scale productions, or at the Court House Theatre, a grand building of Queenston limestone on Queen Street. With a deep thrust stage, the Court House is the smallest of the trio and provides an intimate setting. The Royal George, a classic Greek-style building set amidst Queen Street's shops, retains touches of its glitzy past. The theater was built to entertain Canadian troops during World War I.

For an introduction to the plays, plan to come to the pre-show chats at the Festival Theatre every evening at 7:30. Saturday Conversations on selected Saturdays during the season provide an opportunity to take part in discussions with company members on the Members Terrace at the Festival Theatre. Another event, the Bell Canada Reading Series, presents stage readings by members of the Shaw acting ensemble. In August, you'll find the Shaw Show of Artists and Artisans, an annual juried event showcasing original works by more than 100 artists, on the grounds of nearby Fort George.

DIRECTIONS: I-190 North to Lewiston/Queenston Bridge to Niagara River Pkwy. (becomes Main St.)

NEARBY ATTRACTIONS: Wineries, Niagara Falls, butterfly conservatory

HISTORIC INNS

I often meet other inn visitors who seek out historic accommodations because they're interested in the design, construction, and furnishings of these treasured gems. The innkeepers in this chapter took the time to point out details of restoration and renovation in their properties. I also learned fascinating histories of previous owners from books and photos during my stays. Historic inns give us a glimpse of life in gentler times, but now also provide the modern amenities we come to expect when selecting an inn getaway

It's a joy to find an inn that is harmonious with its environment, and all eight of the inns reviewed here fit that description. The Roycroft Inn in East Aurora, New York, anchors the campus of this early Arts and Crafts community founded by Elbert Hubbard. In the village of Scenery Hill, Pennsylvania, the Century Inn reigns as the oldest continuously operating inn on the National Road and has welcomed many a famous guest, including Andrew Jackson and Henry Clay. The stately White Inn, located on Main Street in Fredonia, New York, is within easy walking distance of fine examples of 19th- and early 20th-century architecture in this western New York village. The National House Inn, located in a National Historic Landmark district, lays claim to the title of Michigan's oldest operating inn. Two of the inns are in mountain settings. Gateway Lodge, a rustic country inn, fits its setting at the edge of Cook Forest State Park in Cooksburg, Pennsylvania, while the Mountain View Inn in the Laurel Highlands of southwest Pennsylvania is set against a backdrop of the Chestnut Ridge Mountains. Deerpark Country Inn, made up of an 18th-century cabin, a turn-of-the-century farmhouse, and a log lodge, is nestled in the hills of West Virginia. In downtown Lebanon, Ohio, the Golden Lamb, Ohio's oldest inn, continues to welcome guests on South Broadway.

With a tradition of hospitality, seven of the inns serve breakfast, lunch, and dinner, with executive chefs at the helm of the kitchens. Look forward to a pleasant dining experience overlooking gardens at both the Roycroft Inn and the Century Inn. A cozy log cabin interior welcomes diners to the Gateway Lodge and the Deerpark Country Inn. Take a table by the wide windows of the Mountain View Inn and look out over beautifully landscaped grounds. At the White Inn, dine on the veranda in pleasant weather or in the elegant formal dining room. Guests of the National House Inn find breakfast, afternoon tea, and cooking classes. It's a short walk from the inn to the renowned Schuler's Restaurant.

The Golden Lamb

A historic hostelry where famous 19th-century literary and political figures once stayed

The United States had been in existence for only 21 years when the Golden Lamb was established in Lebanon by Jonas Seaman in 1803, making it not only the oldest inn in Ohio but also the oldest continuous business in the state. Originally a two-story log building, the first brick structure was built in 1815 and is now the inn's lobby. The second floor and the Lebanon Dining Room were added in 1825. This four-story Federal brick building with white balconies continues to stand proudly on South Broadway.

In the 1800s, travelers who couldn't read depended on signs that innkeepers displayed using animals as illustrations. In southwestern Ohio, they were told to stop at the sign of the golden lamb. It was at the Golden Lamb that guests and local residents attended political rallies, learned of the Shakers' move to the area, and discussed plans for Ohio's canals and roads.

The Golden Lamb has a long list of noteworthy guests, including 10 American presidents. John Quincy Adams stopped at the inn in 1843 when he came to Cincinnati to dedicate the Cincinnati Observatory. Both James A. Garfield and William McKinley stayed there while cam-

Lebanon, OH
27 S. Broadway
513-932-5065
www.goldenlamb.com

RATES & RESERVATIONS:
Hours: 24 hours/day
Season: Year round
Rates: $65–$90
Specials: Sun–Thu $115 for stay & dinner
Reservations recommended
Check, Visa, MC, Disc accepted

ACCOMMODATIONS: 17 rooms w/bath; 1 suite w/bath

AMENITIES: Cable TV, phone in room, Internet, air cond.

MEALS: Breakfast, lunch, dinner; Beer, wine, liquor served

OTHER:
Not fully wheelchair accessible
Parking: On-street

paigning for office. After opening his first campaign for governor of Ohio in Lebanon, Rutherford B. Hayes was feted by local politicians at a dinner at the inn. Other luminaries who stayed at the Golden Lamb include Charles Dickens, Henry Clay, and Harriet Beecher Stowe. While on his tour of America, Dickens stopped at the inn on April 23, 1842, with his wife, her maid, and his secretary. Disgruntled when he learned that the Golden Lamb, known at the time as the Bradley House, was a temperance hotel, he stomped down to the nearest tavern after dinner. Henry Clay was a frequent visitor on his way to Washington or to Lexington, Kentucky. Traveling with her sister, Catherine, Harriet Beecher Stowe visited Lebanon for the purpose of establishing a school.

Today, visitors to the Golden Lamb are invited to come upstairs for a self-guided tour of 18 antique-laden guest rooms. Take a peek into the Dickens Room, the most requested room with its massive reproduction Lincoln bed, marble-top chest, and washstand. The John Quincy Adams Room, with crewel wallpaper, twin spool beds, and framed photos of Adams, looks out onto the corner park below. With a rose settee, wing chair, and flower-sprigged carpet, the Harriet Beecher Stowe Room appeals to women travelers. When you stay at the Golden Lamb, you can't help but think as you touch the worn banister on your way to your room that Charles Dickens also spent the night here.

Continue on to the fourth floor to view the inn's Shaker museum. While Shaker furniture is used throughout the inn, three rooms on this floor have been reserved for displays of the Shakers' simple furnishings. Superb examples of the importance of function in Shaker furnishings are the pine cupboard, Shaker boxes, rocker, and wall pegs lining the pantry. For a nostalgic look back at another era of childhood, take time to see the room occupied by Sarah Stubbs, whose family owned the inn from 1843 to 1914. This room—with a single bed, small chest, doll beds, and a miniature tea set—seems to have remained untouched throughout the years. In 1978, the Golden Lamb was placed on the National Register of Historic Places.

Charles Dickens would be pleased to know that the Golden Lamb management knows how "to keep Christmas well" in the 21st century. Christmas is celebrated every day of December except for the 25th, when the inn is closed. It takes the staff eight months to ready the inn for the special holiday celebrations. Seven trees are decorated throughout the inn, and guests are greeted by a blazing log fire in the lobby. Two guest rooms, the Charles Dickens Room and the John Quincy Adams Room, are given a festive treatment.

Chef Dennis Glosser prepares three Yuletide feasts: a German meal called Frohe Weihnachten, Cratchit's Christmas Dinner to honor Charles Dickens, and a Mount Vernon Dinner as it would have been served in 1789. The recipes and menus used for these dinners were carefully researched by talking with culinary historians and checking cookbooks.

Look for comfort food from your childhood on the menu. Lunch on creamed chicken on a buttermilk biscuit, Shaker beef stew, or Salisbury steak. Leg of lamb, roast duckling with orange sauce, and roast turkey with dressing are dinner features. Two desserts served throughout the year are Sister Lizzi's Shaker Pie and Ohio Lemon Pie.

When making a reservation at the Golden Lamb, you have a choice of four dining rooms. The oldest, the Lebanon Room, dates back to the original inn. Old mottoes such as "Welcome Home" and "Forget Me Not" cover the dark floral wallpaper on one side of the room. Enjoy lunch in the Dickens Dining Room where, seated at a table by the window, you can watch the activity on Broadway. An extensive collection of English prints lines the cream-colored walls. The Shaker Room features kitchen implements and chairs hanging from pegs in true Shaker style, while the Buckeye Room provides a fourth option for dining. For a cozy spot for a snack or lunch, try the Black Horse Tavern at the back of the inn.

THINGS TO DO:

Antique lovers will have a field day in Lebanon. On my March visit, I counted many antique stores, ranging from smaller shops like Exotic Art and Antiques (antique Chinese furniture) and the Lemon Tree (specializing in Fiestaware and Depression glass) to multidealer shops like the Broadway Antique Mall, Hunter's Horn Antiques Center, Miller's Antique Market, and the Shoe Factory Antique Mall. A half block

south of the inn, the Golden Turtle Chocolate Factory offers over 100 varieties of chocolates. Christmastime visitors find the Historic Lebanon Christmas Festival, which kicks off with a parade of horse-drawn carriages. December is also a good time to tour Glendower State Memorial, a red brick Greek Revival mansion done up in period holiday decor.

DIRECTIONS: I-71 to Exit 28

NEARBY ATTRACTIONS: Kings Island, Ft. Ancient, Cincinnati attractions

Gateway Lodge

Escape to this rustic country inn surrounded by forest

The approach to Gateway Lodge on Route 36 through a spectacular old-growth forest provides a tantalizing taste of what awaits visitors to this rustic country inn. Located at the edge of Cook Forest State Park, Gateway Lodge has been listed by *Money* magazine as a "Top Travel Pick" and by *Insider Magazine* as one of the "10 Best Country Inns in the U.S." Tucked into the woodland, suites with decks overlooking the forest offer views of the mist-shrouded Clarion River while the spacious front porch is a prime spot for bird-watchers.

Ray and Beth Griscom built Gateway Lodge in 1934 as a summer retreat for visitors to Cook Forest. Constructed of felled logs of hemlock and pine, the interior of the original inn remains as it was with wormy chestnut walls and wide pine floors. There's a cozy log cabin feel to the living room with a log ceiling, stone fire-

Cooksburg, PA
SR 36
800-843-6862
www.gatewaylodge.com

RATES & RESERVATIONS:
Hours: 7 a.m.–11 p.m.
Season: Year round
Rates: $125 +
Specials: AAA, packages available
Reservations recommended
Check, Visa, MC, Disc, Amex accepted

ACCOMMODATIONS: 8 rooms, 3 with bath; 24 suites w/bath; 7 cottages

AMENITIES: Sauna, pool, whirlpool tubs, phone in room, air cond., fireplaces, picnic area

MEALS: Breakfast, lunch, dinner, snacks; Beer, wine, liquor served

OTHER:
Parking: Lot

place, and small-paned windows. Family pictures and historic documents line the hallway, and upstairs the eight small original bedrooms are done up in antique quilts, calico prints, and rag rugs.

Linda and Joe Burney took over the inn in 1980 and expanded it in 2000. A wide brick hallway, referred to by the staff as "the sidewalk," connects the old section of the inn to the common rooms and suites and provides gallery space for nature photography by local artist Anthony E. Cook. A heated indoor pool and sauna can be accessed from this corridor. The common room, with 30-foot ceilings and a wall of windows reaching 18 feet, is suffused with light. A copper bathtub topped with glass serves as a coffee table for a grouping of green leather sofas around the massive fieldstone fireplace. Eight comfy chairs with ottomans and good reading lights are scattered about the room, making it a reader's delight. Afternoon tea is set out on the sideboard where early risers will also find coffee every morning. Three deer surprised me near the patio doors as I came down for coffee just before 7:00 a.m.

On the upper level, a second common room offers an intimate conversation area and a selection of games and books. An antique carousel horse adds a whimsical touch. The view to the great room below is breathtaking during the holidays, when a 17-foot-tall Christmas tree decorated with 6,000 lights is in place.

Take your pick of one of the luxurious Jacuzzi suites located in the new addition, where individually decorated rooms are named for local historic figures. The Judge's Chamber, honoring the Honorable Anthony Cook, features a four-poster bed so high you might need the small bedside stepstool. The innkeepers have been consistent in placing art that reflects the area or scenes from nature throughout the inn, such as the sketch of Judge Cook's house and early mills.

If you arrive too late for tea, you'll find a welcome gift basket stocked with cider, fruit, crackers, and cheese. A fireside whirlpool tub, small ice cream table and chairs, and refrigerator make the suite an invit-

ing weekend refuge. The Beth Griscom Suite offers a black brass four-poster bed topped with a flowered comforter in pale pinks and greens. The Seneca Suite employs muted greens with Navajo touches.

Settle down for a romantic dinner in the inn dining room, featuring log walls, a wagon-wheel chandelier, and tables centered with kerosene lamps. It's a charming country inn setting with lace curtains at the windows, a high shelf displaying a collection of china and glass, and a table set with pewter chargers and goblets. You can reserve ahead for a four- or seven-course dinner or order from the a la carte menu. Prime rib is a favorite, along with pork medallions and chicken Florentine. Stop in the wine room before dinner to choose a bottle from the inn's collection of 380 different labels. Breakfast features the expected hearty fare of pancakes and egg selections with sides of homemade biscuits and grits, along with some surprise offerings like lemon-pepper catfish. A family-style dinner is served on Sunday from noon to 3:00 p.m.

With a choice of eight rooms, 23 suites, and seven cottages, you can tailor your stay to your interests. Families like the cottages with a choice of bed-and-breakfast stay or "roughing it" by bringing your own linens and cooking utensils. There's a picnic area with a fire ring, with firewood provided. Check out the inn's current packages. Along with romantic stays, a special package unique to this area is the Punxsutawney Phil's Pick, which includes afternoon tea, dinner for two, and a map for the next morning's trip to try to get a glimpse of that problematic groundhog.

THINGS TO DO:

Name a season or a sport you like, and you'll find your pleasure in this area of forests, river, and streams. There's canoeing, tubing, kayaking, and fishing on the Clarion River, as well as hiking, hunting, and cross-country skiing. Pick up a guide to the Cook Forest State Park trails from the ranger's office and take time for a drive along the Clarion River on River Road. Travel south from Gateway Lodge to find Mac-Beth's Discoveries, a tidy cottage filled with handmade items—quilts, smocked children's dresses, hand-knit sweaters, woodcrafts, and antiques. Travel north to stop at Mountain Mercantile, offering home furnishings, gourmet foods, antiques, and penny candy. Feel like a night at the theater? The Verna Leith Sawmill Theatre is just two miles from Gateway.

DIRECTIONS: I-80 West to Exit 62; left on SR 68 to Clarion, through Clarion to Miola Rd. for 11 miles; right on SR 36 to inn.

NEARBY ATTRACTIONS: Cook Forest State Park (National Natural Landmark)

Mountain View Inn

A classic American inn along the Lincoln Highway Heritage Corridor

The Mountain View Inn, set in the Laurel Highlands in southwest Pennsylvania, was buzzing when I visited on an early May weekend. It was hosting the Greensburg Pennsylvania Antiques Show, one of three held yearly at the inn. This classic American inn with its extensive collection of antiques provided the perfect backdrop for the show. Third-generation owners and innkeepers Vance and Vicki Booher showcase their antique collection throughout the inn. In the main foyer, you'll find Grandpa Booher's baby cradle by the stone fireplace and a grandfather's clock owned by the family since 1898. Around the corner, a collection of Christmas plates fills display cases in the hallway. A guide to the Booher's antique collection is available at the front desk.

Opened in 1924 as the Mountain View Hotel, travelers found the inn a welcome stop along the Lincoln Highway (Route 30). The Booher family purchased the property in 1940 and through the years have expanded and improved the inn, skillfully meshing old and new sections. Each of the 89 guest

Greensburg, PA
1001 Village Dr.
800-537-8709
724-834-5300
www.mountainviewinn.com

RATES & RESERVATIONS:
Hours: 24 hours/day
Season: Year round
Rates: $65–$90
Specials: AAA, Musical Weekends, Antique Lover's Getaway, seasonal getaways
Reservations recommended
Visa, MC, Disc, Amex accepted

ACCOMMODATIONS: 89 rooms w/bath; 7 suites w/bath; 3 apartments

AMENITIES: Cable TV, pool, phone in room, Internet, air cond., restaurants, tavern, gift boutique, gardens, room amenities

MEALS: Breakfast (included); Beer, wine served

OTHER:
Parking: Lot

rooms and suites has its own ambience thanks to the selection of furnishings and colors. I stayed in the original inn's historic section. With hardwood floors, marble-top chests, and flowered wallpaper, my room included a comfortable sitting area with a sofa, desk, and TV hidden behind louvered doors. Guest rooms in the Mountain Laurel Wing are furnished with a canopy four-poster queen bed or two double beds and offer views of the mountains or the gardens. Garden suites with a king bed, Jacuzzi, and gas fireplace are named after a favorite garden of the innkeepers. The newest addition, the Loyalhammer Wing, is popular with corporate guests, who find large desks, comfortable chairs, and queen or double beds. All rooms feature high-speed Internet, data port telephone, mineral water, Gilchrist & Soames bath accessories, and a newspaper at the door each morning. For a luxurious stay, book the Giverny Suite with a galley kitchen, den, living room with a grand piano, dining room, and master suite with Jacuzzi. The Dalai Lama, Bernadette Peters, and Harry Belafonte made this suite their home while in the area.

It's the view of the Chestnut Ridge Mountains from the wall of windows in the Candlelight Restaurant that gave the inn its name. The restaurant is a comfortable room with dark wood paneling accented by a collection of Booher family antique plates, a fireplace, and greenery festooned with tiny lights. Fresh flowers and colonial-style lamps on crisp linen set the tone for leisurely dining. The menu offers classic American fare using local products like the lamb cut especially for the inn by the Jamison farm in nearby Latrobe, and depends on artisan growers for fresh produce. Everything possible is prepared in house. Overnight guests have a choice for breakfast in the Candlelight dining room: sit down for a leisurely breakfast ordered from the menu or serve

yourself from the buffet of fruit, cereal, homemade granola, and breads. For special events like Mother's Day, the Candlelight offers an elegant buffet along with traditional family-style sit-down service.

The enticing aroma of popcorn pulled me into the inn's second restaurant venue, 33rd Street. This is the spot for casual dining, with eight large TV screens, an extensive menu of 133 items, and 10 draft beers. Offering 60 of the finest Scotch whiskeys, Mountain View Inn claims bragging rights as Pennsylvania's largest Scotch bar.

The Antique Lovers Weekend getaway package is available for January, April, and November. It includes accommodations for two nights, dinner, breakfast, a gift basket, and admission to the inn's Antique Show and Sale. The last Friday of January, February, March, and October brings the sounds of Benny Goodman, Tommy Dorsey, Artie Shaw, and Glenn Miller to the inn for the Big Band Overnight package. Mountain View Inn is the host hotel for the Ligonier Highland Games on the weekend after Labor Day.

This is the kind of hostelry that easily hosts large groups for corporate retreats, but is also a desired destination for romantic getaways.

THINGS TO DO:

For a pleasant small-town shopping experience, head over to "The Diamond," Ligonier's center green named by early Scotch-Irish settlers. A bandstand built in 1894 for the local cornet band, flower gardens, and benches make it a good spot to take a break. In the mix of shops, Martin's Specialty Shop, a Ligonier business that has been under the same family ownership for three generations, carries sportswear for the entire family. The Needle Nook is a compact shop stocking needlepoint and counted cross-stitch. Master goldsmith John M. Clark offers his own line of jewelry, including Ligonier Bandstand items. Stop for lunch at the Ligonier Tavern, originally the residence of the city's first mayor, or pick up a lunch to go and settle on a bench on the Diamond green.

Ligonier is home to seven antique shops as well as a fantastic toy store, the Toy Box on South Market Street. The annual Fort Ligonier Days take place in October and Antiques on the Diamond draws crowds in June and August.

For those seeking outdoor recreation, there's white-water rafting on the Youghiogheny River and hiking and biking trails nearby. Frank Lloyd Wright's Fallingwater and Kentuck Knob are an easy drive from the inn.

DIRECTIONS: I-80 to PA Turnpike to Exit 7 for Irwin; on SR 30 East.

NEARBY ATTRACTIONS: Fallingwater, Kentuck Knob, Idlewild Park, Historic Ligonier, Seven Springs Ski Resort, Westmoreland Museum of American Art

Century Inn

A historic hostelry along the old
National Road

The Century Inn has had its share of notable guests. Our seventh president, Andrew Jackson, stayed at the inn on the way to his inauguration in 1826. General Lafayette stopped with his retinue for breakfast in May 1825. Wayfarers and wagoners also found a welcome at this sturdy inn built of stone quarried on the property. Century Inn, opened to guests in 1794, is the oldest continually operated inn along the National Road.

During my stay, innkeeper Megin Harrington took me on a tour of the inn's fine collection of antiques. A narrow hallway fans out to rooms of various sizes on the first floor. In the music room, she pointed out a Chippendale highboy that was brought to the area by Conestoga wagon. Across the hall in the McCune Saloon, the only known Whiskey Rebellion flag used at Parkinson's Ferry has a prominent place on the wall. You get a sense of the inn's age as you step down to the dining-room level via a stone threshold worn smooth by shoes and boots over a period of more than 200 years.

Six guest rooms on the second floor offer more antiques. The Albert Gallatin Room, named for the first secretary of the U.S. Treasury, boasts an early American inlaid slant-front desk and a 19th-century inlaid cherry chest of drawers. Special finds in the Andrew Jackson Suite include a Sheraton chest of drawers with pressed glass knobs

Scenery Hill, PA
2175 National Rd. East
724-945-6600
www.centuryinn.com

RATES & RESERVATIONS:
Hours: 24 hours/day
Season: Apr-Dec
Rates: $65–$125 +
Reservations recommended
Check, Visa, MC accepted

ACCOMMODATIONS: 9 rooms w/bath

AMENITIES: Hot tub, air cond.

MEALS: Breakfast, lunch, dinner; Beer, wine, liquor served

OTHER:
Not fully wheelchair accessible
Parking: On-street

and a dovetailed blanket box. Chief Blackhawk's Room is done up in a stunning combination of reds, greens, and blues, with the comforter fabric repeated in the wainscoting and window treatments. A canopied four-poster is augmented by a hired man's bed in this room with space for three guests. The Stephen Hill Suite, with a large sitting room and bedroom, offers comfortable space for a family stay. Antique treasures in this set of rooms include a rare harvest cradle, early English framed engravings, and an American 18th-century walnut stretcher tavern table. A collection of majolica and an Adams-style curved and inlaid mahogany tester bed are found in the David Bradford Room. All the guest rooms in the inn have working fireplaces and private baths. Due to the inn's age and room configuration, bathrooms are small.

Century Inn extends to the property across the street, Zephanie Riggle's House of Entertainment. If Victorian furnishings and decor interest you, this is the place to book a stay. Three spacious suites are filled with Victorian antiques such as the Eastlake dresser in the Fannie O'Brien Room and a Rococo-style mid-19th-century carved Victorian walnut bed in the Kitty Gumbert Suite. The inn's honeymoon suite, the Lilly Beekman, is a luxurious space with a sitting area, bedroom, and extra-large bathroom with a Jacuzzi and a bidet.

Located 35 miles south of Pittsburgh, Century Inn is a dining destination for city dwellers. The Garden Room, one of five dining rooms at the inn, overlooks the back garden where bricked paths lead to the gazebo, the site for summer dining as well as private parties and weddings. Along with lighter fare of salads and sandwiches, the lunch menu offers entrees from earlier times like shepherd's pie and rum tum ditty,

a warming dish of crisp bacon, ripe tomato slices, and cheddar cheese sauce on toast points. I enjoyed an evening meal in the intimate setting of the original kitchen, now known as the Keeping Room. Dried herbs hang from the rafters and early utensils and tools are displayed on the stone wall of the wide hearth.

Heading chef James Shaw's menu are starters like beef Blackfoot, rare tenderloin strips marinated in ginger and soy, mushroom strudel with wild forest mushrooms in puff pastry, crab tomato concasse, and peanut soup. Entrees include petite veal rack Forester with wild mushroom sauce and pheasant stuffed with apricots, chestnuts, and wild rice. Traditional entrees like roast turkey and stuffed pork chops remain popular with those who return again and again. I found the dining rooms to be busy on a weeknight, so reservations are always a good idea. A full breakfast is served in the Garden Room for overnight guests only. While the Century Inn Restaurant is closed to the public from January through mid-March, facilities for special events and business meetings are available year-round, as are the guest rooms.

There are tennis courts on the inn grounds, along with the old-fashioned games of croquet and horseshoes. Century Inn easily accommodates business meetings or corporate retreats with a choice of dining settings. Fax and photocopy equipment is available; audiovisual equipment can be arranged.

THINGS TO DO:

Shopping offerings in Scenery Hill are ever changing. The shops lined up along the National Road are within easy walking distance from the inn. If you're willing to sort through a warren of dusty rooms, quality pieces can be found at Christian Getzendanner's Antiques. He carries country and period furniture dating from the 18th and 19th centuries, as well as transferware, Quimper pottery, and folk paintings. John and Linda Glover opened one of the newer shops, Heart & Soul Gallery, a full-service jewelry and gift shop. John works in both gold and silver; Linda creates etched glass and stained-glass paintings. Take a break during your shopping tour to stop at Jan's Tea Shoppe & 2nd Street Coffee Roasters. Jan stocks a wide selection of teapots along with gourmet coffees and teas. On your way out of town, visit Westerwald Pottery. The studios and gallery showroom, open seven days a week, are situated on a 100-acre llama farm along the National Road. Phil Schaltenbrand founded the company in 1975. Westerwald pottery is known for its traditional blue decoration and gray glaze but has recently added other color choices.

Golfers can head to nearby Chippewa Golf Course or over to Mystic Rock Golf Course at Nemacolin Woodlands Resort.

DIRECTIONS: I-80 East to 70 West to SR 917 South to SR 40 (National Rd.); left on SR 40; on left

NEARBY ATTRACTIONS: Nemacolin Golf Course, Chippewa Golf Gourse, pottery

Roycroft Inn

*An inn from the
Arts and Crafts era*

A brochure I picked up at the Roycroft Inn best describes the inn's history: "Opened to friends in 1905—Restored 1995." "The inn had been closed for nearly eight years when the restoration began," relates innkeeper Martha B. Augat. "In terrible disrepair, it had to be virtually gutted before it could be reconstructed. Period photographs and postcards were used to restore the floor plan to its 1905 design. It was wonderful to see life breathed into this tired old building and watch its splendor unfold." Augat finds that many devotees of the Arts and Crafts style make their way to this historically significant structure from the Roycroft Movement. Others who come as business travelers, or as guests for special events or getaway weekends, leave with a new or increased appreciation of the Movement's style and philosophy.

East Aurora, New York, was home to the Roycroft Arts and Crafts community and their char-

East Aurora, NY
40 South Grove St.
877-652-5552
716-652-5552
www.roycroftinn.com

RATES & RESERVATIONS:
Hours: 24 hours/day
Season: Year round
Rates: $125 +
Specials: Children, AAA
Reservations recommended
Visa, MC, Disc, Amex, Diners Club accepted

ACCOMMODATIONS: 5 rooms w/ bath; 24 suites w/bath

AMENITIES: Cable TV, phone in room, Internet, air cond.

MEALS: Breakfast, lunch, dinner, brunch, snacks; Beer, wine, liquor served

OTHER:
Parking: Lot

ismatic leader, Elbert Hubbard. Fine artisans flocked to this stimulating community based on the English medieval guild system. These artists and craftsmen turned out leather goods, copperware, fine bookbinding, and Mission-style furniture. To accommodate the influx of visitors and newcomers, the Roycroft Inn opened in 1905.

This National Landmark property features Hubbard's mottoes, like the one inscribed on a heavy oak entrance door: "Produce great people—the rest follows." At another entry door, he left this motto: "The love you liberate in your work is the love you keep."

Step into the inn lounge and you find a restored Gothic-style artglass window by Dard Hunter. A series of 12 murals depicting famous cities, temples, and sites by Alexis Jean Fournier above the oak wainscoting in the main salon add a touch of classicism. Simplicity prevails in the spacious public rooms, appointed with Stickley and Roycroft furnishings.

The oak doors of the Roycroft's guest rooms are inscribed with the names of notable guests Hubbard admired from the fields of literature, science, and the fine and performing arts. Famous names include Ralph Waldo Emerson, Elizabeth Barrett and Robert Browning, Richard Wagner, Charlotte Brontë, Henry David Thoreau, and Susan B. Anthony. As you stroll the halls, take a look at the photographs and framed pages from one of Hubbard's publications, "The Fra," which help explain his philosophy and ideals.

The restoration resulted in the inn's 50 original rooms becoming 22 spacious suites. Each suite offers one sleeping area, a changing/sitting area, and a full bath. You can also choose a larger suite of three to five rooms. Beadboard ceilings remain as a reminder of earlier times when sleeping porches were part of the room configuration. Mission-style furniture is softened by wallcoverings and decorative fabrics in the style of William Morris. Accents include Roycroft lamps, wall sconces, colorful throws, green plants, and fresh flowers. Wicker furniture with

Southwest-design pillows and wooden blinds add an informal air. Commodious bathrooms repeat the nature motif of the wallcoverings, with an acorn detail edging the tiles. An adjoining guesthouse with seven rooms and a parlor opened in August 1999. The Roycroft Inn is a member of Condé Nast Johansens Hotels, Inns, and Resorts.

Plan for leisurely dining in exceptional settings at the Roycroft Inn. White linen and reproduction Roycroft china dress the tables, and your waiter wears a flowing black cravat, a trademark of Hubbard's wardrobe. In warm weather dine in the peristyle or "veranda" (circa 1904), which runs the length of the inn, or settle in the Larkin Room overlooking a courtyard perennial garden. On a menu that changes seasonally you might find dinner entrees of rack of lamb, Cornish game hen, tournedos of elk, and sesame-encrusted tuna. Finish with the inn's signature dessert, the Nouveau Craftsman—a stacked confection of crème de cassis whipped cream layered between crisp almond tiles on a brown sugar poundcake, topped by raspberries soaked in Beaujolais. On Friday evenings, enjoy the professional jazz musicians holding forth in the lounge. Inn guests find an expanded continental breakfast set out in the Larkin Room.

THINGS TO DO:

Step out the door of the inn to gift and antiques shops across the way. One shop of interest on the historic Roycroft campus is the Roycroft Potters, located in the original Roycroft furniture and bookbinders building.

Take time to visit the Elbert Hubbard-Roycroft Museum located near the inn on Oakwood Avenue. Housed in a green clapboard and shingled Craftsman-style house built in 1910 for leather artisan George ScheideMantel and his wife, Gladys, the museum offers a treasure-trove of Roycroft furniture and decorative objects. A walk through the house finds a Morris chair by the split fieldstone fireplace in the living room, hand-hammered copper bowls lining the mantle, and leather-bound books throughout. An original lighting fixture with Steuben glass globes hangs over the sturdy Roycroft oak table and chairs in the dining room. One of the upstairs bedrooms used by ScheideMantel for his studio displays tools, reference books, and samples of this master leatherworker's craft. The view from the studio's back window is of an English garden designed in 1920 and cared for today by master garden-ers.

Stroll East Aurora's tree-shaded streets lined with homes from the Greek Revival, Federal, and Victorian periods. Interesting stops along the way include the Town Hall, a medieval building that served as a chapel for the Roycrofters, and the Baker Memorial Church with 17 opalescent glass windows created by Tiffany. Stop at the Millard Fillmore House, a National Historic Landmark, to view the formal Presidential Rose Garden featuring varieties grown before 1840.

You might want to come back to East Aurora the last full weekend in June for the Roycrofters Summer Art Festival featuring highly skilled artisans. A concurrent event is the East Aurora Art Society's outdoor show and sale.

DIRECTIONS: I-90 East to exit 54 (SR 400) to Maple St. exit; right on Maple; left on Main St.; right on South Grove St.

NEARBY ATTRACTIONS: The Roycroft Campus, Millard Fillmore House, Ralph Wilson Stadium, Darwin D. Martin House, Graycliff Estate

The White Inn

A historic inn in a charming boutique village

Stately twin maple trees planted in 1825 by Devillo White flank the brick walk that leads to the entrance of the White Inn. Devillo, son of Dr. Squire White, Fredonia's first medical doctor, replaced his father's frame house on the site in 1868 with a grand mansion built in the Second Empire style, which was essentially absorbed into the core of today's White Inn. Rooms remaining from the original home include the foyer and the University Room on the first floor as well as several guest rooms on the second and third floors. On the third floor, the Lincoln Suite replicates the Lincoln Room in the White House with an ornate walnut headboard with large oval side-by-side panels and an imposing eight-foot-tall bureau with a mirror and marble top. A sitting room with double sofa bed and desk completes the suite. Take a look at the inn's exterior on the west side and you'll spot the arched windows and elaborate brackets from the earlier structure.

Designer reproduction wallpapers and a collection of framed lace can be found throughout the inn's 23 guest rooms and suites. The Wicker Room features a wicker canopy queen bed and a pair of comfortably

Fredonia, NY
52 E. Main St.
888-373-3664
716-672-2103
www.whiteinn.com

RATES & RESERVATIONS:
Hours: 24 hours/day
Season: Year round
Rates: $70–$180
Specials: Children, seniors, AAA
Reservations recommended
Check, Visa, MC, Disc, Amex, Diners
Club accepted

ACCOMMODATIONS: 12 rooms w/ bath; 11 suites w/bath; 1 apartment

AMENITIES: Cable TV, phone in room, Internet, air cond.

MEALS: Breakfast, lunch, dinner; Beer, wine, liquor served

OTHER:
Not fully wheelchair accessible
Parking: Lot

padded wicker chairs set against flowered and beribboned wallpaper. The Presidential Suite offers a living room with fireplace, bedroom with king bed, full bath with whirlpool tub, and powder room. Special packages include the Getaway Extravaganza with a stay in the Presidential or Anniversary Suite, dinner for two, full breakfast, taxes, and gratuities.

The White Inn offers guests a choice of dining in the Garden Room, in the lounge, or on the 100-foot-long veranda. On the summer day when I arrived at the inn, the veranda was busy with folks stopping for tea and dessert or an early dinner. Duncan Hines discovered the White Inn in the 1930s and included it as one of the 50 finest restaurants in his "Family of Fine Restaurants." Favorite items on today's menu include a tangy shrimp appetizer and entrees of lamb a la Madeline and dijon-grilled salmon, while chocolate mousse cake and bourbon pecan pie highlight the dessert menu. The Concord Room provides an elegant setting for dining, with tables dressed in linen with pink table toppers and rose-motif china. Some special items on the country breakfast menu include White Inn crepes, Belgian waffles, and a scrambled egg dish that includes fresh herbs from the inn garden. Children are welcome at the inn and will be happy to find breakfast menu items like chocolate chip or blueberry silver-dollar pancakes and French toast with sauteed apples.

The White Inn proudly displays Dr. Squire White's butler's desk in a foyer corner. Another fine antique in the inn's collection is the Thomas Brooks secretary, almost 10 feet tall with a six-door display cabinet, which has a place of honor in the Garden Room. Antique aficionados will enjoy browsing the selected antiques for sale in the inn's hallways.

The White Inn has been a member of Select Registry since 1989.

THINGS TO DO:

A walking town, Fredonia is one of many western New York villages offering examples of fine 19th- and early-20th-century architecture. Step out the inn's front door and stroll down Main Street past commercial buildings of Italianate, Neo-Colonial, and High Victorian design. The National Grange movement began in Fredonia in 1868, and the village lays claim to "Grange No. 1," a beautiful Academic Revival building at 58 West Main Street. The Barker Common, made up of two green park areas, centers the downtown area and provides a resting place with benches and fountains under a canopy of trees.

On the other side of Barker Common, you'll find early churches, the old Fredonia fire station, and the 1891 Fredonia Opera House with a year-round schedule of concerts, guest artists, and a cinema series. Nearby Fredonia State College offers sporting and cultural events. The Darwin R. Barker Historical Museum is an easy two-block walk from the inn. Gift shops include Time Pieces, around the corner on White Street, with a selection of fine teas, greeting cards, glass friendship balls, garden decor, and country items. In downtown Fredonia, Chautauqua Rare Books and Antiques stocks used and rare books along with Americana and Native American folk art and prints. Tower Gifts & Treasured Dolls is just off the common in a Victorian Gothic house, with one room devoted to porcelain and vinyl dolls. I found the Luweibdeh Shop worth a stop, about two miles west of downtown Fredonia on Route 20. Located in a former tenant farmer's cottage from the 1800s, the shop is filled with art and fine crafts, including wind chimes, handblown Christmas ornaments, wood carvings, silk flowers, and a wide selection of china serving pieces.

Summertime finds the Chautauqua Institution in full swing with its series of lectures and performances. During the winter months, guests of the White Inn have ready access to miles of groomed ski trails. Special events are offered throughout the year along the Chautauqua Wine Trail, with stops at eight wineries.

The Victorian Dazzle Festival takes over the village each July for three days. Horse-drawn carriage rides, a Teddy Bear Picnic, a croquet tournament on Barker Common, and Victorian gift shop open houses take visitors back to the 1800s. One popular festival event is a Victorian ice cream social at the White Inn.

September brings the Red, White & Blues Fest to town, with wine tastings and a national blues band holding forth in the park. In the evenings, blues can be heard in various venues around the village, including the White Inn.

DIRECTIONS: I-90 to Exit 59 for SR 60; left on SR 60; right on SR 20 (Main St.); on right

NEARBY ATTRACTIONS: Chautauqua Institution, Chautauqua County Wine Trail, antique shops, Fredonia Opera House

Deerpark Country Inn

A traditional country inn off the beaten path

S et in the foothills of the Allegheny Mountains, Deerpark Country Inn is the epitome of a traditional country inn. An 18th-century cabin, a turn-of-the-century farmhouse, and a two-story log lodge with twin verandas make up the accommodation.

Miles from a major highway, The Inn is surrounded by woods, meadows, and gardens. Life moves at a gentler pace here. You might spot a herd of white-tailed deer on the hillside in the early morning or watch hummingbirds in the English gardens. Guests find well-stocked ponds and woodland trails. A tree house overlooking the pond is a favorite of bird-watching guests. For many returning guests it's the quiet they savor most.

There are more than 8,000 white pines on the 100-acre property. The Deerpark Country Inn, a proud member of Select Registry Distinguished Inns of North America, has welcomed guests

Buckhannon, WV
Havener Grove Rd.
800-296-8430
304-472-8400
www.deerparkcountryinn.com

RATES & RESERVATIONS:
Hours: 7 a.m.–10 p.m.
Season: Year round
Rates: $125 +
Specials: Children, seniors, singles, AAA
Reservations required
Check, Visa, MC, Disc, Amex accepted

ACCOMMODATIONS: 4 rooms w/ bath; 2 suites w/bath

AMENITIES: Cable TV, phone in room, air cond.

MEALS: Breakfast, lunch, dinner, snacks; Beer, wine, liquor served

OTHER:
Cat living on premises
Parking: Lot

from 37 countries and every state in the Union. Visitors to West Virginia Wesleyan College in nearby Buckhannon find the inn a convenient lodging spot. After a Korean administrator first stayed at the inn while visiting the college, the Hayneses welcomed family and friends of their first Korean guest.

The guest rooms and suites in the house are named for West Virginia counties that touch the inn's own county, Upshur. The style can best be described as American country elegance. It's not the usual country decor, nor is there a trace of heavier Victoriana. There's a masterful combination of antiques and collectibles in this architecturally interesting setting of cozy cabin, farmhouse, and lodge rooms. A personal touch is evident in fresh flower arrangements, ferns, and fine linens. Books are placed throughout the inn's rooms.

The first-floor Randolph Suite, with a view of the cottage flower gardens, is furnished with an antique bedstead, marble-top chest, and a wardrobe that almost grazes the nine-foot ceiling. I found a collection of books on the Civil War in the adjoining sitting room, along with a George Washington desk, a daybed, and an antique opalescent chandelier. There's easy access from the sitting room to a wicker-furnished porch. Some returning guests request the Lewis Suite, an upstairs farmhouse suite done up in jewel tones with two built-in alcove beds, a queen bed, and a sitting room. Antiques in the Upshur Room include a cherry table, hairpin Windsor chairs, and an antique child's bed.

In chilly weather, folks gather in the log-walled lodge's great room by a crackling fire. The Greenbrier Room, with an antique wardrobe, sleigh bed, and writing desk, has French doors that open to the veranda. This is the room to enjoy the mist rising from the pond in the spring and watch the snow fall on the pine forest in winter. The Pocahontas Room features a wood-burning stove and a Sundance king iron bed. Oriental rugs warm the Webster Room, with cannonball beds and windows to the forest. Check out the ancestral photos that line the wall of the lodge's stairwell and hallway.

The ambience of this country inn draws you in when you settle by the fire in the main dining room. Deep wing chairs at tables set with fine china and crystal help establish the mood. For a drink before dinner, pull up a stool to the beautiful cherrywood bar. Other dining options are smaller rooms within this log cabin portion of the inn. In fine weather, diners move out to the terrace.

After enjoying dinner on my March visit in the dining room, I was

served breakfast in the bar area the next morning. It was a gourmet meal served on whimsical china with a village scene pattern. A sweet bouquet of spring flowers centered the table.

The staff is kept busy catering special events at the inn—weddings, reunions, small corporate retreats. They have catered events for as many as 400. On a summer afternoon, the lawns are dotted with white tents, gazebos, and a dance floor for a wedding celebration. Sydney, the resident cat, can be spotted wandering among the crowd. For informal retreats, guests spill out to the lodge's wraparound porches.

THINGS TO DO:

Visit the West Virginia Wildlife Center, where you can view animals in their natural habitat. Plan to spend time hiking or swimming at Audra State Park or catch one of the local festivals. Head into Buckhannon, highly ranked in Norman Crampton's book *The Best Small Towns in America.* Visit the West Virginia Wesleyan campus and, while in town, check out the shops that line Main Street. Have lunch at Aesop's Cafe and browse the selection of books at this coffeehouse cum bookstore.

DIRECTIONS: I-79 to Exit 99 for SR 33 East to Buckhannon; left on SR 151, right on Havener Grove Rd.; on right

NEARBY ATTRACTIONS: Antiquing, whitewater rafting, heritage festivals

National House Inn

Michigan's oldest inn in the heart of Marshall's National Historic Landmark District

The massive Williamsburg-style beam-and-brick open-hearth fireplace in the entryway of the National House Inn in Marshall, Michigan, provides a warm welcome for visitors. Returning guests know that the scent of woodsmoke will greet them from September through April and that they'll find a bowl of marshmallows for toasting. It's one of innkeeper Barbara Bradley's special touches that make the inn a favorite of many. Built in 1835, the National House Inn, listed on the National Register of Historic Places, reigns as Michigan's oldest operating inn. The structure served originally as a stagecoach stop, subsequently as a hotel during the railroad era, then as a factory that produced windmills and wagons, and finally as an apartment building. Local restorationists rescued the building in 1976 and presented it to the community as a bicentennial gift.

Marshall, MI
102 S. Parkview
269-781-7374
www.nationalhouseinn.com

RATES & RESERVATIONS:
Hours: 24 hours/day
Season: Year round
Rates: $125 +
Specials: Children, seniors, singles, AAA
Reservations recommended
Check, Visa, MC, Amex accepted

ACCOMMODATIONS: 13 rooms w/ bath; 2 suites w/bath

AMENITIES: Cable TV, phone in room, air cond., Internet

MEALS: Breakfast, afternoon tea

OTHER:
Not fully wheelchair accessible
Parking: Lot

The sign above the front door, "Traditional Overnight Lodging," best describes the National House Inn. Exploring the inn, I found it to be a well-loved and carefully tended home with a fine collection of antiques and decorative art. During a stay you'll discover attention to details in the form of luxurious linens, feather ticks, fresh flower arrangements, and afternoon tea.

Choose from 15 guest rooms themed to Victorian, country, and romantic styles. No two rooms are alike; you find Williamsburg bouquets in one and primitive art in another. Named for historic personages in Marshall's history, each room has a short paragraph with information about these public figures posted outside. I settled in a corner room, the Charles T. Gorham Room, a true Victorian bedchamber with a magnificent walnut armoire, marble-top cherry chests, and cherry bedstead. My window presented a view of the Brooks Memorial Fountain on the center green. The fountain, of Greek Doric design, put on a colorful water show later in the evening.

When I return to the National House Inn, I'll do what many B&B guests do—have the fun of selecting a different room. There's the Anne J. Ellis Suite done up in blue and white with sheer curtains at the window and an old printer's bench at the side of the bed. Often requested, the country-style H. C. Brooks Room has flowered wallpaper with a white iron queen bed, fireplace, and claw-foot tub overlooking the courtyard gardens.

Breakfast at the inn is taken in a cheerful setting with candlelight, wooden shutters, and shelves displaying a collection of antique china and glassware. Tables for two or four are centered with flowering plants, and each is set with a different china pattern. Choose from a buffet of fruit, juices, the National House strata, and freshly baked goodies like jam tart cake or apple tart prepared by the inn baker, Dorothy Collins (Barb's mom).

Browse a while in the adjacent Tin Whistle Gift Shoppe, filled with

country items, Victorian reproductions, and small antiques, or spend some time in the courtyard gardens.

Barbara has created some tempting specials, such as a package that pairs a tea, a night's lodging, and breakfast with cooking lessons at a popular downtown bistro, Malia's. Another regular event is a package that includes dinner for two at Schuler's Restaurant, lodging, breakfast, and a tour of the Honolulu House across the center green from the inn. February brings the Candle Light Tour weekend with a stay from Friday evening to Sunday noon. Guests are treated to a fireside cocktail party with entertainment, a gourmet dinner by candlelight, and a chance to tour three historic area homes.

The National House Inn has been a member of Select Registry Distinguished Inns of North America since 1978 and is also a member of Thinkabout Inns.

THINGS TO DO:

The National House Inn is situated in Marshall's National Historic Landmark District, which offers an amazing 850 structures and 45 historical markers. History and architecture buffs can have a field day exploring this neighborhood, which represents one of the finest cross-sections of authentic 19th-century architecture in the United States. Ask a staff member for a walking or driving guide to the district. One of the most remarkable structures is the Honolulu House, built in 1860 for Judge Abner Pratt. The tropical design is a surprising architectural style for a Michigan city. The house boasts nine bay porches, a raised veranda, and an observation platform. Pratt served as U.S. Consul to the Sandwich (Hawaiian) Islands and upon his return to Michigan built the Honolulu House to resemble the executive mansion he had loved in the islands.

You need only one thin dime to feed the parking meter in downtown Marshall, home to a mix of boutiques, antique stores, florists, and eateries lined up along Michigan Avenue. Stop at Malia's, an Italian eatery, for fine continental fare at lunchtime or dinner where a blackboard lists new daily specials along with creative pasta and seafood offerings. Another favorite of locals and visitors to the city is Schuler's, a restaurant founded in Marshall 93 years ago. You may feel you've stepped into an old English inn when you enter the half-timbered Centennial Room with colorful murals of historic Marshall buildings ringing the walls and famous sayings inscribed on the beams. Prime rib is a longtime menu favorite along with regional specialties like Grand Traverse Bay chicken and Great Lakes whitefish. All breads, crackers, and desserts are made fresh daily in house. Old World apple strudel, Michigan cherry crisp, and malt ice cream top the dessert list.

Head up to Marshall the first weekend after Labor Day for the granddaddy of historic home tours in the Midwest. October brings the Marshall Scarecrow Festival, when scarecrows appear all over town. Festivities include a costume parade and a grand harvest celebration. Marshall bills itself as Michigan's "Christmas City," with an annual parade and an open house in the business district. The G.A.R. Hall and the U.S. Postal Museum are worth a stop, and devotees of prestidigitation will find the world's largest collection of magic memorabilia at the American Museum of Magic.

DIRECTIONS: I-95 to Exit 110 for SR 27 South; left on Michigan Ave.; on corner of Michigan and Parkview

NEARBY ATTRACTIONS:

CASTLES AND VILLAGES

Have you ever stayed at a castle? Why not pretend to be a "royal" for a night or a weekend and book a stay at an Ohio castle built as an inn. You'll find Ravenwood Castle, a romantic medieval castle designed in the 12th-century Norman style in Ohio's Hocking Hills. Stay in a room or suite in the castle or book one of the sweet pastel-hued houses in the medieval village of Bryn Raven on the property. Other lodging options are quaint European-styled Gypsy Wagons or the Celtic Legend Cottages. Dine in the castle's Great Hall and find a menu featuring Old English fare.

Entrance to Landoll's Mohican Castle near Loudonville is via a winding road on the 1,110-acre estate. Along the way, catch glimpses through the trees of the towers and turrets of this fanciful castle with Renaissance influences. Take your choice of a suite or a VIP cottage and walk down the hill for a fine dining experience at the on-site restaurant, Legends at the Castle. Explore the estate's 30 miles of trails that wind through the forest and come back to the luxury of your suite.

A third option for a castle stay is the GreatStone Castle in Sidney, Ohio. Built by a Sidney business leader, this massive home with 18-inch-thick walls, turrets, and porte cochere is typical of the castle-like style of home favored by prosperous Americans in the late 1800s.

In contrast to the castle inns reviewed in this chapter, I included three inns in historic villages in Ohio. First stop was the Roscoe Village Inn, a canal-era inn in Coshocton with its guest rooms done up in simple Shaker style. The inn restaurant, King Charley's, offers a choice of dining in a colonial-style dining room or a casual bar. Take a self-guided tour of the Living History buildings of this restored 19th-century canal town or hop on the horse-drawn canal boat for a trip through a portion of the Ohio and Erie Canal.

I traveled next to Zoar, a village settled in 1817 by German Separatists. Plan to stay at the Zoar Tavern & Inn with a choice of rooms in the historic inn or luxurious suites in the Zoar Tavern Guest House. Settle down for dinner in the cozy tavern and next morning take a walking tour of Zoar, with stops at the German-style houses and shops.

My final stay was at the Sauder Heritage Inn in Archbold. Opened in 1994, this newer inn welcomes with an oak-framed lobby and extra spacious rooms. Walk to the Barn Restaurant for lunch or dinner, then take a self-guided tour of the 37 buildings in Sauder Village and find costumed interpreters along the way.

Inn at Roscoe Village

A country inn in a restored 19th-century canal town

The Inn at Roscoe Village borrows its architectural style from the canal-era structures lining Whitewoman Street. In this village of Greek Revival buildings, with brick walkways edged by ivy and pocket gardens, the inn harmonizes with its surroundings. Enter the lobby and you get a sense of an earlier time. It's a cozy setting with a fireplace flanked by loveseat, sofa, and chairs, accented with baskets, wreaths, and selected antiques on the mantle.

Shaker style and a subdued color scheme of blues, cream, green and touches of red are used in the 51 guest rooms. It's simple and charming, with Shaker pegs on the walls, folk art, and watercolors of Roscoe Village scenes. Recent additions include four-poster king beds in 13 rooms and a new suite with a king-size Murphy bed. Once the Murphy bed is tucked away, this large space can function as a meeting room with a compact food preparation area and an adjoining king guest room. The inn has two wheelchair-accessible rooms: one with two queen beds and one with a king bed.

A traditional full-service country inn, the Inn at Roscoe Village is

Coshocton, OH
200 N. Whitewoman St.
800-237-7397
740-622-9310
www.roscoevillage.com

RATES & RESERVATIONS:
Hours: 24 hours/day
Season: Year round
Rates: $65–$90
Specials: Children, seniors, AAA
Reservations recommended
Check, Visa, MC, Disc, Amex, Diners Club accepted

ACCOMMODATIONS: 51 rooms w/ bath; 1 suite with bath

AMENITIES: Cable TV, phone in room, Internet, air cond., hair dryers, irons & boards, in-room coffeemakers

MEALS: Breakfast, lunch, dinner; Beer, wine, liquor served

OTHER:
Parking: Lot

popular with both leisure travelers and conference planners. Meeting space easily adapts to family reunions or company retreats. Groups can select the Canal Level Room, with maps of the Ohio and Erie Canal system covering the walls, or the Parlor, with wooden peg tables, wing-back chairs, a fireplace, and a grand piano. Another option is the James Calder Room.

Renovation is an ongoing process. If you've stayed at the inn in the past, you'll recall King Charley's Tavern, a casual dining spot with en-tertainment on the weekends, and the more formal Centennial Room. Now combined, the new inn restaurant is simply called King Charley's. Located on the second floor, the restaurant's bar area has paddle fans, a green-tiled bar, booths along two walls, and a good-sized captain's table. The traditional portion of the room features fireside dining by candlelight. The lunch menu continues to offer inn classics like the Gabby Crabby and King Charley's burger, along with salads, Reubens, and subs. There's a continental flair to the dinner menu, with lamb, veal, and beef entrees. Favorites on the dessert menu include chocolate spoon cake and crème brûlée. Inn guests find a full breakfast buffet with omelet bar, fresh fruit, breads, juices, hot cereal, and Belgian waffles.

Come to the inn in February for the "Straight from the Heart" pack-age and you'll find chocolates, champagne, and a single rose in your room. Dinner and breakfast for two along with a gift certificate for the Shops of Roscoe Village are part of the package. From Memorial Day through Labor Day, bring the family for the AAA Family Fun package with overnight lodging, breakfast, and tickets for the aquatic fun center. Explore the village with the kids and then cool off in the waterpark.

THINGS TO DO:

Historic Roscoe Village has been named by *Midwest Living* as one of the Midwest's best historic vacation sites. Pick up your ticket at the Roscoe Village Visitor Center for a tour through this restored 19th-century canal town. During June, July, and August, self-guided tours take you into the Living History buildings. Learn about daily life in the 1800s as you chat with one of the crafters or artisans at work—the broom squire, cooper, weavers, and blacksmith. As you make your way through the village, a cast of first-person interpreters help tell the story. At other times of the year, call to arrange a guided tour. The kids will love the 45-minute narrated trip through a restored section of the Ohio & Erie Canal on an authentic horse-drawn canal boat, the *Monticello III.*

The nationally recognized gardens at Roscoe Village are a highlight for many visitors. Ivy-covered stone walls, ground covers, and planted pots complement the Greek Revival buildings. Gardeners look forward to the "garden strolls" offered by the landscape staff from March through November.

You can feather your nest with a few hours' shopping in the village. Royce Craft Baskets carries maple baskets handwoven in Coshocton. The Village Soap & Candle Shop is filled with locally made crafts, Yankee Candles, and Crabtree & Evelyn products. The tin ceiling and fixtures in the Roscoe General Store reflect the selection of old-time items available there. Behind the general store, woodcarver Sam Chow can be found in his little shop, the Sandpiper, where he carves feathered friends. For home decor and Cat's Meow pieces, the Canal Company

is the place. Stop at the John Dredge Bookstore to browse the selection of children's, local history, gardening, and culinary books. Wildwood Music, located next to the Roscoe Village Visitor Center in the lockkeeper's house, carries more than 500 new handcrafted acoustic string instruments.

Each year in May, sweet sounds fill the air when the village hosts the Mid-Eastern Regional Dulcimer Championships at the Coshocton Lake Park Pavilion. June brings the Annual Heritage Craft & Olde Time Music Festival, when folks come to watch traditional craft demonstrations, browse the Coshocton Art Guild Show and Sale, and take part in old-time music workshops. Military battles and drills take center stage during the Civil War Reenactment in July, and the commemoration of the landing of the first canal boat, the *Monticello*, is marked with the annual Coshocton Canal Festival in August. Come to Roscoe Village the first three weekends of December for the traditional Christmas candlelighting ceremony. It's a Christmas-card scene brought to life, with lights in every window, a 35-foot Christmas tree, strolling carolers, carriage rides, and cookies and hot mulled cider.

DIRECTIONS: I-77 to Exit 65 for US 36; west on US 36 to Coshocton

NEARBY ATTRACTIONS: Lake Park Campground and Aquatic Center, Amish country, golf, horseback riding, bike trails, wineries

Landoll's Mohican Castle

A fanciful castle in Ohio's Mohican region

Jim Landoll started building Landoll's Mohican Castle in 1996, but the idea for this American castle with Renaissance flourishes came much earlier in his life. During military service in Germany in 1963-65, Jim traveled extensively in Europe and picked up ideas for the mélange of towers, balconies, peaks, dormers, and turrets he built in Ohio's Mohican region. An environmentalist, Jim and his crew gathered cherry, walnut, red oak, and hickory from windblown storms on the property for the floors, beams, and moldings of the castle suites. Stones cleared from fields or used for fences by early settlers were utilized in the castle's construction, keeping a stonemason busy for six years on the grounds. Ornamental chimneys from 17th-century European buildings add a whimsical touch to the castle roofline.

Loudonville, OH
561 Twp. Rd. 3352
800-291-5001
419-994-3427
www.landollsmohicancastle.com

RATES & RESERVATIONS:
Hours: 24 hours/day
Season: Year round
Rates: $125 +; Specials: Children, seniors, singles, AAA, groups
Reservations recommended; Visa, MC, Disc, Amex accepted

ACCOMMODATIONS: 15 suites w/bath

AMENITIES: Hot tub, sauna, spa, cable TV, pool, phone in room, Internet, air cond., game rooms, fitness center, massage center

MEALS: Breakfast, lunch, dinner, brunch, snacks; Beer, wine, liquor served

OTHER: Parking: Lot

Entrance to Landoll's Mohican Castle takes visitors through the forested estate via a winding road. Along the way, catch glimpses of charming buildings such as the on-site restaurant, Legends at the Castle. At the crest of the hill, you come upon the castle proper with its peaked roofs and trademark Landoll dormer windows. It's truly an inn for all seasons. Arrive in spring for a show of 100,000 daffodils and in summer for flower gardens and lush ferns. Come back in the fall when the woodlands are ablaze with color and during the holidays when a million sparkling lights outline the castle.

Look forward to a luxurious stay in one of the 11 suites bearing family names. You'll find fresh flowers, overstuffed sofas and chairs, Oriental rugs on hardwood floors, gas fireplaces, bathrooms with imported Italian tile floors that warm up with the flick of a switch, a Jacuzzi, and glass-enclosed showers. Guests say that the beds, covered with sumptuous linens and comforters, give them the best night's sleep they've had in a long time. Attention to detail—from the hand-applied faux finish on walls and ceilings to the Gothic-style doorways—contributes to the feeling of living in a grand style, if only for a weekend. Once they arrive, some guests don't want to leave their posh sanctuary and order their meals from the castle restaurant. Amenities include satellite television, a fully equipped kitchen and dining area, and computer access in each suite. DVD movies are available at the front desk.

The design studio from Pine Tree Barn in Wooster provided the interior design for the suites, which are done in classic and timeless style. The rich, deep colors—gold, navy, green, and burgundy—complement the royal architecture. Settle in the Lawrence Suite, a two-room chamber finished in rich cherry with a two-sided fireplace, and you'll have a view of the woodlands garden. Make your way to the Landoll Suite via a spiral staircase to a rounded tower at the top of the castle and find yourself more than 50 feet from the ground with a grand view of the peaks and valleys that make up the castle roofline. This multilevel accommo-

dation with pitched ceilings that repeat the castle's architectural style has a private balcony. You'll get a child's-eye view from little windows as you ascend the stairway to the Miller Suite. There's an attic feel to this suite, with dormer windows looking out to the estate's woodlands. Interior details include upholstered cornices and window treatments. An antiqued leather chair and ottoman, along with a queen sofa bed in the sitting room, invite relaxation. The ground-level Hess Suite is perfect for guests who require wheelchair access.

In addition to the suites, two VIP cottage suites offer a two-floor, two-bedroom, two-bath plan. Upper and lower decks, an efficient kitchen, queen beds, a double Jacuzzi, and a sofa bed make this a comfortable accommodation for families. Children under 14 stay at no additional cost. Weekends at the castle must be booked at least three months in advance. There is no minimum stay requirement.

One of the joys of a full-service inn is that you don't have to leave the place to enjoy fine dining. Legends at the Castle, located down the hill from the castle, serves lunch and dinner as well as providing room service. A wall of windows in the main dining room looks out to the castle grounds. A larger dining room with tapestries and murals is the setting for special events and the Sunday brunch. The smell of woodsmoke from the native stone fireplace that centers the main dining room and music from the Renaissance set the scene for leisurely dining. The chefs use herbs and produce from the Landoll estate greenhouse and blueberries from their own Blueberry Hill. Try the organic blueberry vinaigrette on the spinach salad, and don't miss the signature dessert, blueberry piefin, a blending of a variety of blueberries topped

with a sweet, crispy streusel. A pastry chef bakes eight varieties of bread daily in the restaurant's wood-fired baking ovens. If you find a favorite, you can pick up a loaf from the gift shop located on the other side of the fireplace in the restaurant. Note the trees left undisturbed on the decks of the restaurant. Jim Landoll, always the environmentalist, insisted the decks be built around the trees.

THINGS TO DO:

Jim and Marta Landoll love the solitude and beauty of their 1,100-acre estate and decided to share this magnificent spot near Mohican State Park with others. Guests find 30 miles of trails to hike or explore by mountain bike or golf cart. The trails wind through virgin forest, and along the way you find boulders from the Ice Age, a pioneer cemetery, deer, wild turkeys, and box turtles. Reserve ahead for a picnic lunch to take along on your exploration of the estate grounds.

You don't have to forgo your usual exercise regimen while a guest at the castle. Head up to the indoor pool and fitness center, located just above the castle. It's a tropical setting with a cascading waterfall and mist-shrouded small cave in the pool. In addition, you'll find a hot tub, sauna, and tanning bed. A spacious billiard room completes the facility.

DIRECTIONS: I-71 South to Exit 165 for Butler-Bellville SR 97 to SR 3; straight across SR 3 to Twp. Rd. 629; left on Twp. Rd. 3352

NEARBY ATTRACTIONS: Malabar Farm, Mohican State Park, Amish country

Zoar Tavern & Inn

*Historic lodgings in a village
founded by the Separatists*

A group of German Separatists who came to Ohio in 1817 and settled this village. The tavern building originally a home and office for the village doctor, and later served as an early tavern, followed by a series of eateries. It became the Zoar Tavern in 1984. In 1990 the owners purchased the Homestead Restaurant next door and joined the two buildings to provide banquet rooms and additional kitchens. The rooms above the restaurant had served as an apartment and were converted into five guest rooms. In the renovation process, original stone and brick were discovered hidden beneath the plaster walls. It was a labor-intensive project as workers scraped away the mud, horsehair, and straw that had been used for insulation in the original building. Beautiful hand-hewn beams remained and were given a dark stain. Saved artifacts include a framed Zoar wedding cloth displayed in the hallway at the base of the stairs to the inn rooms.

Zoar, OH
162 Main St.
888-874-2170
330-874-2170
www.zoar-tavern-inn.com

RATES & RESERVATIONS:
Hours: 8 a.m.–10 p.m.
Season: Year round
Rates: $90–$125
Reservations recommended
Check, Visa, MC, Disc, Amex accepted

ACCOMMODATIONS: 9 rooms w/ bath; 3 suites w/bath

AMENITIES: Hot tub, cable TV, phone in room, Internet, air cond., fireplaces, Jacuzzi suites, massage therapist on staff

MEALS: Breakfast, lunch, dinner, snacks; Beer, wine, liquor served

OTHER:
Not fully wheelchair accessible
Parking: Lot

You can take your choice of a room in the inn proper or in the Zoar Tavern Guest House. History aficionados will appreciate the inn's five compact guest rooms furnished with Ohio antiques. There's an authentic feel to the rooms, accented by a collection of early kitchen tinware, pottery, and various implements used by the Zoarites. Rope beds have been converted to standard double beds. Ask for a room with the exposed brick and stone walls from the original structure. I stayed in the largest room, with space for two antique bedsteads and a small table and chairs. A welcoming bowl of fruit centered the table and crisp white curtains top the dark-stained wood shutters. Antique pieces include a tall oak wardrobe and samples of the tinware collection. Around the corner, a common room is stocked with coffee, tea, hot chocolate, and a small refrigerator. A genuine European breakfast consisting of assorted cheeses, meats, a basket of breads, granola, yogurt, juices, coffee, and table settings for two is brought to the room.

Take a short stroll behind the inn past the Zoar Post Office to find the Zoar Tavern Guest House. It's a romantic and quiet getaway with four spacious suites and a common room. All the rooms have a gas fireplace, king pillow-top beds, color television, and Internet access. There's a pleasing mixture of antiques and reproduction pieces like the cherry Shaker-style beds set under bay windows in the two Jacuzzi suites. The two standard suites, with furnishings in oak, offer an extra-large shower for two.

It's a true tavern-like atmosphere at the Zoar Tavern, with a solid oak bar, early advertising signs on the walls, red-and-cream checked curtains, and cushions on the wood booths that line one wall and the rustic benches that hug the opposite wall. Tables augment the overflow crowds I found at lunchtime on a perfect fall day. Folks come back to the tavern for steaks served with Davey's sauce, German favorites like chicken schnitzel and Holsteiner (veal) schnitzel with sides of sau-

teed spaetzles and cabbage, and the local bratwurst, char-grilled and topped with sauerkraut. Lighter fare at lunch includes a Georgia peanut chicken salad of romaine hearts tossed with peanut-encrusted chicken, roasted peanuts, grapes, and goat cheese.

There's a tempting array of desserts, including chocolate silk pie, but don't miss the trademark Zoar gingerbread. It's a toothsome plate of slices of rich dark gingerbread topped with a special amber sauce and vanilla ice cream.

The Zoar Tavern offers special menus throughout the year, like the Cajun food you'll find two weeks preceding Ash Wednesday. But the real showstoppers are two November events—the Beaujolais Nouveau dinner, celebrating the first wine crush, and the Alsatian wine dinner. In February, the Alsatian Winter Night celebration is a welcome break in the dark, cold month of February. It's a grand seven-course meal with accompanying wines for each course, along with beautiful table settings and food presentation. Holidays bring special menus for banquets and parties.

THINGS TO DO:

Many visitors come to Zoar to explore the 10 restored houses owned by the Ohio Historical Society. Buy a ticket at the Zoar Store and take a walking tour of the village, with stops at the German-style structures furnished with items made and used by the Separatists. You'll find costumed guides in some of the buildings. Stop at the Garden House between Main and Park Streets and ask about the significance of the giant Norway spruce surrounded by 12 junipers in the large community garden.

August brings the Zoar Harvest Celebration to the village, with a juried folk art show, antiques sale, music, and entertainment. There's open-fire cooking, apple-butter stirring, and a beer tent featuring local microbrewers for the Apfelfest in October. In late October, take a Lantern Tour of the Ghosts of Zoar. It's a haunted stroll through the village by candlelight with guides sharing tales of Zoar's resident spirits. The year closes with Christmas in Zoar, a German-style holiday celebration.

Hikers find the Ohio & Erie Canal Towpath a short walk from the inn. The inn's staff are happy to arrange tee times for golfers at three nearby courses.

DIRECTIONS: I-77 to Exit 93; follow SR 212 East to Zoar; on right

NEARBY ATTRACTIONS: Zoar Village State Memorial, Ft. Laurens, Ohio & Erie Canal, golfing

Sauder Heritage Inn

Stay in a living history village

Archbold, OH
22611 SR 2
800-590-9755
419-445-6408
www.saudervillage.org

RATES & RESERVATIONS:
Hours: 24 hours/day
Season: Year round
Rates: $90–$125
Specials: Seniors, AAA
Reservations recommended
Check, Visa, MC, Disc, Amex accepted

ACCOMMODATIONS: 31 rooms w/ bath; 4 suites w/bath

AMENITIES: Cable TV, phone in room, air cond., room fridges, exercise room, game room, lobby w/fireplace

MEALS: Breakfast, lunch, dinner (at adjacent Barn Restaurant on property)

OTHER:
Parking: Lot

The four-mile drive from Exit 25 on the Ohio Turnpike to Sauder Village takes you past solid farmhouses and barns that anchor this fertile farmland. It's an unwavering canvas of field and sky that stretches ahead until Sauder Village appears on the horizon. Early cabins and shops circle the central village green. Larger buildings house a welcome center, restaurant, and exhibition hall. Sauder Heritage Inn, a two-story gray frame hostelry, is situated at the edge of this rural village.

Erie Sauder had a vision of creating a living history village so that future generations could learn about this area of northwest Ohio known as the Great Black Swamp. When Amish and Mennonite groups came to the region in 1834, these tenacious settlers tamed the forbidding environment of dense forests and swampland by cutting back the forest and digging drainage ditches. Today's rich farmland is the result. To tell their story and that of the Indians who preceded them and the European settlers who arrived later, Erie bought property north of Archbold and set about amassing cabins, tools, and farm implements. Sauder Village welcomed its first guests in June 1976.

To accommodate visitors to the village, the Sauder Heritage Inn was built in 1994. The inn's oak-framed lobby reaches up two stories, resulting in a pleasing convergence of arches and crisscrossed beams. Hand-forged lamps and ironwork railings created by former Sauder Village ironsmith Mike Bendele contrast with the wood. Green plants and groupings of comfortable overstuffed chairs warm this vast lobby space. On cool evenings, a wood fire burns in the lobby's brick fireplace. Colorful quilts and two skylit atriums with live plants, trees, and small goldfish ponds brighten inner hallway areas. The inn has two wheelchair-accessible rooms, with an exercise room, guest laundry, and game room on the lower level.

The Sauder Heritage Inn's 35 rooms and suites are larger than most found in country inns. Each oversize room has either two queen beds or one king, a reclining chair, refrigerator, and small dining table and chairs. Twenty-seven rooms look out to the surrounding countryside or a view of the courtyard. The largest, the Founders Suite, comprises a living room, full kitchen, bedroom, and lovely rattan-furnished sunroom. Come down to the lobby in the morning for an expanded continental breakfast. The breads, donuts, bagels, and rolls are made from scratch in the village bakery, the Doughbox, known for its "Bellystickers," a local specialty. The serve-yourself coffee bar is open 24 hours.

Erie Sauder was a collector and proponent of the adaptive reuse of materials. The Barn Restaurant was built from timbers salvaged from a barn built in 1861 on a nearby farm. Enjoy family-style dining in the restaurant's cozy dining room with wagon-wheel lights and waitresses in long gingham dresses topped by aprons. Order from the menu or line up for the hearty buffets served daily at noon and in the evening. It's a child-friendly environment with children charged per year for the buffet or family-style dinners. In a hurry? Visit the Village Cafe, with soup, salads, sandwiches, and homemade pie served cafeteria style.

THINGS TO DO:

"Visitors to historic Sauder Village can enjoy a leisurely visit at their own pace," says Kim Krieger, spokesperson for the village. "It's not a guided tour, so visitors are free to enjoy the historic homes and shops, and to take time to talk to the craftsmen they meet." This living history museum recreates daily life in the Great Black Swamp in 1803-1920. As you make your way through the village's 37 buildings, you might happen upon a craft demonstration, a hymn sing, or be invited to take part in a spelling bee. Stop to watch the full-time historical farmer work with a team of horses, or interact with costumed interpreters in the "Natives & Newcomers" addition to the village which honors the Native Americans and Europeans who lived together in the Black Swamp. Small heirloom gardens with plants and vegetables specific to the period are found near each historic house.

Sauder Village appeals to all ages. Intergenerational groups of grandparents, parents, and children find plenty to do. The youngest visitors have a new place all their own that asks them to "Please Touch." It's the Little Pioneer Homestead, with Mary Ann's Cabin and Miller Barn scaled to their size. Preschoolers find child-size furniture, pretend food, dishes, and a fireplace in the cabin. Out in the barn, they can milk a full-size fiberglass cow.

Special events draw visitors to Sauder Village throughout the year. The Annual Quilt Fair in April brings quilters for a six-day show with demonstrations and workshops. The exhibition space, Founders Hall, is hung with more than 400 quilts. The Traditional Rug Hookers Exhibition in August is considered one of the country's best such exhibits. Rug hookers come from 10 states to display their work.

Each season brings a chance to spend time down on the farm. In May, come to see the baby animals or help plant a garden. In July, take a look at early 20th-century farmlife and make ice cream or wash clothes on a scrub board. Music is part of the celebration, with fiddlers gathering for a youth fiddle competition. The Woodcarvers' Show and Sale is a two-day event in October. Master carvers present demonstrations, vendors offer carving supplies, and you can get in some early Christmas shopping.

Shop year-round at Sauder Village. Lauber's General Store stocks old-fashioned wares like penny candy, marbles, paper dolls, kazoos, enamelware, harmonicas, and McGuffey Readers. Quilters stop at the Threads of Tradition shop for quilting supplies. Volunteer quilters demonstrate hand quilting in the shop from May to October.

DIRECTIONS: I-80/90 to Exit 25 for SR 66; south on SR 66; left on SR 2

NEARBY ATTRACTIONS: Historic Sauder Village

GreatStone Castle

*A castle-like mansion
more than 100 years old*

The GreatStone Castle, a limestone mansion built by Sidney businessman William Henry Collier Goode in 1892-95, is typical of the architecture of the time, with three turrets lending it a castle-like appearance. Walls that measure 18 inches thick, a porte cochere to protect guests alighting from their carriages, and a wraparound porch with an arched window and short columns are other regal characteristics. Set on two acres of lawn with gardens and 100-year-old oaks, the home is listed on the National Register of Historic Places as the Whitby Mansion, after the ancestral home of the Goode family in Whitby, England. Frances Goode, Goode's daughter from his first marriage, lived in the mansion until her death in 1973. Fourth owners Frederick and Victoria Keller purchased the property in 1994.

The castle entry through front doors with original stained-glass windows takes you into the

Sidney, OH
429 N. Ohio Ave.
937-498-4728
www.greatstonecastle.com

RATES & RESERVATIONS:
Hours: Mon–Sat 9 a.m.–9 p.m., Sun noon–9 p.m.
Season: Year round
Rates: $90–$125
Specials: AAA, weekday business travel specials
Reservations required
Check, Visa, MC, Amex accepted

ACCOMMODATIONS: 2 rooms, 1 with bath; 2 suites w/bath

AMENITIES: Hot tub, spa, cable TV, Internet, air cond., three in-room fireplaces

MEALS: Breakfast, snacks

OTHER:
Dog living on premises
Not fully wheelchair accessible
Parking: Lot

vestibule and on through a second set of doors to the reception hall. Throughout the mansion you'll find exquisite woods like the red African mahogany in this large reception area, highlighted by gold lincresta wallcovering and parquet floors. Straight ahead at the end of the hall is the spectacular dining room. A 10-foot built-in oak breakfront with leaded glass and beveled mirrors dominates one wall. The original dining table and 13 chairs with red velvet upholstery, willed by Goode to stay with the house, center the room under a crystal chandelier. A marble fireplace with oak surround is one of 10 working fireplaces in the mansion. Also emanating from the reception hall is the grand ballroom—with carved white mahogany woodwork, a tapestry original to the home, and portraits of the Goode family—used for wedding receptions, dinners, and parties. Across the hall, the parlor provides a quieter space for entertaining.

In a private home with vast spaces, I appreciate finding a more intimate room like the GreatStone Castle's library. Padded window seats and built-in benches in inglenook style by the corner fireplace make it a cozy place to read or chat. The Kellers have filled the library's maple glass-fronted bookcases with Mr. Goode's business records and family memorabilia. The atrium conservatory is another charming smaller room where inn guests gather for breakfast. It's one of the turret rooms, and a round table and cushioned window seat neatly fit the space. Start the day in this sunny, plant-filled room with a house favorite—caramelized cream-cheese French toast or a strata served with a tray of fresh-cut fruit, nut breads, and cinnamon coffeecake.

The GreatStone Castle is a popular setting for Victorian weddings, the sweeping stairway providing the perfect grand entrance for brides. Wedding photographers often utilize the trio of stained-glass windows on the stairway landing as a backdrop for keepsake photos. The Kellers open their home in late November for the Shelby County Historical

Society's Victorian Celebration. Victoria Keller delights in decorating the mansion in Gilded Age style for this holiday event. Guests come to tour the beautifully decorated rooms, dine in the ballroom, and enjoy seasonal music after dinner.

Goode used more exotic woods in the four bed-and-breakfast rooms on the inn's second floor. I stayed in the Goode's guest room, finished in bird's-eye maple woodwork with furnishings in the same honey-hued wood. Curly birch, also known as tiger wood, was used in the master bedroom. Both of these rooms have generous-size bathrooms and gas fireplaces, and showcase some of the Kellers' antique collection. With five children in the family, a governess was part of the Goode household. Her room across from the nursery has a Victorian bedstead, a leather wing chair, an in-room sink, and an adjoining bath with a claw-foot tub. The fourth smaller bedroom is often used by families when they book one of the larger guest rooms.

Stay at the GreatStone Castle and you can indulge in spa treatments on the mansion's lower level in what was once the servants' quarters. The Kellers transformed this area into the GreatStone Castle Spa. The brick arched entry hallway to the treatment rooms has a Tuscan feel, with insets for flower arrangements, heated tile floors, and translucent handblown lights from France. Certified aestheticians offer a wide range of treatments. Popular services include relaxation massage with aromatherapy, a peppermint sea twist wrap, and a European seaweed facial. Bridal parties enjoy special wedding packages for pre-wedding pampering.

The Kellers offer an alternative accommodation to GreatStone Castle: Canal Lake Lodge, the historic site of the Monarch Rod & Gun Club. Perfect for business meetings, retreats, parties, receptions, and weddings, the lodge offers a casual getaway in a stone and log building overlooking the lake. Leisure activities include boating, fishing, hiking, shuffleboard, horseshoes, and trapshooting.

THINGS TO DO:

The Sidney County Courthouse anchors the square, which has been designated a National Registered Historic District. Two other outstanding buildings are the People's Federal Savings and Loan, designed by renowned architect Louis Sullivan in 1927, and the Monumental Building honoring the county's Civil War dead. Fort Loramie State Park offers a 1,700-acre lake with boating and a swimming area. Summer events include the Country Concert at Hickory Hill Lakes in July and the Shelby County Fair in August.

With prior arrangements, you can dine at the GreatStone Castle. One couple came back to celebrate their wedding anniversary with a private fireside dinner. The Spot, a downtown Sidney tradition, is the kind of dining experience many remember fondly. The jukebox is free and folks line up at the counter to order hamburgers, malts, and home-made pie, or order from their cars behind the restaurant. For a unique dining experience, it's worth the drive to the Inn at Versailles. The interior decor is French country to match the town's heritage; the menu, home-cooked regional fare along with specialties like the inn's French onion soup, chicken Aluette, and choucroute.

DIRECTIONS: I-75 to Exit 92 for SR 47; continue through 6 lights; left on West Ave. for 3-1/2 blocks to back of inn for parking.

NEARBY ATTRACTIONS: Dayton Air & Space Museum, Neil Armstrong Space Museum, antiques

Ravenwood Castle

Escape to a romantic realm

New Plymouth, OH
65666 Bethel Rd.
800-477-1541
740-596-2606
www.ravenwoodcastle.com

RATES & RESERVATIONS:
Hours: 24 hours/day
Season: Year round
Rates: $125 +
Specials: Seniors, seasonal discounts
Minimum stay 2 nights on weekends
Reservations recommended
Check, Visa, MC, Disc accepted

ACCOMMODATIONS: 6 rooms w/ bath; 2 suites w/bath; 7 cottages

AMENITIES: Air cond., Jacuzzis, kitchenettes

MEALS: Breakfast, lunch, dinner, snacks; Beer, wine served

OTHER:
Dog, cat living on premises (outdoors)
Parking: Lot

My directions for visiting Ravenwood Castle included turning off Route 93 onto Bethel Road. Within a short distance, I came upon a small sign directing me to turn onto a winding gravel road through heavy forest that culminated in a clearing. Here I came upon Ravenwood Castle. English ivy creeps up the walls and flags line the parapet of this romantic medieval castle designed in 12th-century Norman style. After entering via a drawbridge ramp, I rang the bell to be admitted into the Gothic-inspired entrance hall.

Ravenwood Castle, built by Sue and Jim Maxwell, was first opened to guests in 1995. The Maxwells' inspiration came from frequent trips to Britain. Details like the single beds of medieval box-style design are evidence of their careful research. Interior wood shutters are pulled back to allow light but can be closed for complete privacy. Castle rooms boast gas fireplaces with antique mantles, whirlpool or garden tubs, and usually a balcony or deck. The Henry VIII Suite, located in one of the castle's lower corners, accommodates up to six guests with a king bed on the first floor and an an-

tique English double bed plus two singles on the upper level. Guests who must avoid stairs can book the first-floor Duke & Duchess Room, which offers two queen beds and an oversize bath with garden tub and shower. Of course, there's a Rapunzel's Tower in this castle. Rapunzel invites you into her aerie, furnished with a queen four-poster canopy bed with floral comforter.

"We ask our guests to leave the modern world behind for a day or a few," says Sue Maxwell. "Ravenwood Castle is the place to come to find peace, quiet, and romance. It becomes an oasis of relaxation and provides a setting that helps recharge your life." There are no phones or TVs to disturb the castle environment. Not even my cell phone allowed outside communication, but there is the assurance of a guest phone in the castle hallway.

Ravenwood's gardens help warm the castle grounds. Three kinds of climbing plants—trumpet vine, English ivy, and Virginia creeper—are beginning to cover the castle walls. In the early spring the drawbridge is flanked by the blue flowers of ajuga. Between the castle and the Coach House, a gate opens to the courtyard garden with herbs and edible flowers for the kitchen. Behind the castle, the boxwood parterre, watched over by a statue of Pan, was developed by a student intern from an English horticulture college.

Wildflower and perennial gardens border the path through the medieval village of Bryn Raven, where six pastel-hued old-world cottages blend into the landscape. Along the way, you come upon the fairy garden—planted, Sue says, with lilies and small flowers to attract elves and fairies. When I came upon a costumed storyteller and an attentive group of young children seated on benches, I truly began to believe in the magic of this setting.

The pink Silversmith's House with towers and turrets is the largest and sleeps six. Stay in the king bedroom with a red-heart whirlpool tub in the tower bath. Decorative accents in the Merchant's Cottage include English brass, chintz, and china, and the interior of the Old World Clock Tower features leaded and stained glass.

While the eight castle rooms generally are reserved for couples, Ravenwood is a family-friendly place. The innkeepers have developed a special package, "Royal Family Summer Adventure," good on two-night stays Monday through Thursday nights in June, July, and August. Families can opt to lodge in the Gypsy Wagons, a kind of 19th-century camper. The highly decorated wagons, in combinations of yellow, green, and pink, nestle under trees across from the castle front. Think camping style for these cottages on wheels and bring along the ice chest. Two queen-size air mattresses are provided, and you join other guests for breakfast at the castle.

Another option for families or couples is the Celtic Legends Cottages. The six cottages, discovered by the Maxwells at the Mount of Praise Campground near Circleville, were destined for bulldozing. They moved the buildings to a meadow at Ravenwood, undertook extensive renovations, and themed the interiors to aspects of Celtic life.

Guests gather for breakfast and dinner in the Great Hall, a 50-foot-long room with a wall of stained-glass windows anchored by a massive limestone fireplace. The Great Hall glows with candlelight for the 7:00 p.m. dinner, which often features Old English fare. Breakfast is buffet-

style, and on my summer visit a bountiful spread of melons, a hot entree, homemade granola, chocolate chip/pumpkin muffins, and juices was set out on the sideboard. Stop for lunch or tea a few steps from the castle at the Coach House Tea Room, reminiscent of a cozy English tearoom with pale green walls highlighted with white latticework and tables covered with flowered cloths. The cream tea is generous enough to serve two. A popular lunch item is the Ploughmans' Lunch, with homemade bread, cheese, salad, and chutney.

Romantics find Ravenwood to be just the place for a private wedding in the woodsy pavilion or the grander Great Hall. The September Gold package offers seniors a special rate, and anniversary celebrants find a midweek stay a good buy year-round. For a winter getaway, book the "Fuzzy Slippers" weekend. No need to dress up. Bring your fuzzy slippers and enjoy a casual soup supper by the fire. Ravenwood also offers a Fly-Drive special. Land at the Vinton County Airport and the castle shuttle will pick you up for lunch or an overnight stay.

THINGS TO DO:

There's a full schedule of events at Ravenwood, including the Annual Medieval Faire, Holiday Madrigals, and Murder Mystery Weekends. Lake Hope State Park, Ohio's first state park, is nearby and the Hocking Hills area beckons with hiking, bird-watching, rappelling, and rock climbing.

DIRECTIONS: I-71 South to I-70 East to SR 33; south on SR 93

NEARBY ATTRACTIONS: Hocking Hills and Lake Hope State Parks, scenic railway, antiquing

SPA STAYS

The European tradition of spas as part of an inn accommodation is gaining popularity in the United States. We come to these centers of tranquility because we're stressed or seeking an alternative approach to preventative medicine. Today's spas are as much about wellness as they are about pampering. Guests arrive from their busy everyday lives seeking rejuvenation and renewal. Awakening to a day of spa treatments in a serene environment becomes an important component of a spa getaway.

In my search for spa/inns, I discovered an infinite variety of settings. Come to stay at Glenroth in western New York and you can pretend you're at a European country house on the inn's 104 acres of meadows and woodland. Settle into the Buhl Mansion in Sharon, Pennsylvania, and take pleasure in the art collection in this beautifully restored historic home. You'll find a peaceful Zen-like atmosphere at the spa at Nemacolin Woodlands Resort in Farmington, Pennsylvania, along with a choice of sumptuous accommodations. Take a trip to Niagara-on-the-Lake in the heart of Niagara's wine country and stay at the Pillar and Post where the treatment rooms are themed to exotic places. I found a rustic setting at Heartwood Place in Adrian, Michigan, a new home built specifically as a spa inn, set on 10 acres of woodland. Close to home, there's a hidden gem in Aurora at the Spa Sanctuary at Mario's in an 1800s renovated barn located across the highway from the main spa. Spa cuisine is offered at all six of the inns for breakfast, luncheon, and healthy breaks. Some have on-site dining or recommend nearby restaurants for evening meals.

The menu of spa services at these inns offers as much variety as the settings. Get ready to be massaged, scrubbed, wrapped, toned, and oiled in quiet surroundings with flickering candles, the scent of aromatherapy, the calming sounds of water. Take a yoga class. Check out color therapy or sample sound and scent therapy. Have a Reiki treatment or take time for a fitness assessment. Pamper yourself with a pedicure and get a new hairstyle. And after reaching a desired state of well-being, explore the unique environment of your inn, walk the grounds, shop the boutiques, golf or cross-country ski depending on the season, or retreat to the quiet of your room at the inn.

Check out special spa packages for couples, girls' getaways, anniversaries, or design one of your own. To keep on schedule during your stay, remember to get to your spa appointments 15 minutes before the scheduled time.

Spa Hotel at Mario's
International Spas, Hotels, and Inn

An internationally recognized spa in a historic hostelry

Aurora, OH
35 E. Garfield Rd.
800-444-6121
330-562-9171
www.marios-spa.com

RATES & RESERVATIONS:
Hours: 24 hours/day
Season: Year round
Rates: $90–$125
Specials: AAA, Monthly Spa & Inn specials; Reservations recommended
Check, Visa, MC, Disc, Amex, Diners Club accepted

ACCOMMODATIONS:
14 rooms w/bath; 1 suite w/bath

AMENITIES: Hot tub, sauna, spa, cable TV, pool, phone in room, Internet, air cond., indoor and outdoor pools, tennis courts, several restaurants

MEALS: Breakfast, lunch, dinner, brunch, snacks; Beer, wine, liquor served

OTHER: Parking: Lot

Mario and Joanne Liuzzo love century buildings and antiques. When the Luizzos were looking for a site for a European-style spa, they found an old stagecoach stop from the 1840s known as the Grey Hotel at the intersection of Routes 82 and 306 in Aurora. After a two-year renovation, the facility was opened in 1979 as the Aurora House Spa. To answer increased requests for overnight stays, the Liuzzos purchased another century home adjacent to the spa property. A four-bedroom guesthouse became the first accommodation for spa visitors. Today's guests find a 14-room spa hotel, part of a hotel complex totalling 84 rooms at the Aurora location.

There's an old-world ambience at Mario's International Spa and Hotel, with art and antiques in the hallways and guest rooms. A range of guests—groups of women on spa getaways, midweek business travelers, and couples seeking a romantic weekend stay—find rooms with one king or two queen beds. All rooms feature down comforters, feather pillows, and Italian-tile baths with enclosed whirlpool tubs. A third-floor suite includes a fireplace. Selected antiques and a different color palette make each room unique.

Along with antique furnishings, the Liuzzos blended architectural artifacts into the hotel interior, including the beautiful reception desk in the foyer. This area connects to a comfortably furnished lobby that in turn takes you into the Cabin Restaurant, which offers another interesting bit of Western Reserve history. Originally a sugarhouse, the Cabin's stone fireplace remains in use and heavy beams reinforce the structure's rustic style. To authenticate the Cabin's history, check the black-and-white photograph of the original sugarhouse on the wall. The ceiling was raised to cathedral heights, a bar added, and more dining space provided during the renovation process. Spa guests in robes and slippers find a connecting hallway from the spa to the dining room where they can dine in privacy. The menu features fine continental cuisine with Northern Italian influences. Homemade bread served with olive oil and Parmesan cheese accompanies soups and salads. Wood-fired pizza and pastas star on the menu. Favorite main courses include beef tenderloin topped with lobster claws, along with fresh tomatoes over roasted potatoes and braised Swiss chard. A woodfire-roasted swordfish entree is served over artichoke hearts, asparagus, marinated tomatoes, and fennel in a seeded mustard vinaigrette. Pastries, sorbets, and gelatos are made in house.

Mario's International Spa has been nationally and regionally recognized by *Condé Nast Traveler, Allure, Self, Cleveland Magazine, Pittsburgh Magazine, Midwest Travel,* and *Cleveland & Akron Family*

Health as "Best Spa." Choose from among 125 treatments and services, including three specialized therapies: microdermabrasion to exfoliate the skin, Endermologie to fight cellulite, and Panthermal, a European treatment to de-stress and detoxify. The spa menu offers scrubs, masks, wraps, foot and hand therapies, hair styling, and makeup application.

The best-kept secret at Mario's Aurora location is the Spa Sanctuary. Tucked behind the Realty One office in a white colonial-style building on Route 306, across from the main spa, the Sanctuary offers a holistic environment. It's a quiet setting from the moment you open the door. Touted as "An Oasis for the Mind, Body, and Spirit," the Sanctuary is situated in another of the Luizzos' finds, an 1800s barn on the property. The barn's heavy doors remain, along with feeding troughs now fitted with zinc sinks. In the Yoga Room on the main floor, whitewashed walls and fireplace contrast with rough-finished barn doors and beams. This is the place for hatha yoga sessions and guided or self-guided meditation. A low table is set for a healthy spa lunch, which may be onion soup, whole-wheat bread, and asparagus salad one day, and hot Korean vegetables, urud dal, and rice the next. Take the stairs to the spacious Environmental Loft, the setting for private massage therapies, complete with fireplace, bubbling fountains, candlelight, the distant sound of chimes, and the scent of aromatherapy. Indulge in raindrop therapy, ayurvedic therapy, or the Shiro Dhara, a mystical "third eye" treatment with a pressure-point massage finished with warmed oils released to the ajua marma point on the forehead.

A visit to the Sanctuary can be tailored to your needs. Like many who come to the spa, I arrived with my usual "to do" list and a busy

agenda for the rest of the day. Dressed in robe and slippers, I started my visit in the Yoga Room seated by the fire on a blustery winter day. A blanket was placed on my knees and a cup of tea offered based on the Dosha Charting questionnaire I had completed on arrival. The combination of warm fire, tea, and quiet space brought total relaxation. I moved next to the Environmental Loft for LaStone therapy. Following a massage with alternating hot basalt stones and cold marble stones, I was offered a tray of fresh fruit, muffins, and tea or spa elixir. Some guests opt to begin or end their treatment sessions with yoga or the steam shanti, a detoxifying warm steam bath.

The Spa Sanctuary is a popular destination for couples. Privacy is ensured and couples can enjoy side-by-side massages. Packages include the Serenity Stay, with one overnight in the hotel, a three-course dinner, full breakfast, and a schedule of steam shanti, personal fireside meditation, and a relaxation massage, champagne, wine, tea, or elixir tonic. Come for a daylong Spa Sanctuary Experience and partake of a steam shanti and shower, personal meditation, basalt stone thermal massage, reflexology, and a health lunch.

THINGS TO DO:

Aurora Premium Outlets are a five-minute drive from the inn. Nearby specialty shops include Three Elysabethe's with a stock of gifts, fine linens from France and Italy, furniture, and art; Amanda's Loft, a children's boutique; Chet Edwards with general home furnishings; and Antiques of Aurora.

DIRECTIONS: I-77 South to 480 East to 422 East for SR 306 exit; right (south) on SR 306; left (east) on E. Garfield St.; on left

NEARBY ATTRACTIONS: Geauga Lake, Aurora Premium Outlets, antique shops

Nemacolin Woodlands Resort & Spa

Rejuvenate your body and spirit

Farmington, PA
1001 LaFayette Dr.
800-422-2736
724-329-8555
www.nemacolin.com

RATES & RESERVATIONS:
Hours: 24 hours/day
Season: Year round
Rates: $125 +
Specials: Children, seniors, AAA, packages and special offers
Minimum stay on weekends in summer
Reservations recommended
Check, Visa, MC, Disc, Amex, Diners Club accepted

ACCOMMODATIONS: 335 rooms w/bath

AMENITIES: Spa, cable TV, pool, phone in room, Internet, air cond.

MEALS: Breakfast, lunch, dinner, brunch, snacks; Beer, wine, liquor served

OTHER:
Horses at equestrian center
Not fully wheelchair accessible
Parking: Lot (fee)

At the Nemacolin Woodlands Resort in the Laurel Highlands Mountains of western Pennsylvania, the Woodlands Spa offers a stunning architectural presence. Designed by world-renowned designer Clodagh and constructed of natural materials found on the resort property, the spa is situated across from the French Renaissance-style Chateau LaFayette. Entrance to the spa via a wooden bridge takes you over a reflecting pool bordered by rocks and trees. You soon become aware of the elements of Feng Shui (balancing the harmony between heaven and earth; connecting the body, spirit, and soul) incorporated into the spa environment. Open the wide doors and the senses are alerted by the sound of cascading water, the scent of aromatherapy, the placement of flickering candles, the touch of trained therapists. The Woodlands Spa has garnered its share of honors, including a listing among the Top 10 Spas in the United States by *Travel & Leisure* and being named by *Elle* magazine as one of the Top 20 Spa Getaways.

A staff of 120 at this European spa offer massage treatments, body scrubs, hydrotherapy, body rituals, facials, and body kurs (treatments based on the use of thermal mineral water, algae, mud, essential oils, and herbs). Experience the Woodlands Hot Stone Shirodhara, a combination of hot stone massage, ayurveda, and Reiki, and emerge from the treatment in a tranquil state. For deep relaxation, try the Ayurvedic Rebalancer, which utilizes specific Indian oils and herbs to bring mind, body, and spirit back to balance and create a deep sense of well-being. After your treatments, settle down in the relaxation lounge, a calming space with spare, clean lines and a massive copper-hooded fireplace. Sit awhile, sip a cold drink, and reflect on your day at the spa. A full-service salon offers hair design, as well as Woodlands signature stone manicures and pedicures. Stop at the Spa Boutique to pick up spa treatment products, gifts, and swim and fitness apparel.

A fitness assessment at the Woodlands Spa is an invitation to get in touch with your body. A take-home fitness program based on your interests, fitness level, and lifestyle is prescribed for you by a fitness specialist. Spa packages include the Laurel Dreams, with a choice of a personalized facial or hot stove Swedish massage, reflexology, spa lunch, and gift. Weekend packages require a two-night minimum stay.

Plan to have tea in the Chateau LaFayette's Tea Lounge, a sunny room reminiscent of a conservatory with French-inspired furnishings and touches of yellow contrasting with green plants. Two-story Palladian windows look out to the formal Lafayette Gardens. Enjoy a pot of tea served with a tray of tea sandwiches and freshly baked scones with Devonshire cream and strawberry preserves. Tea is served daily from

3:00 to 5:00 p.m. against a background of classical music played by the resident pianist.

Look forward to gourmet spa cuisine in the Seasons Restaurant, which maintains the Zen-like atmosphere of the spa with the use of wood and stone in the dining room. A sushi bar faces the open kitchen, and Stefan Pegani's dazzling chandelier—Falling Leaves—centers the space, which at certain times during the day sends reflected sunlight throughout the room. The top of the menu suggests selecting portions for the Hunter, the Gatherer, or the Vegetarian appetites. Dinner might include starters of miso soup, followed by Cantonese duck in rice paper, an entree of seared salmon with soft millet polenta, or Coleman beef and wild boar medallions and conclude with a Seasons dessert like scarlet orange flan or crispy chocolate hazelnut Napoleon. There's a wide choice of dining venues at Nemacolin Woodlands Resort, ranging from the formal Lautrec, a French bistro featuring lighter French cuisine, to family-friendly spots like the Caddy Shack. For those hungering for steak and seafood, the Golden Trout is the place.

Book a room at the classic Chateau LaFayette and find an elegantly appointed room with vaulted ceilings, traditional furnishings, and a marble bath. The English Tudor-style Lodge, the original accommodation at the resort, features oversize rooms done up in English country cottage style. Popular with families, couples, and groups of women who come to Nemacolin for a girls-only outing, the Links Townhouses with one or two bedrooms, a full kitchen, dining area, and living room provide space to spread out. In this secluded setting, a patio balcony looks out onto the golf course. Or choose to stay at one of the private luxury

homes—the Cottage at Grouse Glen, the funky modern Graceland, or Walden Pond, set in a wooded hollow overlooking a pond. A shuttle service is available to whisk you to any of the resort facilities.

THINGS TO DO:

If you're spending a few days or a week at Nemacolin Woodlands Resort, you can stay busy without ever leaving the premises. Take a leisurely tour of the Hardy Family Art Collection located in the Chateau LaFayette on your own or join the guided tour offered every day at 3 p.m. This multimillion-dollar collection is the personal property of Nemacolin Woodlands' owners Joseph A. Hardy, Sr. and his daughter Maggie Hardy Magerko. Art is also showcased outdoors, as I discovered when I came upon contemporary sculpture during a drive through the grounds.

Love to shop? Take a stroll along the Heritage Court Shoppes, a street of retail shops with storefronts replicating landmark buildings along Route 40, the "Nemacolin Trail" from Cumberland, Maryland, to Scenery Hill, Pennsylvania. Settle down on a bench next to a seated bronze sculpture of Mark Twain and watch the sculptures of General George Washington and Delaware Indian Chief Nemacolin come to life.

There is a Toy Store at Nemacolin, but don't expect to find a present for a young child. Featuring a collection of antique and rare automobiles, it's a store for the big boys who love cars. In a hangar just off the resort's airstrip, you'll find Steve McQueen's pride and joy, a 1931 Pitcairn PA-8. Other amenities include the Equestrian Center, offering one-hour trail rides and two PGA-rated championship golf courses.

For a half-day trip, visit Frank Lloyd Wright's Fallingwater, designed for the Edgar J. Kaufmann family in 1935, and the smaller, charming Kentuck Knob. Both are within a 12-mile drive of the resort.

DIRECTIONS: I-80 to I-76 to Exit 8 for SR 119 South; SR 199 through Connelsville to SR 40 East; on left

NEARBY ATTRACTIONS: Fallingwater, Kentuck Knob, golf, skiing, shopping

Buhl Mansion Guesthouse and Spa

Escape to a mansion with a world-class spa

The history of Buhl Mansion is a rich and colorful one. Frank H. Buhl built this castle-like mansion of native ashlar sandstone in the Sharon Hills for his wife, Julia, in 1890. A grand home in the Richardson Romanesque style, with arches, columns, finials, and turrets, the Buhl Mansion was a showplace in the Shenango Valley. Like many houses from the Victorian era, when it was no longer a private family residence the mansion was used at various times as a French restaurant, a beauty school, and apartments. Ultimately, the property was condemned and became one of those VOV properties—vacant, open, and vandalized. A vagrant moved in, causing irreversible damage to the main floor. That's when Jim and Donna Winner stepped in to bring this fine old home back to its original glory.

Sharon, PA
422 E. State St.
800-782-2803
724-346-3046
www.buhlmansion.com

RATES & RESERVATIONS:
Hours: 24 hours/day
Season: Year round
Rates: $125 +
Reservations required
Check, Visa, MC, Disc, Amex accepted

ACCOMMODATIONS: 10 rooms w/bath

AMENITIES: Hot tub, Sauna, Spa, Cable TV, Pool, Phone in room, Air Cond., Fireplaces

MEALS: Breakfast, afternoon tea; Beer, wine, liquor served

OTHER:
Not fully wheelchair accessible
Parking: Lot

Today this magnificent mansion's elegantly appointed rooms showcase the Winner Art Collection of statuary and oil reproductions, including works by Monet, Manet, Renoir, and Van Gogh. Pick up a guide at the front desk to help identify the works throughout the mansion and coach house. One of two bed and breakfasts in the United States to receive the coveted AAA Five Diamond Award, the Buhl Mansion is a member of Select Registry Distinguished Inns of North America and is listed on the National Register of Historic Places.

The motto inscribed on the mantle of the fireplace in Frank Buhl's library—"Good Friends, Good Food, Good Cheer"—reflects Frank and Julia Buhl's hospitable nature. When the mansion was completed, the Buhls threw a party for 100 with an orchestra and a catered meal. Throughout their lives, the Buhls generously contributed to the Sharon community, establishing a hospital, the F. H. Buhl Club, the Julia A. Buhl Girls Club, and the F. H. Buhl Farm, which today is Buhl Park.

The coffered ceilings in the library and the dining room as well as the walnut window frames in the music room survived the damage that befell the first floor. On the second floor the beautiful original woodwork remains intact. A stained-glass window on the landing of the grand oak staircase replaces an original Tiffany window. Take the steps to the third floor and you find a hand-painted mural with cherubs, swans, and formal garden scenes.

Look forward to being spoiled when you come to Buhl Mansion. Afternoon tea is served daily in the music room, and on weekends an informal reception gives guests a chance to chat with the staff and check out area activities. Chocolates are left at bedside and linens freshened at evening turndown service. Upon arrival, guests find in their rooms a welcome tray of fresh fruit, cheese, and a bottle of champagne. All the guest rooms feature gas fireplaces, Jacuzzis for two, separate showers, Egyptian linens, down featherbeds, and TVs in both guest room and bathroom.

It can be a dilemma to decide which of the 10 rooms at the Buhl Mansion to reserve. There's the Grand Turret for starters. Once part of the 1940s ballroom, the turret comfortably houses a round Jacuzzi for two. A focal point of the bedroom is a king-size replica of a bed from the Hearst Castle. The original hardwood floors are covered with Oriental carpets. In contrast, the Artist Loft has a lighter feel, with pickled oak floors, wall coverings with imprints of Michelangelo's famous "Creation of Adam," and a king-size copper and iron bed. I found Mr. and Mrs. Buhl's rooms of interest. Her namesake room is light and airy in blues and yellows with French furniture, a sparkling chandelier, and wallpaper with flowers and cherubs. His room is definitely a masculine retreat with greens and browns dominating, a cooper-like ceiling, a desk, and dark woodwork. For a room with a view, book the Steel Magnate, a stunning room in neoclassical style that overlooks the gardens, greenhouse, and waterfall.

During a stay at the Buhl Mansion, treat yourself to breakfast in bed. Guests find a room-service breakfast menu to slip under their door with gourmet choices of traditional eggs Benedict, seared strip steak served with eggs and hash browns, buttermilk pancakes, or the house specialty, plantation eggs. You can opt to dine in the cheery breakfast room with windows that open onto a view of gardens, pond, and a Victorian greenhouse. It's a gracious dining experience with white linen, silver, and impeccable service. Samples from the Winner Art Collection—familiar Degas and Monet reproductions—grace the walls.

At the Buhl Mansion Spa, a world-class facility with six treatment rooms on the mansion's lower level, you're invited to indulge your

senses, relax your mind, and revive your body and soul. It's a calming environment with a color scheme of cream, white, and peach. A corner fountain, artwork, and a large room with fireplace invite relaxation between treatments. Revive in the monsoon shower with 13 showerheads or step into the steam room or sauna, amenities that are also available to houseguests. Have a facial in the turret room or select from the menu of massage therapy and hydrotherapy. Two popular therapies are the hot basal lava stone massage, combining massage with deep heat therapy, and the moor mud wrap for rejuvenating tired muscles, followed by a Vichy shower.

Allow four hours for the Mansion Magnifique Package of aromatherapy massage, anti-aging facial, your choice from the bath menu, and a spa cuisine lunch, or treat yourself to the Trumpeter Swan Package with manicure, pedicure, neck, back, and shoulder massage, and a spa cuisine lunch.

THINGS TO DO:

Arrive early enough to take the tour offered hourly to gain an overview of the guest rooms, sample the art collection, and learn a little of the Buhl Mansion's history. On weekends, a limo will take you to the Winners' other property, Tara, to dine in Ashley's Gourmet Dining Room or Stonewall's Tavern.

Shops just steps from Buhl Mansion include the Flamingo Rose Tea Room & Gift Shop and Daffin's Candy. The Winner, touted as the world's largest off-price fashion store, and Reyer's Shoe Store are in downtown Sharon.

DIRECTIONS: I-80 to Exit 4B; north on SR 18; west on Business 62; on left.

NEARBY ATTRACTIONS: Tara—A Country Inn, The Winner department store, Daffin's Candy

Glenroth Inn & Well Being Center

Relax in a country manor house

Westfield, NY
6534 S. Portage Rd.
888-523-5885
716 326-6462
www.glenroth.com

Picture a European country house set on 104 acres of meadows and forest. You could be in Austria or the South of France but this sanctuary, Glenroth, is in western New York. Both an inn and a center for well-being, Glenroth was created by Kathleen Bittner Roth and her husband, Dr. Hans Roth. The inn's name comes from a combination of the glen you pass as you enter the property and the owner's last name.

Kathleen Bittner Roth, an internationally known leader in the human potential movement, has appeared on over 850 radio and television shows nationwide. An intuitive consultant, Kathleen had a dream more than a dozen years ago of creating a well-being center where she could offer classes, seminars, and retreats to help others gain a better understanding of their lives. She thought of it as an environment where guests could relax in the comfort of a country manor house. At the time, she lived in Texas and never thought of finding the right location in western New York. Both Kathleen and Hans wanted a four-season climate

RATES & RESERVATIONS:
Hours: Daily checkout 11 a.m., check in 2 p.m.; reservations taken 8 a.m.–9 p.m.
Season: Year round
Rates: $90–$125
Specials: Children, seniors, singles, extended stay
Reservations recommended
Check, VS, MC accepted

ACCOMMODATIONS: 4 rooms w/ bath; 1 suite w/bath

AMENITIES: Cable TV, air cond., spa services

MEALS: Breakfast (full), lunch, dinner, snacks

OTHER:
3 dogs, pair of black swans living on premises
Not fully wheelchair accessible
Parking: Private lot

and while visiting a friend in New York they discovered a property bordering Little Chautauqua Gorge. The Roths say they literally found their dream place. They transformed an Alpine ski lodge already on site into their country house. At Glenroth, you can ski the groomed woodland trails in winter and in warmer weather hike the graded footpaths. Glenroth is just three miles from Chautauqua Lake and Lake Erie and within easy driving distance from Buffalo, Cleveland, and Pittsburgh.

As a guest in late June, I discovered Glenroth offers spectacular views. I awoke to the morning calls of birds and looked out in one direction to Lake Erie, in another to the hills of western New York, and in a third to the pond. A gentle breeze moved a hammock, and benches near the pond offered a promise of a quiet spot to sit later in the day. Flower gardens border the house and the well-kept lawns extend to the woodland.

The Roths have furnished their home with an eclectic collection of antiques from Europe and Asia. Two five-foot hand-carved Buddhas look down on the great room from a ledge. In this room with 20-foot ceilings, tapestries and Persian rugs in deep shades of burgundy and gold warm the vast space. Soft luxurious suede and leather chairs and sofas form conversation groupings and antique chandeliers from Austria add a touch of European elegance in the great room and over the dining table. There's a glamorous bathroom on the main floor with handblown crystal sconces from the Czech Republic flanking an over-sized gilt mirror. Hans Roth is Baron of Burrane, Germany, and you first spot his coat of arms over the red entry doorway to the house and again over the fireplace in the great room.

I stayed in the Crown Room, part of a larger suite. Sunny yellows and golds dominate the room and a fabric treatment over the bed supports a gold crown. A highly detailed Chinese armoire conceals a TV and a good selection of reading material. The Roths have carefully organized the guest room space to adapt to groups who come for seminars or to leisure travelers looking for a country inn stay. Book the Crown Room and you have use of the bedroom, a private bath, and the adjoining sitting room with woodstove, wet bar, and walls of windows to those fantastic views. If a group of four reserves the suite, the loft above this room offers two additional single beds. The Venetian Room with a king bed and a day bed sleeps three. The Country French Suite is made up of a small sitting room and a bedroom with a rustic feel. Angel art and sculpture, gifts from Kathleen's students and guests, adorn the suite which opens to a private patio. When groups come for seminars, they find the best value by staying in the dorm rooms that sleep eight.

Meals at Glenroth feature fresh foods and no preservatives in the Taoist tradition, resulting in 80 percent alkaline and 20 percent acid. Breakfast is served in the formal dining room or in warm weather on the deck. I started the morning with fresh whole-grain bread, natural preserves, yogurt, juice, and soft-boiled eggs. Lunch is buffet style and the menu typically includes a rice salad, salmon mousse, and green salads with homemade dressings. Dinner might be eggplant lasagna, salad, and vegetables in season.

Some of the seminars and classes offered at Glenroth include first-level and advanced Reiki classes, an all-day seminar on Sound and Scent Therapy, Creating Sacred Spaces, and the Making of a Mandala.

A popular fall retreat, A Map of the Soul, brings guests to Glenroth during New York's beautiful fall foliage season. Those who have experienced Kathleen Bittner Roth's classes say they will make the pilgrimage to Glenroth again.

Massage therapy, Reiki treatments, and private consultations are available by appointment. Treatment rooms are on the lower level of the home and in a red cottage by the pond. Step into the cottage and you're transported to Morocco with a tented ceiling, Moroccan hanging lamps, and cobalt blue walls accented with fabrics of fuschia and gold.

During your stay, you're sure to meet the friendly pair of Hamish McDuff, a West Highland White Terrier, and Bear, a Great Pyrenees. Bear guards the grounds and Hamish McDuff keeps him company on his rounds.

THINGS TO DO:

There's a fine collection of regional art at the nearby Portage Hill Gallery housed in a 1830s Greek Revival home on Route 394. A few miles from Glenroth, you'll find the Wool Works, showcasing textile products from all over the world made with the finest natural fibers. Follow the Chautauqua-Lake Erie Wine Trail along the southern shore of Lake Erie with stops to tour the vineyards and taste the wines. In season, visit the world-famous Chautauqua Institution. Antiquers will want to explore the shops in Westfield. For gourmet dining, make a reservation at the nearby William Seward Inn.

DIRECTIONS: I-90 East to Exit 60 for Westfield to 394 East (S. Portage Rd.); through Westfield to top of hill; on left

NEARBY ATTRACTIONS: Chautauqua Institution, Lake Chautauqua, Lily Dale, Panama Rocks, Lake Erie, Rails to Trails, wine trail, antiquing, boating, fishing, horseback riding, Amish country

Heart Wood Place

A spa sanctuary in the woods

Adrian, MI
3723 Wisner Hwy.
888-200-5126
517-265-3550
www.heartwoodplace.com

RATES & RESERVATIONS:
Hours: 7 a.m.–11 p.m.
Season: Year round
Rates: $75–$115
Minimum stay 2 nights on race weekends
Reservations recommended
Check, Visa, MC, Disc accepted

ACCOMMODATIONS: 4 rooms w/bath

AMENITIES: Hot tub, Internet, air Cond.

MEALS: Breakfast, lunch, snacks

OTHER:
Not fully wheelchair accessible
Parking: Lot

Set in 10 wooded acres near Adrian, Michigan, Heart Wood Place combines a bed-and-breakfast stay with holistic spa treatments. This wellness center offers peace and serenity in a smoke-free, alcohol-free, pet-free environment.

The approach to the bed and breakfast via a gravel road takes you past a pond with a resident family of ducks. Owner Mary Alice Thompson, a licensed practical nurse and massage therapist, planned the large gray house with burgundy shutters to incorporate areas for spa services along with guest rooms. The plan works. You can come for a day or two of spa treatments and stay in one of the comfortable guest rooms upstairs. Family antiques, historic documents, and photos are worked into rooms aptly named Peace, Harmony, Serenity, and Tranquility. Each has a view of the woods or pond. Quilts in tulip, star, and autumn leaf patterns cover the antique wood and brass bedsteads. On the main level, guests relax in the living room with a gas fireplace, games, books, and puzzles.

A long porch fronts the house and offers a place to sit and commune with nature. Gardens border the porch and it was here I came upon the first angel, carved from a tree trunk by a woodcarver who was a guest at the inn. There seems to be an angelic presence in Heart Wood: A mural with smiling cherubs graces the wall on the stairway to the lower level, and I continued to find angels randomly placed throughout the interior. A wood deck circles the back of the house and is a favorite spot for bird-watchers. Walkers find some paths cut through the woods or can follow the gravel road to the farm. With prior arrangement, Mary Alice's husband, Ray, will take guests on a horse-drawn ride in his vis-à-vis carriage. Ask Ray if you can take a peek at his classic 1958 crystal blue Corvette lovingly stored in the garage.

The holistic concept of balancing body, mind, and spirit guides the wide range of services available at Heart Wood Place. Prevention and wellness are the key for the staff of massage therapists, a certified healing touch practitioner, and cosmetologists. A typical day at the spa includes steam tube with aromatherapy, herbal facial massage, herbal body wrap, full body therapeutic massage, vegetarian lunch, hot-tub time, and hair styling or paraffin dipping. Additional options include Reiki and healing touch sessions. The main floor houses two massage rooms along with a hot-tub room with one-way windows that provide a view of the natural landscape. On the lower level, three more treatment rooms await. Solace is a wet room for herbal wraps, moor mud wraps, seaweed wraps, exfoliation treatments, and herbal facial massage. Fulfillment, the aromatherapy room, combines essential oils with steam for relaxing therapy.

A favorite of many women who come to Heart Wood Place is the Reflection Room, where a framed print says it best: "Sometimes Heaven is just a hot bath." For all those moms who can never find time for a bath without interruptions, this room—tiled in pink and beige with an extra-large tub set on a dais surrounded by pink candles—is the

answer. The staff prepares the tub with appropriate oils and salts or a bubble bath if you prefer. The lower level permits wheelchair access.

A spa lunch might include homemade vegetable soup, spinach salad, a meatless sandwich, and one of Mary Alice's special desserts—miniature cream puffs with hot fudge sauce or fruit pie. Breakfast is served in the dining room, where a ruby-red glass chandelier hangs above the dining set that belonged to Mary Alice's grandparents. On my November visit, we enjoyed an egg/cheese dish, tasty meatless sausage, date-bran muffin, baked apple, and gourmet coffee. A serve-yourself buffet is set up with herbal teas, hot water, and baked items for anytime snacks.

This place inspired one guest to write a poem in the guestbook and another to leave a suggestion to future guests to be sure to try the herbal wrap. Romantic stays include anniversary and birthday celebrations. Women have discovered Heart Wood Place and come for mother/daughter reunions, group getaways, and a scrapbookers' workshop. There's meeting space for off-site training sessions and seminars.

THINGS TO DO:

There's live theater in Adrian at the historic Croswell Opera House with an interior of beautifully restored Italian plasterwork. Early performers who graced the opera-house stage, the oldest continuously operating theater in Michigan, include Tom Thumb and John Philip Sousa, and lecturers Ralph Waldo Emerson and Susan B. Anthony. Today's patrons find nine shows a year and can enjoy the theater's art gallery upon arrival or during intermission.

Adrian is home to Adrian College, which offers a series of performances by the Adrian Symphony Orchestra. I stopped to tour Siena Heights University and found nature paths and a labyrinth.

You'll find Zelda's Tip Top Cafe, with its dineresque interior, a great place for lunch. I wasn't surprised to learn that owner Ami Jo Walters was an English major before her culinary career and named her eclectic cafe after Zelda Fitzgerald. In nearby Tecumseh, chocoholics line up for treats at the Chocolate Vault, an old-fashioned ice cream parlor and candy store located in a restored 1849 bank.

DIRECTIONS: I-90 West to US 23 to US 223; right on Main St.; left on Bent Oak Hwy.; left on Hunt Rd.; right on Wisner Hwy.; on right

NEARBY ATTRACTIONS: Croswell Opera House, Adrian College, Siena Heights University, Hidden Lake Gardens

Pillar and Post

A country inn in the heart of Niagara's wine and fruit region

Settle down in the Cannery, an on-site restaurant at the Pillar and Post, a country inn in Niagara-on-the-Lake, Ontario, and you get a sense of the inn's history. Heavy beams and posts remain from the inn's beginnings in the late 1890s as a canning factory. The exposed brick walls showcase gleaming copper kettles and artifacts like a crusher from the days when peaches and tomatoes were canned in this space known as "Factory 13." After 60 years as a cannery, the factory closed in 1957 and a basket manufacturer took over the site, followed by a few years as a restaurant and craft center. In 1972, the first guest rooms were built and the building was officially renamed the Pillar and Post Inn.

Arrive at the Pillar and Post on an autumn day and you're greeted by masses of flowers from the entrance into the expansive lobby, where chrysanthemums in yellows and golds bank the stairway to the restaurant. Straight ahead in the skylit lobby, more flowering and green plants are interspersed with comfy groupings of sofas and chairs by the fireplace. Afternoon tea is served in the sunroom, which is also a good spot to linger over coffee and the morning paper.

No two rooms are alike at this traditional country inn. Look for-

Niagara-on-the-Lake, Canada
48 John St.
888-669-5566
905-468-1362
www.vintageinns.com

RATES & RESERVATIONS:
Hours: 3 p.m. check in; 11 a.m. check out
Season: Year round
Rates: $125 +
Specials: AAA
Reservations required
Visa, MC, Disc, Amex accepted

ACCOMMODATIONS: 123 rooms w/bath; 8 suites w/bath

AMENITIES: Hot tub, sauna, spa, cable TV, pool, phone in room, Internet, air cond., WiFi Internet access in public areas

MEALS: Breakfast, lunch, dinner, brunch; Beer, wine, liquor served

OTHER:
Parking: Lot

ward to elegant appointments in the 123 rooms—plush duvets, rich antiques, luxurious fabrics, deluxe whirlpool baths. In my king premium room, shades of pink, rose, and green predominated in the four-poster canopy, comforter, and window treatments. A deep rose chaise longue to the side of the bed and a grouping of sofa, wing chair, and easy chair flanking the dark wood fireplace invite relaxing. I found a beautiful hand-painted wash basin in the oversize bath and the expected amenities of a four-diamond/five-star accommodation like plush robes, an illuminated makeup mirror, and fine toiletries. As a member of the Vintage Inn Group, known for hospitality, turndown service includes a card with the temperature for the next day and a rose on the pillow.

Enter the 100 Fountain Spa, and you're in another world. A swimming pool is set amidst lush tropical foliage contrasting with the traditional brick walls and rattan seating along the pool's perimeter. The 12 treatment rooms take you to exotic destinations around the world. Step into the wood-paneled room from Sweden and you feel you're in a sauna. Japanese screens highlight the Japan room, a calming space for a massage. A trompe l'oeil mural sets the scene for the treatment room from France, and you'll find Egyptian art and charts in the Egypt room used for reflexology.

Select from a repertoire of European spa treatments at the 100 Fountain Spa to find balance in body, mind, and spirit. Start with the GM Collin collagen facial. After cleansing and exfoliation, a pure collagen mask is applied which, according to a group of women on a spa getaway, brings instant results. Another innovative treatment is the LaStone Sole Connection, which utilizes hot basalt and marble stones during the 75-minute treatment. Submit to Cleopatra's Delight and relax with gently applied oils and warm moist towels while undergoing the healing touch of reflexology, or treat yourself to the Ultimate Body Rejuvenator, an all-encompassing body treatment that includes exfoliation, algae wrap body mask, and oil application. Check out the spa's midweek special offers.

For a light lunch or tea, head down to the lower-level lounge. Multiple rows of lion-head fountains along the wall lend the calming sound of flowing water to the space. Glass doors lead to the popular year-round outdoor hot spring pool with cascading waterfall.

The Pillar and Post Inn, Spa and Conference Center has received the CAA/AAA Four Diamond Award for both accommodations and dining. The inn was designated a Five Star Resort by Canada Select. Sample superb theater with the Shaw Festival Theatre package, which includes two tickets for the Shaw, breakfast, lunch, and dinner, or treat your love to the Romance package with a dozen roses, a bottle of local sparkling wine, and a horse-drawn carriage tour through Niagara-on-the-Lake. Come to the Pillar and Post during the holidays and enjoy festive meals offered for Christmas Eve, Christmas Day, and New Year's Eve.

Enjoy fireside dining at the Pillar and Post. The comfortably casual Cannery and the elegant Carriages dining rooms offer a contemporary menu featuring the freshest of regional products. The evening I dined in the Cannery, main course choices included prime rib with Yorkshire pudding, pine nut-crusted lamb rack with roasted potato and feta salad, and penne with caramelized mushrooms and European bacon

in a bourbon tomato cream sauce. A sumptuous breakfast buffet awaits overnight guests.

The charm and warmth of this country inn extends to conference and reception rooms. For private dinners or small weddings, the Olde Library is the perfect setting with rich wood paneling, bookcases, and a wood-burning fireplace. A larger open-concept room, the Gallery, provides space for meetings and workshops. Business travelers find a state-of-the-art fitness center and a business center open round the clock.

THINGS TO DO:

The Shaw Festival brings theatergoers to Niagara-on-the-Lake for a season of plays that run from early April through November. There is also superb shopping on Queen Street, a short five-minute walk from the Pillar and Post. Spend some time at the cozy Old Niagara Bookshop, check out festival merchandise at the Shaw Festival Shops, browse the Angie Strauss Art Gallery for prints, paintings, and cards, or pick up some of Greaves famous jams and marmalades.

Plan to have lunch or dinner at one of the nearby wineries. I stopped at Terroir La Cachette located within Strewn Winery. Featuring French Provençal cuisine using the best local ingredients and an all-Ontario wine list, meals are served on the patio or in the dining room with a view of the Niagara countryside.

DIRECTIONS: I-90 to Lewiston/Queenston Bridge to Niagara River Pkwy. (becomes Main St.); left on King St.; right on John St.; entrance on right.

NEARBY ATTRACTIONS: Fort George, golf, wineries

AMISH STAYS

What is it that draws us to Amish country? The beauty of the hilly backroads where you might come upon an Amish farmer and a team of Percherons or Belgians pulling a plow to turn over the dark earth on a spring day? Amish schoolchildren engaged in a ballgame on the grounds of a small Amish school, or perhaps a procession of black buggies on the way to a funeral? The excitement of auction day or pulling into a driveway of an Amish farm after spotting a "Quilts for Sale" sign in the yard? It's all part of discovering the Amish way of life, and on each visit to these pockets of 18th-century life, I learn something new.

For this collection of inns in Amish country, I first stayed at three Ohio inns and then moved on to northeastern Indiana and western Pennsylvania to explore other Amish settlements. No matter the location, I found reassuring scenes of windmills on the horizon and neat farmhouses bordered by flower and kitchen gardens. Many of the same family names—Mast, Miller, Raber, Troyer, Yoder—appear on mailboxes and businesses in Indiana, Ohio, and Pennsylvania. I also came upon surprises like the brown Amish buggies spotted in Lawrence County in western Pennsylvania.

The influx of tourists to the areas of Amish settlements created a need for larger accommodations beyond the existing bed and breakfasts. Two Ohio inns, the Inn at Amish Door in Wilmot and the Carlisle Village Inn in Walnut Creek, and two Indiana inns, Essenhaus Country Inn in Middlebury and the Farmstead Inn in Shipshewana, fill that need with 50 rooms or more. All four of these larger inns have dining on site or within an easy walk. The Inn at Amish Door and Essenhaus Country Inn are located in a village setting with shops as part of the complex. When you stay at the Carlisle Village Inn, you can step out the door and find shops across the street. The Farmstead Inn is a convenient accommodation for those coming to the Shipshewana Auction, and other shopping options are nearby.

For travelers looking for smaller accommodations, I included two in this roundup of inns. Holmes With a View, a trio of octagon-shaped buildings near Charm, Ohio, offers spacious units and spectacular views. If you want to sample the great shopping in Volant, Pennsylvania, the Candleford Inn is located around the corner from the shops lined up along Main Street.

Take it easy and watch for slow-moving vehicles on your visits to Amish country. Keep in mind that most businesses are closed on Sunday.

Holmes With a View

Rooms with a view

Millersburg, OH
3672 Township Rd. 154
330-893-2390
www.holmeswithaview.com

RATES & RESERVATIONS:
Hours: 8 a.m.–10 p.m.
Season: Year round
Rates: $125 +
Minimum stay 2 nights preferred
Reservations required
Check, Visa, MC accepted

ACCOMMODATIONS: 7 suites
w/bath

AMENITIES: Hot tub, satellite TV,
air cond., full kitchens, private gas
fireplaces, decks, entertainment
centers

MEALS: Breakfast (Continental),
snacks

OTHER:
Parking: On-street

When Miriam and Paul Grossi were searching for land to build their hillside homes near Charm, they found one of the most beautiful vistas in Holmes County. Three octagonal houses with floor-to-ceiling windows ringing the great room allow for a panoramic view of the hills and valley below. On my early May visit, I looked out to a patchwork of freshly plowed fields, green pastures, and the white buildings of nearby Amish farms. It's the kind of scene you find on calendars picturing the Amish countryside. I watched the sun break through silver and gray clouds, culminating in a sparkling spring morning. Two hours later it was a different view with black-and-white Holsteins in one pasture, horses grazing in another, and a thin ribbon of highway in the distance. A line of trees on the highest hills frames the view. Guests enjoy spectacular evening sunsets in every season. In the winter, pull a chair to a window to see snow-covered hills, or move outdoors to the wraparound deck in warmer months to watch the brilliant orb slide behind the now-green hills. This is the kind of place where you want to linger an extra day.

When I first met Paul Grossi, I detected an East Coast accent and learned he hails from New York City, while Miriam grew up in Holmes

County. Through the years of living away from Ohio, they both found they loved coming back to the area and decided to retire and return to Holmes County to start a bed and breakfast.

Holmes With a View's three octagon-shaped buildings house six suites: four with one bedroom and a bath, and two with two bedrooms and two baths. Each suite is different. Floors are hardwood oak in one, distressed pine in the next, and stained cherry in yet another. All the suites have a whirlpool tub, gas fireplace, and entertainment center.

The contemporary exterior belies what you discover once you open the door to rooms furnished with antiques mixed with comfy pieces like the oversized chair by the fireplace in Suite 3, where I stayed. Paul and Miriam brought some antiques from Florida and Virginia to the bed and breakfast. They found the rest of the pieces within a 100-mile radius of their home—the tall walnut wardrobe and shabby chic distressed wall-hung coat rack in the great room and an oak mirrored wardrobe in one of the pie-shaped bedrooms. Soft furnishings are in subdued florals and contrasting solids. Architectural interior effects like crown moldings, a cathedral ceiling in the great room, and creative use of colors give the place a classic feel.

Suite 3, one of the larger units with 1,250 square feet, is the kind of accommodation that can easily handle a family visit or two couples traveling together. A daughter gave her mother the gift of a stay together as a Mother's Day gift. Guests from sunny California enjoyed Ohio's snow-covered landscape in January, and a group of cousins and sisters stayed for a mini-family reunion. There's a dining table situated for a view of the valley and a kitchen stocked with every utensil, pan,

and table setting needed for meals. The Grossis seem to have thought of everything you might want, including packets of hot chocolate, popcorn, tea, and coffee. I found a loaf of freshly baked cinnamon bread on the kitchen counter and, in the Sub-Zero refrigerator tucked into a lower cabinet, breakfast items like orange juice and homemade jam.

The suites at Holmes With a View house the best of cutting-edge electronic equipment in the entertainment center by the fireplace. For the technically challenged, finding a TV, DVD, surround sound, and lots of dials can pose problems. But you'll find detailed instructions left by the hosts. There's a good selection of CDs (ranging from oldies to classical), magazines, and books on architecture and interiors. If you're immersed in reading, watching TV, or listening to music, you needn't leave the comfort of the fireside sitting area, as there's an ice-maker nearby.

Special packages include a midweek year-round package and a romantic getaway in winter months. Golf specials for two-night stays in both single and double suites, midweek and weekend, include tee times scheduled for 18 holes with cart at Black Diamond or Fire Ridge golf courses in Millersburg. The package also offers a continental breakfast in the suite and gift certificates for area restaurants.

THINGS TO DO:

While the location of Holmes With a View on Township Road 154 off Route 557 allows easy access to Millersburg and Berlin for shopping and dining, the village of Charm is closest—and it's a good place to start your exploration of Amish country. New businesses have arrived in

Charm, but it retains the air of a place not too touched by tourism. Your first stop might be Guggisberg Cheese, famous for the original baby Swiss cheese. You can watch the cheese-making process and purchase items to take home. Continue the Swiss experience across the highway at Chalet in the Valley, where the menu features Swiss and Austrian dishes. Miller's Dry Goods is chock-full of fabric, quilts, and wall hangings. You'll find handmade country apparel, candles, and wrought iron items at Old Mill Crafts. Stop for lunch or dinner at a favorite of both locals and visitors, the Homestead Restaurant. Plan ahead in the busy seasons to dine here, because there is often a waiting line. The Grossis offer another suggestion: dining with an Amish family. Contact information can be found in each suite. Looking for well-made Amish furniture? Stop at Ole Mill Furniture in Charm and Farmerstown Furniture to the east. Antiquers will want to continue on through Charm on Route 557 to find Hershberger Antique Mall.

DIRECTIONS: I-71 South to Wooster/Lodi exit; SR 83 out of Wooster to Millersburg

NEARBY ATTRACTIONS: Amish country, shopping, golf, horseback riding, antiques, farmers markets, flea markets

Carlisle Village Inn

A traditional inn overlooking a beautiful valley in Ohio's Amish country

Driving along Route 39 between Sugarcreek and Berlin in Ohio's Amish country, you come upon the Carlisle Village Inn perched on a hilltop in Walnut Creek. The inn takes its name from the original name of the community, New Carlisle. As you approach it, one of the first things you notice are the porches and decks that gird the beige inn accented with Victorian hues of green and burgundy and a bit of white gingerbread trim. The Carlisle Village Inn has received the AAA Four Diamond Award every year since opening in August 1993.

The inn's interior is gracious and welcoming. To the right of the reception area, the fireplace room—with a Thomas Kinkade painting over the mantle, a grand piano, and Victorian decorative accents—proved to be a popular gathering place on a February evening. A group of women on their annual getaway played cards in one corner, while other guests found a wing chair or a cozy spot by the fire to read. Cookies and hot chocolate were set out for an evening snack.

Each of the 52 guest rooms in the inn has its own ambience and opens to a porch or deck. Most of the furnishings were made by folks

Walnut Creek, OH
4949 Walnut St.
877-422-7547
330-893-3636
www.carlislevillageinn.com

RATES & RESERVATIONS:
Hours: 24 hours/day
Season: Year round
Rates: $90–$125
Specials: Children
Reservations recommended
Check, Visa, MC, Disc, Amex accepted

ACCOMMODATIONS: 52 rooms w/bath; 4 suites w/bath

AMENITIES: Hot tub, cable TV, phone in room, Internet, air cond.

MEALS: Breakfast, Sunday evening meal

OTHER:
Parking: Lot

from a local Amish cabinet shop. On the first floor, the wood trim and furniture is done in oak, while cherry is the featured wood on the second and third floors. In Alma's Quilts Room, named for one of the owner's family members, pale floral quilts in pinks and rose cover the queen beds and framed art depicting peaceful Amish scenes reflect the area. The larger standard rooms have a bathroom and a separate spacious dressing area with sink. The Scenic Valley and King's View Rooms do indeed offer views of the Genza Bottom Valley, a beautiful Amish valley dotted with farms. In the two-bedroom suites, a living room joins the two bedrooms and each has a private bath. A four-poster cherry king bed with a lace canopy, a Jacuzzi tub, and a VCR are special amenities in the Honeymoon Suite. All rooms are equipped with a small refrigerator, while suites and executive rooms have a microwave, coffeemaker, refrigerator, and large private decks. One of the six executive rooms, the Sherwood Manor, a many-windowed room with views in two directions, offers a spacious sitting area and a whirlpool tub. The Carlisle has one barrier-free room and an elevator. A continental breakfast is available for guests in the Wicker Room on the inn's second floor. Corporate guests find high-speed Internet connections, a morning newspaper, and an efficient and helpful front desk staff.

Guests of the Carlisle Village Inn can walk to the adjacent Der Dutchman for lunch or dinner. In business in Walnut Creek since 1967, the Der Dutchman menu offers traditional Amish family-style dinners with a choice of meat, real mashed potatoes, stuffing, gravy, corn or green beans, and salad bar. Other house specialties include Manhattans: hot roast beef, pork, or turkey sandwiches served with mashed

potatoes or stuffing, and smothered with gravy. With 20 varieties of pie on the dessert list, manager Ivan Miller told me the cream pies are most popular—with peanut butter cream pie topping the list. During the busy season, folks line up on the wide porch or rock a while until their turn comes to settle down in the dining room for an Amish meal. The view from the dining room windows of the Genza Bottom Valley—or Goosebottom Valley, as the locals call it—is worth the wait.

Most area restaurants are closed on Sundays, so the Carlisle offers a light meal. Homemade soups, hot roast beef sandwiches, creamed chicken, coleslaw, and assorted cheesecakes are set out for guests between 5:00 and 7:00 p.m. on Sunday evenings. After the meal, guests gather in the Fireplace Room for musical entertainment. Returning guests say this kind of comfortable atmosphere is one of the reasons they come back to the Carlisle Village Inn.

THINGS TO DO:

It would be easy to spend an afternoon or an entire day exploring the shops within walking distance of the Carlisle Village Inn. Across the street, the Carlisle House is known for its Thomas Kinkade Showcase Gallery. Carlisle House also carries R. A. Lang gifts, English china, lace, Seraphim angels, and Crabtree & Evelyn products. On the lower level, Ten Thousand Villages, sponsored by the Mennonite Central Committee, offers gifts from Third World countries. Next door to the Carlisle House, the Farmer's Wife Gift Shop occupies one of the older houses in Walnut Creek and carries country decor, Boyd's bears, candles, and garden accessories. If you have warm memories of an old-fashioned

candy store, stop at Coblentz Chocolate located just beyond the Carlisle and you'll find glass cases brimming with hand-dipped chocolates, homemade fudge, and fresh roasted nuts. Step over to the store's viewing gallery to watch the candy being made.

Antiquers will want to browse the Walnut Creek Antique Mall, located next to the town's water tower. For a light lunch or coffee break, stop at the nearby Peppermint Mill.

While staying at the Carlisle Village Inn, take time to explore the area. Visit Yoder's Amish Home located two miles from the inn. On this 116-acre working farm tour a circa 1886 Amish/Mennonite house and a 10-room present-day Old Order Amish home. Travel over to the Mennonite Information Center near Berlin to take a guided tour of Behalt, a spectacular 265-foot cyclorama painted by Heinz Gaugel that traces the history of the Amish and Mennonites. On your way home, pick up some cheese and locally made Trail Bologna at the new Walnut Creek Cheese on Route 39.

DIRECTIONS: I-77 South to Exit 83 for SR 39; on corner of SR 39 and SR 515

NEARBY ATTRACTIONS: Shopping, Amish country

Inn at Amish Door

Step out the door to shop

Wilmot, OH
1210 Winesburg St.
888-264-7436
330-359-7996
www.amishdoor.com

RATES & RESERVATIONS:
Hours: 24 hours/day
Season: Year round
Rates: $90–$125
Reservations recommended
Check, Visa, MC, Disc, Amex, Diners
Club accepted

ACCOMMODATIONS: 50 rooms
w/bath; 9 suites w/bath

AMENITIES: Hot tub, cable TV,
pool, phone in room, air cond.,
fitness room

MEALS: Breakfast; Beer, wine,
liquor served

OTHER:
Parking: Lot

The Inn at Amish Door in Wilmot is part of a village setting with four shops, a bakery, and the Amish Door Restaurant. Milo and Kathryn Miller, the inn's owners, started business in 1977 at this site with a small restaurant seating 48. As the popularity of their Amish Door Restaurant grew, they added a rustic-style barn with a loft for additional dining space. In 1992 the present restaurant, seating 450 guests, was built in the style of a large white Amish house. The final addition to the village was the Inn at Amish Door, which opened in 1997 with 50 guest rooms. The inn offers a smoke- and alcohol-free environment.

Located in Stark County near the Holmes County line, this part of Amish country has thankfully retained open spaces. I couldn't get over the views from the inn. I first looked out from the bay window in my room to U.S. Route 62 snaking along in one direction and an Amish buggy on a country lane in the opposite direction. On a snowy January morning, guests found the breakfast room bathed in sunlight and had yet another chance to savor this scene stretching out over four counties.

The wide front doors of the Inn at Amish Door open to the lobby area with a grand staircase and beautiful woodwork, including fine scrollwork surrounding the fireplace, an architectural decoration repeated in the reception desk. Locally made traditional cherry, oak, and mahogany furnishings fill the guest rooms and suites done in Victorian or Shaker style. Rooms range from a standard garden-themed room with hand-painted furniture and garden-oriented decorative items to deluxe rooms and honeymoon or family suites. In the deluxe suite, I found a king bed, a generous sitting area with sofa and chairs, a Jacuzzi tub, VCR, and kitchenette. The expansive third-floor honeymoon suite is a joyful space done in violet-sprigged wallpaper with a pale green striped chair rail. A gas fireplace is the sitting area's focal point. Three sets of windows allow views from the kitchenette area, from the formal mahogany dining table, and from the bedroom where a four-poster king bed centers the room, also done in violet and pale green hues. The two-room bath boasts a corner Jacuzzi in one room and twin sinks in a separate area. The Inn at Amish Door offers two wheelchair-accessible rooms and an elevator.

Enjoy breakfast in a setting of flowered-cushioned wicker and glass-top tables. The expanded continental menu brings pastries from the Amish Door Bakery next door, including those decadent apple fritters we always find down in Amish country.

Settle down for lunch or dinner at the Amish Door Restaurant and you might overhear conversation at the next table about farming or the chatter of a young family on vacation. The wait staff in flower-print aprons bring generous family-style dinner portions of ham, chicken, or beef, or the homey favorite: a hot turkey sandwich platter with a side of gravy-smothered mashed potatoes. It's hard to resist such bountiful meals, but health-conscious diners can stay on track with the Heart

Healthy menu listings. Homemade pies, apple dumplings, and date pudding with butterscotch sauce and whipped cream highlight the dessert menu. The restaurant schedules special luncheon or dinner concerts with Southern gospel groups or barbershop quartets.

There are getaway packages for special days throughout the year. Book a stay on weeknights from November through March for the "Get Lost, Jack Frost" winter getaway. Families fill the inn during Christmas and spring break. The guest laundry room is appreciated by those who come for longer stays. The inn's public spaces—a large conference room, extra-wide hallways furnished with comfortable sofas, chairs, and reading lamps, the reception area, and the breakfast room—easily accommodate business meetings, family reunions, and retreats.

THINGS TO DO:

You don't have to leave the Amish Door Village to shop: step out the inn's front door and you'll find a variety of options at the Amish Door Shoppes. Browse the Wooden Toy Shop for handcrafted toys and oak accessories or Grandma's Pantry for bulk food, candles, spices, and kitchen accessories. Fans of country decor enjoy exploring the Country Loft. Vintage Collections fills two floors of an 1880s house with Victorian decorative items and gifts.

A half mile west of the inn, the Barn Shops of Amish Door are set up with multiple dealers offering furniture, glass, pottery, and tools. Grandpa's General Store takes over the second floor with a line of log cabin furniture along with NASCAR, Harley-Davidson, and western items. On the third floor, colorful quilts hang from the rafters in a new shop, Seams So Simple, stocked with fabrics, notions, and kits.

Carriage rides around the village can be arranged on Friday and Saturday from May to October, led by George or Ralph, the Amish Door Clydesdales.

Close-by activities include inn golf packages at Fire Ridge Golf Course near Millersburg. Hikers find nature trails and a new interpretive center at the Wilderness Center, located a mile west of Wilmot just off U.S. 250. Aficionados of Shaker furniture will want to stop in Wilmot at Mulheim & Son Furniture, a small family business that takes pride in building traditional Shaker-style pieces on the premises. In the nearby community of Winesburg, the Winesburg Antique Mall in Kinsley's General Store, built in 1895, showcases a range of antiques and folk art.

DIRECTIONS: I-77 South to 250 West to 62 West

NEARBY ATTRACTIONS: Amish country

Candleford Inn

Laze away a summer afternoon on the front porch

Volant, PA
225 Mercer St.
724-533-4497
www.candlefordinn.com

RATES & RESERVATIONS:
Hours: Reservations 10 a.m.–10 p.m.; check-in 4–8 p.m. or by arrangement
Season: Year round
Rates: $65–$90
Specials: Frequent guest discount (7th night free); extended stay (8 or more nights 20% off)
Reservations required
Check, Visa, MC, Disc, Amex accepted

ACCOMMODATIONS: 3 rooms w/ bath; 1 suite w/bath

AMENITIES: Hot tub, air cond.

MEALS: Breakfast

OTHER:
Not fully wheelchair accessible
Parking: On-street

Sometimes a destination invites a stay. Visit the tiny borough of Volant, Pennsylvania, for a few hours and you wish you could linger longer to explore the 30 shops lining Main Street or fish the trout-stocked Neshannock Creek. You're in luck, as Howard and Carolyn Moss opened the Candleford Inn on Mercer Street in April 2002.

A roomy, foursquare gray house with white trim, the Candleford Inn is steps away from the Main Street shops. The Moss family relocated from a Pittsburgh suburb and purchased an existing bed and breakfast in 2001. They spent the next four months renovating the property, adding bathrooms, air-conditioning, and general updating. The easy informality of their inn-keeping style attracts travelers. One notable guest was Martin Sheen, from the cast of TV's *The West Wing*. Sheen stayed at the Candleford when he was in the area for an episode's filming.

Innkeeper Howard Moss says the generous size of their late 1800s home's front porch allows two groups to have their own conversations or play a game without disturbing each other. It's the kind of porch perfect for lazing away a summer afternoon, with wicker furniture, a porch swing, and a table and chairs for snacks or a game of cards or chess. Guests come back from a shopping tour and find lemonade or iced tea on a hot day. On a summer evening, the Mosses' porch is the place to watch holiday fireworks or sit in quiet conversation. Amish farms are just down the road from the inn, and the clip-clop of passing horse-drawn buggies provides a reminder that you've left your fast-paced life behind.

The three guest rooms on the second floor have queen beds, ceiling fans, hardwood floors, rag rugs, a rocking chair or an easy chair, and antique chests. The Amish Room is centered by a bent-hickory, queen-size four-poster bed. The blue and white of an Amish-made quilt is repeated in the sponge-painted walls and woodwork. In the Wildflower Room, a silk patch quilt in deep tones covers the brass bed. The Rose Room flower motif is found in the wallpaper and linens. Both the Wild-flower and Rose Rooms sport new bathrooms with pedestal sinks and whirlpool tubs. The best space for families or older guests coming to the Candleford Inn is the first-floor suite. The sitting room has a sleeper sofa and shelves stocked with games. A bedroom with a sleigh bed and a bathroom with a steam shower complete the unit.

One of the things frequent inn-goers love is waking up to the aroma of breakfast being prepared by someone else. Carolyn Moss is a gourmet cook and guests leave rave reviews of her breakfasts. On a late January morning, I sat down to a breakfast of grapefruit, homemade blueberry muffins, bacon, and a made-to-order omelet. A lovely table setting and chatting with Carolyn over the meal added to the pleasure. Carolyn is happy to adjust the menu to special dietary requirements if

you let her know when booking
a room.

THINGS TO DO:

When you come upon an
Amish buggy in the rolling countryside of Lawrence County in
western Pennsylvania, you may
take a second look. Instead of the
all-black buggies we see in Ohio,
Indiana, and the Lancaster settlement in Pennsylvania, the buggy
tops in this area are brown.

Shopping enthusiasts rejoice
at the prospect of 30 shops right
outside their door when they stay
at the Candleford. One inn guest
wrote that she had "a shopping
good time." And there is variety
in the lineup of Main Street shops. During a morning shopping spree, I
managed to stop at eight stores. Tole N Trinkets carries a delightful collection of home decor items—primitives, quilts, rag dolls, lampshades,
and candles. The first floor of the Kitchen Shoppe has kitchen gad-
gets, cutlery, and seasonal items. Head up to the second floor for china,
linens, and cookbooks. 1906 Mercantile & Doll Company, located in
a century home, is filled with curtains, prints, cupboards, wallpaper,
rugs, and tinware. You'll find the Soap Dish, carrying natural body-care
products, in a brightly painted train car just off Main Street. Volant
Miniature Shop stocks a large selection of handcrafted dollhouse furnishings and accessories. In the Volant Depot, I found K. C.'s Collectible & Rubber Stamp Heaven for the rubber stamp enthusiast, and Native American and nature art, jewelry, pottery, and weavings at Native
and Nature. A welcome surprise in this town of shops was the Music
& Art Gift Shoppe, with sheet music, fine art, CDs, and music boxes.
For a coffee break or lunch, stop at Brua's Dumplin Haus. Famous for
its dumplings, this cozy eatery serves cinnamon rolls as big as a soup
plate. The Neshannock Creek Restaurant is known for home cooking
with a menu of soups, sandwiches, and salads. For fine dining, there's a
choice of restaurants in nearby Mercer—Springfield Grille, Iron Bridge
Inn, and Rachel's Roadhouse.

One of Volant's annual events is Trout Stocking Day, when 15,000
trout enter Neshannock Creek at approximately 1:00 p.m. The nearby
Neshannock Creek Fly Shop, a fly-fishing pro shop, is authorized to sell
Orvis products. A short drive takes you to Teena's Quilt Shop, offering

more than 100 quilts, Amish crafts, and wall hangings. Note that this Amish-owned shop is not open on Sundays. The Cheese House, near New Wilmington, carries domestic and imported cheeses, Amish jams and jellies, and German-made Black Forest cuckoo clocks, nutcrackers, and beer steins.

Volant gets a head start on celebrating July 4 by staging its Independence Day celebration on the Saturday before the holiday. Classic cars are on display, shops are open, and an area band plays rock-and-roll. The day is topped off by a fireworks display. Fall brings the Autumn Pumpkin Festival with a harvest market, apple butter making, and craft demonstrations. Santa arrives for the Christmas On Main Street celebration in mid-November.

DIRECTIONS: I-80 to SR 60 to SR 208; left on Mercer St.; on left

NEARBY ATTRACTIONS: Grove City College, Westminster College, shopping

Essenhaus Inn
& Conference Center

A charming country inn in the heart of Indiana's Amish country

Built to resemble a large white Amish farmhouse, Essenhaus Country Inn opened in 1986 with 33 rooms and has become a favorite getaway for all ages. On my late fall visit, I found a girls' reunion weekend in progress on the sunporch. In the large atrium sitting room, couples chatted, played board games, or settled in rocking chairs to read or knit by the black potbellied stove embellished with nickel-plated trim. The atrium reaches up three floors, with a white picket fence and flower boxes on the second floor lending a cottage-like ambience to this casual space. A replica of an old-fashioned schoolhouse functions as a small conference room on this level. During the holidays, the picket fence is festooned with evergreens and a 15-foot Christmas tree holds a place

Middlebury, IN
240 U.S. 20
800-455-9471
574-825-3471
www.essenhaus.com

RATES & RESERVATIONS:
Hours: 24 hours/day
Season: Year round
Rates: $90–$125
Reservations recommended
Check, Visa, MC, Disc, Amex accepted

ACCOMMODATIONS: 95 rooms w/ bath; 9 suites w/bath

AMENITIES: Hot tub, cable TV, pool, phone in room, Internet, air cond.
MEALS: None

OTHER:
Parking: Lot

of honor. Coffee and homemade cookies are set out on the counter where overnight guests find a generous continental breakfast.

Warm pine furnishings handcrafted by local Amish artisans fill the inn's individually decorated guest rooms and suites. In the Country Living Room Suite, an old-fashioned teacup motif is carried through the rooms—from the border in the bedroom to teacup prints in the bathroom. On the second floor, the Heritage Suite, a VIP kind of space with a cathedral ceiling, offers a living and dining area, kitchenette, fireplace, king bed, and whirlpool-jetted tub. A wheelchair-accessible room is on the first floor.

You might stay in the "Dawdy Haus," a replica of the kind of home lived in by grandparents on Amish farms. This authentic Amish dwelling with seven guest rooms, a kitchenette, and common area with deck adapts easily for gatherings like family reunions. The Dawdy Haus Suite has a private porch and a Jacuzzi tub.

At times, the line snakes out the door for meals at Das Dutchman Essenhaus Amish Country Kitchen. Touted as Indiana's largest family restaurant, Das Dutchman has grown from the Millers' original small eatery seating 125 to a building that now can handle 1,100 diners daily. Essenhaus Foods makes up to 13 tons of noodles each week, and the record set for pies baked in one day is 2,000. You can dine family-style or order from a menu. The all-you-can-eat meal includes those Amish staples of real mashed potatoes and gravy, homemade bread dressing, green beans or corn, and made-from-scratch noodles, served with a choice of chicken, ham, or beef. Warm apple dumplings are a specialty, along with a choice of 29 pies. I talked to guests leaving the restaurant after the evening meal who wouldn't miss sitting down the next morning for the Thresher's Breakfast buffet.

Essenhaus Country Inn will expanded with the opening of a new Inn and Conference Center offering 50 additional rooms, 4,000 square feet of conference space, a kidney-shaped pool, hot tub, kiddie pool, fitness center, and game room with ping-pong, pool, and air hockey. To allay any fears by longtime devotees of the original Essenhaus Country Inn, inn manager Jeff Miller promises that it remains the "quiet place in the country" returning guests have come to love. A hallway

and elevator allow guests of both accommodations to gather in the new second-story breakfast room with a fireplace. Families and conference groups find generous-size guest rooms and suites with views of the pond and Sunshine Farm, a family-owned property across the way from the inn. The oak-furnished family suites have a central living room with bedrooms on either side. Some rooms open to balconies or patios; the third floor features cathedral ceilings. A nice country touch is the multicolor carpeting in a quilt design in the new inn's hallways and common rooms.

THINGS TO DO:

Das Dutchman Essenhaus is a one-stop destination offering lodging, dining, and shopping at the Essenhaus Village retail shops. During the Christmas season, it becomes a fairyland village with white lights outlining the trees and buildings. When the Millers acquired an adjoining farm in 1984, they converted four old farm buildings into shops and have since added two more. Shop at the Clothesline for fashions, jewelry, and hats that the Red Hat Society ladies love. It's Christmas all year long at the Cabin, where you'll also find nature-themed gifts. Hoosiers shop for Indiana items at the Corn Crib, while Dutch Country Gifts offers cottage and Victorian items. Quilters flock to the Quilt Shop, filled with quilting supplies, hand-stitched quilts, and wall hangings. Take home a peanut-butter pie or apple butter from the Essenhaus Bakery. Before dinner, peruse the variety of Amish gifts, John Deere and Coke collectibles, and kitchenware in the lobby area of the restaurant building. After a shopping spree, relax with a full-service tea at Extravagant Grace, a French/European tearoom.

The Essenhaus Village grounds are beautifully landscaped and maintained. A windmill, flower gardens, a pond bordered with willow trees, and an old farm wagon overflowing with flowers make it a pleasant place to walk or shop. Carriage rides in season take you over the covered bridge on the inn property. Families and groups find an 18-hole miniature golf course at Sunshine Farm.

The first weekend in October brings the Amish Country Harvest Festival to the grounds of Das Dutchman Essenhaus. Enjoy a hometown parade at the annual Middlebury Summer Festival the second Friday and Saturday in August. To watch the cheese-making process, plan to visit the nearby Deutsch Kase Haus.

DIRECTIONS: I-80/90 to Exit 107 for US 20; south on US 20

NEARBY ATTRACTIONS: College Football Hall of Fame, South Bend, Shipshewana, Das Dutchman Essenhaus

Farmstead Inn

*A rambling country inn
in Indiana's farmland*

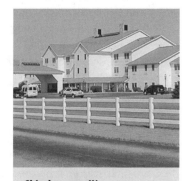

If you come to Shipshewana for the outdoor flea market, considered the Midwest's largest, or for the Shipshewana auctions of antiques, livestock, ponies, and horses, check your bags at the Farmstead Inn. Located across Route 5 from both venues, the inn is the most convenient lodging location for exploring Shipshewana.

The rambling white inn, framed by fields of corn and beans on my August visit, presented a perfect late summer scene in Indiana's Amish country. A red barn with a silo is attached to the inn. While you have easy access to the flea market and auctions during a stay, the Farmstead Inn is set apart from all the activity. It offers a smoke- and alcohol-free environment.

A massive fieldstone fireplace, the centerpiece of the inn lobby, reaches up three stories. Quilts and quilt panels enliven the lobby walls, and green plants on each level break up the vast space of the sky-lit atrium. Antique laundry equipment—old double washtubs, wringers, and washboards—and Amish clothing are displayed on the third-floor walls. An expanded continental breakfast is served in the lobby, with seating at tables for four or at larger harvest tables for families or groups.

The inn's 85 spacious guest rooms are furnished with locally crafted oak furniture, and many offer views of the surrounding farmland. All rooms have either one king bed or two queen beds. The decor is simple

Shipshewana, IN
370 S. VanBuren St.
260-768-4595
www.tradingplaceamerica.com

RATES & RESERVATIONS:
Hours: Check in 3 p.m.; check out
11 p.m.
Season: Year round
Rates: $70–$140
Reservations recommended
Check, Visa, MC, Disc accepted

ACCOMMODATIONS: 154 rooms
w/bath; 4 suites w/bath

AMENITIES: Hot tub, cable TV, pool,
phone in room, air cond.

MEALS: Breakfast

OTHER:
Parking: Lot

and fresh, using hunter-green fabrics and carpeting set against white walls. I found a nice collection of framed photographs of farm and Amish scenes in the guest rooms. There's a casual seating arrangement with good lighting on either side of the center fireplace on each floor, offering a quiet area for reading or chatting.

Holidays and vacations bring many families to the inn. It's not unusual to look out the window and discover a touch football or volleyball game in progress. A pleasant park-like area borders the protected wetlands behind the inn.

The red barn houses conference rooms, a swimming pool, kiddie pool, hot tub, indoor quarter-court basketball court, and a children's playroom. There's easy access from the inn to the recreation area in all kinds of weather through a connecting hallway. The playroom is inviting to the preschool set, with a patterned rug in bright colors. You'll find the hot tub in the silo. A group of high school kids on a church retreat were making good use of the indoor basketball court during my stay. The Farmstead Inn hosts conferences, retreats, seminars, and family reunions. The inn staff can help with planning details, and on-site catering is available.

The Blue Gate Restaurant & Bakery, located in the Riegsecker Marketplace, is an easy two-block walk from the inn. Traditional Amish meals are served family-style. There are daily specials, and folks come back for the deep-dish chicken potpie, beef and noodles, and Blue Gate's signature dish, home-style meatloaf. Apple butter and an Amish peanut butter spread are served with homemade bread at all meals. Along with the tempting Amish feasts, the Blue Gate offers a good selection of salads, soups, and grilled entrees. The "old" Blue Gate Restau-

rant was replaced by a new building in 2001. Typical of the neighborliness of this small town, the Blue Gate owners invited the entire town of Shipshewana, population 521, to dinner at the new restaurant. Five hundred folks came to dine. The Blue Gate also offers a matinee and evening entertainment series featuring musical theater and comedy performances.

THINGS TO DO:

You can walk across a small covered bridge from the Farmstead Inn to Menno-Hof, the Mennonite-Anabaptist Interpretive Center. Menno-Hof tells the fascinating and often tragic story of Mennonite and Amish history through 24 interactive exhibits and recreations. Take a close look at the Menno-Hof barn built by Amish workmen using rough-sawn oak beams fastened together by knee braces and wooden pegs.

The Shipshewana auction started in 1922 as the Shipshewana Livestock Auction. Now every Wednesday, year-round, the antique auction starts at 8 a.m. with 11 rings of auctioneers selling at one time. The hay auction is next at 10 a.m., followed by the livestock auction. Fridays bring the horse, pony, and tack auction, which starts at 9 a.m.

From May 1 through the end of October, the flea market is open, with more than 1,000 vendors. Name it and you'll probably find it at this open-air marketplace. Displays of fresh farm produce share the space with tables of collectibles, tools, furniture, antiques, toys, baked goods, and auto accessories. For a break in your shopping or for a meal, find a seat at the Shipshewana Auction Restaurant located on the grounds.

For antique lovers, Trading Place Antiques Gallery is located just north of the Farmstead Inn. More than 100 dealers offer primitives, furniture, pottery, glassware, textiles, toys, and china in this two-story facility patterned after an Early American farmstead.

While waiting for your table at the Blue Gate, browse the shops at Riegsecker Marketplace. The Craft Barn displays Riegsecker custom-crafted hardwood furniture along with a full line of Lang cards and gifts. Dad's Toys carries hundreds of model cars, trucks, tractors, NASCAR memorabilia, and hard-to-find nostalgic tools. Quilters will find thousands of fabric bolts at Yoder Department Store's fabric center.

Come the first weekend in May for the Shipshewana Mayfest and the second week of October for the Shipshewana Fall Crafter's Fair.

DIRECTIONS: I-90 East to Exit 107 for Middlebury south on Hwy 13; east on Hwy 120; south on Hwy 5; on right

NEARBY ATTRACTIONS: Menno-Hof Mennonite Visitor Center, Hoosier Buggy Shop, Deutsch Kase Haus (cheese factory), Amish shopping

FAMILY STAYS

Family-friendly inns are in! On my travels for this second inn guide, I found more inns that welcomed families than on previous trips to scout out new accommodations. Innkeepers and hotel managers are reaching out to family groups with room arrangements that adapt to various family sizes—connecting rooms, suites, and cabins as well as rooms built specifically for family stays. Budget-conscious parents appreciate finding microwaves and refrigerators for quick, convenient meals and snacks. Plan to take the family for a meal in the dining room of the three largest inns reviewed and you'll find menu items with kid appeal like macaroni and cheese, kid-size burgers, and good old peanut butter and jelly. Most inns offer a convenient, buffet-style breakfast. I found essentials for a family stay—cribs, a rollaway, a list of certified baby sitters—at all these destinations.

Select an inn that fits your family from this chapter with choices ranging from stays at a farm, a cottage in Ohio's Hocking Hills, a water park, an inn within walking distance of museums, a family ski destination, and a comfortable country lodge.

Visits to family farms remain a warm memory for many and we'd like our children to have that experience. A stay at Weatherbury Farm, a working farm near Avelia, Pennsylvania, invites today's kids to sample farm life. They can accompany Farmer Dale on his morning rounds to feed the animals or to explore the farm. Plan to visit Ohio's Hocking Hills and stay in a cottage at the Bear Run Inn. The kids can fish in the farm ponds or the entire family can enjoy a hay ride or take off on the trails on the inn's 550-acre spread. Make the Dearborn Inn your base for exploring the Henry Ford Museum and Greenfield Village and stay in a historic replica home honoring a famous American. Spruce Hill Inn and Cottages located next to Snow Trails Ski Resort is an ideal destination for a family ski getaway. Spruce Hill offers family cottages along with two larger accommodations for families traveling together or family reunions. Mom and Dad might get a little time on their own with a stay at the Cherry Valley Lodge in Newark. Cherry Valley offers an excellent program for children—Camp Cherry Berry during the summer months and year-round activities in the lodge. Guest rooms at Cherry Valley are planned for families. What kid doesn't love the idea of playing in water? At Great Bear Lodge, you can let your children experience the fun of water play in a safe environment. The rustic suites at Great Wolf Lodge appeal to the imagination of all who have a romanticized notion of staying in a log cabin.

Spruce Hill Inn & Cottages

Bring the family to stay in a Victorian home or cozy cottage

Families come to Spruce Hill Inn and Cottages in the hills of Possum Run Valley in the wintertime for alpine skiing at the adjacent Snow Trails Ski Resort. In warmer months, they come back to bike the Richland B&O Rail Trail, canoe the Mohican River, or watch the races at the Mid-Ohio Sports Car Course.

Owner Craig Donley developed the Spruce Hill property and opened it to guests in 2001. Craig placed all utilities underground, allowing for unobstructed views from the hillside setting. Extensive landscaping and a pond add to the beauty of this quiet getaway. Select from a range of accommodations at Spruce Hill: the main inn (Victorian Manor), the Rustic Lodge, or 28 cottage units.

The neat tan cottage units with green trim adapt easily to individual family groups. Parents like the versatility of the two-unit cottages. One half has a bedroom with queen bed, bath with Jacuzzi, and separate shower connected to a twin unit on the opposite side. Children can be nearby, yet it al-

Mansfield, OH
3230 O'Possum Run Rd.
419-756-2200
www.sprucehillinn.com

RATES & RESERVATIONS:
Hours: 7 a.m.–11 p.m.
Season: Year round
Rates: $90–$125
Specials: Seniors, AAA
Minimum stay (except for special event dates)
Reservations recommended
Check, Visa, MC, Disc, Amex accepted

ACCOMMODATIONS: 2 suites w/ bath; 28 cottages

AMENITIES: Cable TV, phone in room, air cond., Jacuzzis in all cottages. Two 4-bedroom homes also available for nightly rental.

MEALS: Breakfast (Continental)

OTHER:
Guest pets allowed
Not fully wheelchair accessible
Parking: In front of each cottage

lows privacy for Mom and Dad. A choice of cottage floor plans provides either a deck or more interior space with a gazebo-style bay window.

Two cottages have room for a dinette. Families appreciate finding a small refrigerator, microwave, coffeepot, and cable TV. Rollaways are available, and Spruce Hill has one wheelchair-friendly cottage.

The warm maple Arts and Crafts-style bedroom furnishings in the cottages were custom made. Rooms are light and bright, with vaulted ceilings and additional light from a sizable dormer window. On the spacious grounds, families enjoy horseshoes and volleyball, and summer evenings find folks gathering around a campfire. When you check into the Carriage House, pick up games to take to your cottage. The next morning, come back for a continental breakfast.

Two larger accommodations at Spruce Hill are often booked for family reunions, weddings, and church retreats. The contemporary-style Rustic Lodge sleeps eight, with four bedrooms, a full kitchen, dining area, two bathrooms, large recreation room, and a living room that opens to a wraparound deck. A gracious setting for family get-togethers, the popular Victorian Manor is reserved two years ahead for Christmas gatherings. Multigenerational groups can spread out in this Victorian beauty done up in traditional Victorian hues of burgundy and green, with hardwood floors and reproduction lighting. The manor has a formal living room with gas-burning fireplace, a cozy family room, study, wet bar, gourmet kitchen, and a dining table large enough to gather the family around for a Thanksgiving or Christmas dinner. The manor's four bedrooms include a twin-bedded room, one queen room with stairs to a skylit loft the kids will instantly claim as their own, and a second queen room. The bath in the master suite located on the first floor has a step-up Jacuzzi and separate shower. Relax on the sunporch

off the family room or in warm weather move out to the patio.

Spruce Hill packages include the Ski Escape available December through March, with a one-night stay in a Jacuzzi cottage and two all-day lift tickets to Snow Trails. Some guests ski from the front door of their cottage to the slopes. Book the Family Fun package anytime and you'll find a family pass to the Art & Discovery Center in Mansfield, four Carrousel Park tokens, a $15 activity voucher for nearby venues, and a Malabar Farm coloring book along with a night's stay in a Jacuzzi cottage.

During my mid-January visit, the adjacent Snow Trails Ski Resort with 16 trails and seven lifts was humming with activity. A family-friendly ski destination, Snow Trails offers the Jiminy Cricket Program for children ages 3 to 8, with instruction on the slopes and indoor activities. The snowboarding park, Mountain Dew Outer Limits Terrain Park, has been recognized as one of Ohio's most aggressive and challenging parks. Staff and volunteers at Snow Trails offer an adaptive ski program for the physically challenged.

THINGS TO DO:

During a stay at Spruce Hill, plan to spend some time in downtown Mansfield where there's a number of venues that families enjoy. Start at the Richland Carrousel Park and experience a bit of yesteryear when you hop on one of the carrousel's hand-carved animals and ride to the old-timey music of a band organ. The kids will have fun picking out their favorite: Along with 30 magnificent horses, there's a choice of 22 menagerie animals—including bears, ostriches, cats, rabbits, goats, and

a giraffe, lion, tiger, and zebra. Don't miss the pirate cat, complete with eye patch, pistol peg leg, saber, and bag of gold. In the summer months, the next stop might be Carousel Magic, a carousel carving company where you can watch craftsmen carve wooden ponies and learn the history of American carousels. Explore the Carrousel District, a Victorian neighborhood with a mixture of shops offering antiques, books, gifts, fine foods, and home furnishings. And be sure to take the kids to the Arts and Science Discovery Center at the Richland Academy.

Attend an outdoor historical drama at the Johnny Appleseed Heritage Center, located near Charles Mill Dam south of Mifflin, to learn about Appleseed's life. If it's time for lunch or dinner, pull into the nearby Cabin Restaurant, where you can dine in the cozy log interior or on the patio or deck. Known for great steaks and ribs, the Cabin's menu also offers salads, sandwiches, pastas, and a children's menu.

Take off to bike, walk, or skate the Richland B&O Rail Trail or visit the Mid-Ohio Sports Car Course with auto races all summer long. Louis Bromfield's Malabar Farm offers wagon tours in the summer months. How about taking the kids fishing in the four stocked farm ponds? There's no charge for the fishing poles. Stop for a meal at the historic 1820 Malabar Inn Restaurant featuring down-home cooking. Note that the restaurant is open seasonally.

DIRECTIONS: I-71 to Exit 169; southeast on O'Possum Run Rd.; on right

NEARBY ATTRACTIONS: Kingwood Center, Malabar Farm, Mid-Ohio Sportscar Course, Old Ohio State Reformatory, Mansfield Motorsport Speedway, Mohican State Forest

Bear Run Inn Cabins & Cottages

A family getaway deep in the Hocking Hills

I t seemed a natural next step in the lives of innkeepers Marcia and Bud Myers to open their country home deep in the Hocking Hills as the Bear Run Inn in 1992. During the years they had spent serving in a Lutheran mission in the Philippines, Marcia recalls a revolving-door existence as their family of five welcomed Peace Corps volunteers, the ill, and sometimes the homeless.

While on home leave in 1972, the Myerses purchased a 34-acre farm that included a house without electricity, plumbing, or running water. They set about updating the house and adding rooms incorporating part of the original log cabin into today's parlor. Over the years, the Myerses added land and accommodations to their inn business, which now offers three guest rooms in the inn, four cabins, and a cottage on 550 acres of woodland, ponds, and meadows. Their children and families have moved back to the farm and joined them in the business.

I arrived later than planned on a stormy November evening and

Logan, OH
8260 Bear Run Rd.
800-369-2937
740-385-8007
www.bearrun.com

RATES & RESERVATIONS:
Hours: 9 a.m.–8 p.m. (reservations 24 hrs.)
Season: Year round
Rates: $90–$125 + (Cabins $155+)
Specials: off-season rates; weekday specials in winter, spring
Minimum stay for cabins 2 nights (3 nights on holidays)
Reservations required
Check, Visa, MC, Disc, Amex accepted

ACCOMMODATIONS: 4 rooms, 2 with bath; 4 cabins; 1 cottage

AMENITIES: Hot tub, Cable TV, Internet, Air Cond., CD players, gas fireplaces, grills, fire rings, fishing ponds, hay & sleigh rides

MEALS: Breakfast

OTHER:
Not fully wheelchair accessible
Parking: Lot

was welcomed by Marcia with tea and cookies in the great room. Three guest rooms await on the inn's second floor. The Four Seasons Room has windows in three directions to the rolling hills and woods. Open the curtains and it's a prime spot for watching the sunrise or, on the night I stayed, a sensational lightning show. This room easily accommodates a family as there are two beds—a king bed for Mom and Dad and, to the children's delight, another king bed high in an alcove, accessed by three steps. The Four Seasons Room provides a comfortable space with a platform rocker, loveseat, satellite television, and a large desk overlooking the pond. The Capiz Room contains reminders of the time the Myerses spent in the Philippines, including a beautiful mother-of-pearl inlaid trunk at the foot of a four-poster canopy bed, capiz shell lampshades, and island artifacts like a tuba gatherer on the wall. Romantics love the Victoriana Rose Room, a study in pale shades of peach, rose, and beige with a corner Jacuzzi garden tub, sparkling chandelier, Florentine pattern chair, and queen four-poster bed. An in-room massage can be arranged.

Marcia serves a gourmet breakfast in the great room with windows to the beauty of this southeast Ohio hill country. Nature photographs from the Hocking Hills area line the opposite wall. Breakfast includes a hot egg dish like the hash brown quiche served during my stay, homemade bread or pastries, fresh fruit, and juices. Our breakfast finished with a cinnamony bread pudding studded with raisins. For anytime snacks, there's a hospitality bar with coffee and tea and a guest refrigerator.

Two of the cabins, the Red Bud and the Red Oak, easily accommo-

date 12 guests. Popular with families who come for vacations, family re-unions, and holiday celebrations, the Bear Run Inn & Cabins also host corporate groups. The recently built Red Bud cabin has a master suite on the upper level with a king bed and corner Jacuzzi. Marcia selected linens for the guest rooms in earth tones; some feature rustic themes, such as the one with a log-cabin design. The great room with a gas fireplace adjoins the dining area and fully equipped kitchen. Three ad-ditional bedrooms, rollaways, and three bathrooms provide the space groups appreciate. You can relax in a hot-tub room with a view and a stereo. This cabin's large covered deck looks out to a spectacular spring-time show of redbuds in bloom. Across the road from the Red Bud, the Red Oak cabin offers four bedrooms, a cheerful sunporch, hot tub, gas fireplace, and fully equipped kitchen. There's a shelter house by the pond. Two smaller cabins, the Sugar Maple and the Aspen, are just the right size for a small family or a romantic stay for Mom and Dad. Both cabins offer a fully equipped kitchen, gas fireplace, Jacuzzi, king bed, and queen sofa sleeper.

Families find plenty to do at the Bear Run Inn. Marcia says some young guests are happy to fish all day at one of the ponds stocked with bass, bluegill, and catfish. Bud grew up on a farm down the road and enjoys taking guests on a hayride around the acreage with a running narration on the flora and fauna. He also points out ecological mea-sures taken to conserve the land. You might be treated to a tour in one of the three Amish buggies or a wintertime ride in a one-horse open sleigh. There's a trail map in the in-room directory as a guide for ex-ploring the property. While the Myerses no longer raise farm animals,

kids will find chickens, two ponies named Midnight and Twilight, a llama named Cocoa, and BF the goat down on the inn farm.

Returning guests say the Myerses welcome them back like family. Some guests like to settle in a rocking chair on the large wraparound porch; others remember the hot tub under the stars. The Bear Run Inn has been listed in the magazine *Inn Traveler* as:

One of the Top 15 Inns in North America

Best Inn Where Kids Are Welcome

Best Inn for Viewing Fall Foliage

Reservations are suggested two months in advance during busy seasons; for October, book a year in advance.

THINGS TO DO:

Meal options include fixing lunch or dinner over the campfire by the pond's shelter house near the inn. For an Amish-style meal, head into nearby Logan to the Olde Dutch Restaurant at Rempels Grove where you can also play the 18-hole miniature golf course or enjoy an old-fashioned ice cream soda. You'll find Great Expectations Cafe and Bookstore in a restored 1892 Victorian home in Logan. Visit the children's reading room or browse their selection of best-sellers, general-interest publications, and Ohio books. Have lunch at the store's Cafe & Espresso Bar and check out the gifts and antiques. Next door to the bookstore, Homespun House offers eight rooms filled with giftware, home decor, collectibles, and antiques.

DIRECTIONS: I-71 to Columbus to I-70 to SR 33 to Logan; north on SR 93; left on Bear Run Rd., on right at top of hill

NEARBY ATTRACTIONS: Hocking Hills State Park, antiquing, golfing, fishing, swimming

Great Wolf Lodge

Ohio's only indoor waterpark

Sandusky, OH
4600 Milan Rd.
888-779-2327
419-609-6000
www.greatwolflodge.com

RATES & RESERVATIONS:
Hours: Indoor waterpark open daily
9 a.m.–10 p.m.
Season: Year round
Rates: $125 +
Specials: See website for ongoing specials
Minimum stay 2 nights during some peak periods
Reservations required
Check, Visa, MC, Disc, Amex accepted

ACCOMMODATIONS: 271 suites w/bath

AMENITIES: Hot tub, cable TV, pool, phone in room, Internet, air cond.; all suites include waterpark passes

MEALS: Breakfast, lunch, dinner, snacks; Beer, wine, liquor served

OTHER: Parking: Lot

The holidays are over and everyone needs to get out of the house. Or it's spring break in northeast Ohio and you can only get away for a few days. You're longing for a place that's warm and not too far from home— a destination that appeals to everyone in the family. Head over to Great Wolf Lodge in Sandusky and settle into the warmth—it's 84 degrees year-round—and varied activities at Ohio's only indoor waterpark.

Friends with young children raved about this watery retreat, so I planned a stay with my visiting granddaughters, Lydia (age 8) and Mary (age 10). For a child's-eye view of the experience I asked the girls and my friend's young children to describe their favorite part of Great Wolf Lodge. The kids said: "So much fun and you can stay as long as you like in the waterpark" . . . "Cool—you get to dump water on everyone on the ground" . . . "I liked sleeping in the cabin with the bunks." Their parents said: "We savored the warmth on a chilly March weekend" . . . "The kids get plenty of physical exercise" . . . "The waterpark was so clean, safe, and well guarded." General consensus was that the lodging and the waterpark provide an ideal family togetherness experience.

The fun of this Northwoods adventure begins when you arrive at what appears to be a giant four-story log cabin in Sandusky. The structure is fronted by brightly painted totem poles that extend above the roofline. As you're checking in, glance around the Great Wolf Lodge lobby and you find a microcosm of those who come to stay at this waterpark. It's a never-ending parade of families through the door—parents pushing strollers, toddlers clutching teddy bears, kids pulling along their own suitcases, teenagers with backpacks. Across the lobby, a busload of middle-school kids arrives, representative of the many groups who come for school programs or church retreats.

After check-in, it's time to find your room. Actually, at Great Wolf Lodge it's more than a room—it's a suite. Six suite choices range from four- to eight-person occupancy. Six can stay in the Family Suite with two queen beds, one sofa bed, and a semi-private living area. In a Kid-Cabin Suite, the kids have their own "log cabin" within the suite with a bunk and twin beds; Mom and Dad have a king bed. Three suites have fireplaces, including the largest with three queen beds (one in the loft) and a double sofa sleeper. The newest room style is the Wolf Den Suite with a specially built "den" that gives kids their own cave-like environment. All suites feature a microwave, mini-refrigerator, coffeemaker, and private deck or patio. The room decor continues the rustic theme found throughout the lodge with artwork by North American artisans. Check for specials and package plans.

The kids can't wait to get to Wolf Track Landing, the 33,000-square-foot, five-story waterpark. Take your choice of waterslides: Alberta Falls thrills with two tube slides that twist inside and outside of the lodge and

drop you into a plunge pool; Totem Towers features two body slides. The little ones can enjoy three kiddie slides and a pool of their own. Take it easy and drift down Caribou Creek River or play in the large activity pool. Fort MacKenzie, a five-story interactive tree-house water fort, seems the favorite of all ages. As you climb the tower, you're surprised by devices like pipes that shoot water, funnels and buckets that dump more water, suspension bridges, cargo nets, and web crawls that invite exploring along the way. At the top, help to dump water from a 48-foot tipping bucket that releases 1,000 gallons onto everyone 48 feet below. A warning bell goes off every few minutes to alert guests to the huge splash that is about to happen.

For a quiet break from all the frenetic activity of the waterpark, kids can come to the Cub Cabin Activities Room for make-and-take crafts. At eight o'clock each evening, it's storytime by the fireplace in the lobby, a three-story atrium with conversational seating areas. Other alternative activities include a new climbing wall for children and adults. There's a choice of games in Northern Lights Arcade. Pick up something to remember the trip in the Buckhorn Exchange Gift Shop off the lobby or the gift shop located inside Bear Track Landing.

The fun continues at mealtime at Great Wolf Lodge. Bring the kids to Lumber Jack's Cook Shanty for an easygoing family-style meal. It's a cozy logging cabin interior with red-and-white checked curtains and lantern lights. A diorama with raccoons breaking into a cabin gets the kids' attention near the entrance. Entrees come to the table in black skillets with utensils in a tin pail. Kid favorites include macaroni and cheese, spaghetti and meatballs, popcorn shrimp, mini corn dogs, and

waffle fries. Come back in the morning for a family-style breakfast that offers good variety and is the answer for a family that's in a hurry to get back to the waterpark or start for home. If you have time, the full breakfast is a hearty repast, with juice, fruit, scrambled eggs with cheese, sausage, biscuits, and breakfast potatoes. Other breakfast options are the omlete station and fruit-and-pastry station.

Step into the Gitchigoomie Grille, a casual eatery that takes its name from the Chippewa name for Lake Superior, and you're in a 1940s Canadian fishing lodge. A 1947 Piper Tri-pacer float plane hangs over the bar, and fishing memorabilia covers the walls and fills the shadowbox tabletops.

While Great Wolf Lodge has become a popular destination during Ohio's wintry weather, the lodge is open year-round and guests often combine a stay with visits to other summer attractions in the area.

DIRECTIONS: I-80 to Exit 118 for SR 250 North; just north of SR 2

NEARBY ATTRACTIONS: Cedar Point, Lake Erie islands, lighthouses, museums, shopping, golf

Cherry Valley Lodge

Enjoy the arboretum and gardens at this family-friendly inn

Come to the Cherry Valley Lodge and you may be greeted upon arrival by Cherry or Berry Bear, the lodge's friendly mascots. Kids love this rustic resort with those fuzzy walk-around bears and plenty of fun things to do. Parents appreciate the planned programs for their children, as well as the accommodations, which easily adapt to a family group of any size.

Settle into a spacious guest room and you begin to notice the carefully selected amenities that make a family stay easier. Parents with infants can request a crib, rocking chair, and baby swing. A special package with baby-care necessities will be in the room when they arrive. Crayons, coloring books, board games, and family videos can be picked up at the front desk.

A popular room configuration is the double-double, with two queen beds in an L-shaped layout. An armoire separates the two sleeping areas so parents can watch TV on one side while children sleep on the opposite side. All rooms have refrigerators and coffeemakers. The lodge also offers king rooms, wheelchair-accessible rooms, and Jacuzzi suites.

Newark, OH
2299 Cherry Valley Rd.
800-788-8008
740-788-1200
www.cherryvalleylodge.com

RATES & RESERVATIONS:
Hours: 24 hours/day
Season: Year round
Rates: $125 +
Specials: Children, seniors, AAA
Reservations recommended
Check, Visa, MC, Disc, Amex accepted

ACCOMMODATIONS: 184 rooms w/bath; 16 suites w/bath

AMENITIES: Cable TV, pool, phone in room, Internet, air cond.

MEALS: Breakfast, lunch, dinner, brunch, snacks; Beer, wine, liquor served

OTHER:
Dog and cat living on premises
Guest pets allowed
Parking: Lot

Explore the lodge and you find indoor and outdoor heated pools, along with basketball and volleyball courts. Toddlers can play safely inside a fenced play yard, and a giant green Funbrella is the center for arts and crafts. Get out and stretch your legs with a hike or borrow bikes (with or without baby seats) and take off on miles of scenic bike paths easily accessed from the lodge. When bedtime rolls around, the kids can come to the lobby in their pajamas and sit by the fireplace to hear bedtime stories. Cherry and Berry Bears stick around for this special time, ready to give out bear hugs. The older kids will love the game room with its pool table and large-screen TV.

Enjoy nature close up in the Cherry Valley Arboretum and Botanical Gardens located in the lodge's central courtyards. Stroll the paths and you find a butterfly garden, bluebird and purple martin houses, hummingbird feeders, and sunflowers that attract birds and wildlife to this beautiful natural setting. It won't take the kids long to spot the ducks, so pick up some duck feed at the desk before exploring the arboretum. The Cherry Valley Lodge is thought to be the only U.S. hotel to be designated an official arboretum and botanical garden by the American Association for Arboreta and Botanical Gardens.

A popular summertime activity at the lodge is Camp Cherry Berry Adventure Playground located across the street from the lodge. "This is the way we played when we were kids," parents have been heard to remark. It's all about using your imagination at this day-camp setting. It's not Disney and nothing is plastic. The planners of Camp Cherry Berry provided the props for a "let's pretend" playtime with frame buildings that look like the kids helped to construct, down to a few misspelled

words on the Frontier Town facade. A man-made pond, actually a giant mud puddle, is the big attraction. You can slide into the water and you're allowed to get muddy if you feel like it. Moms can relax: the camp directors have an outside shower for rinse-off and extra play clothes if needed. One lazy July afternoon I watched a gleeful group of boys, ages 8 to 10, jump into the pond and make their way to a platform resembling a battleship, where they took command until pushed off by the next group. They could have been pirates or outlaws as they clambered out of the water and climbed the frame Frontier Town, where they had a shoot-out. Back in the water, on rafts in Huck Finn style, the boys made their way across the water under their own power using a large pole. The adventuresome try Remington's Raccoon Ride, a tire-seat zip slide. A multilevel tree house gives the young set a bird's-eye view of all the activity on the ground below. Children under age 5 must be accompanied by Mom and Dad, who can find a cool spot under the trees to watch the kids at play. The Camp Cherry Valley program also offers games and crafts both on-site and back at the lodge. On Friday and Saturday evenings, the family can come back to roast hot dogs and marshmallows around a bonfire. Be sure to check the activities board in the lobby for event times.

Like everything else at Cherry Valley Lodge, the menu offers kid-friendly items. Think smiley-face French fries, chicken nuggets, mac and cheese, and peanut butter and jelly sandwiches.

Cherry Valley Lodge offers a series of all-American getaways on summer holiday weekends, starting with Memorial Day and continuing through the Fourth of July and Labor Day. The package includes a

classic American barbecue, continental breakfast, and free accommodations for children. On Saturday mornings of those holiday weekends, kids are invited to have breakfast with Cherry and Berry Bears.

THINGS TO DO:

For a family excursion, plan to visit the Wilds while staying at the Cherry Valley Lodge. On a tour of this 10,000-acre wildlife conservation park, you'll see rhinos, giraffes, and antelopes. You can come very close to the wildlife from scenic overlooks or from your safari transport as you travel the open-range grassland and wooded areas. The safari vans are wheelchair accessible.

Other nearby destinations might tempt Mom and Dad to line up one of the skilled child-care providers listed at the inn for time to do something on their own. Visit Longaberger Homestead, catch a summer parade on Main Street, and stay on to shop or dine. The Longaberger Golf Course, designed by Arthur Hills, offers a tournament-caliber 18-hole course named "America's Best New Upscale Public Course of 2000" by *Golf Digest*. At Dawes Arboretum, you can take the 2.5-mile auto tour or set off on your own to hike the marked trails.

DIRECTIONS: SR 16 East to Cherry Valley Rd.; right on Cherry Valley

NEARBY ATTRACTIONS: Granville, Longaberger, Dawes Arboretum, Ye Old Mill, The Wilds

Weatherbury Farm

Far from the madding crowd
—a family farm destination

Avella, PA
1060 Sugar Run Rd.
724-587-3763
www.weatherburyfarm.com

RATES & RESERVATIONS:
Hours: 9 a.m.–8 p.m.
Season: Year round
Rates: $90–$125
Specials: Children, discount for
2-night stays, Weatherbury Farm
kids program
Reservations recommended
Check, Visa, MC, Disc accepted

ACCOMMODATIONS: 3 rooms w/
bath; 3 suites w/bath

AMENITIES: Pool, air cond.

MEALS: Breakfast

OTHER:
Farm animals nearby
Not fully wheelchair accessible
Parking: Lot

Weatherbury Farm, set in the rolling hills of southwestern Pennsylvania, takes its name from the most pastoral of Thomas Hardy's novels, *Far from the Madding Crowd*. Innkeepers Marcy and Dale Tudor discovered the joys of staying at bed and breakfasts and pensiones while on assignment for Dale's company in Germany. They loved the feeling of being treated as one of the family on their weekend and vacation stays throughout Europe and decided to start their own farm B&B in the United States. The bucolic setting of this 100-acre farm just three miles from the West Virginia border and 45 miles southwest of Pittsburgh is indeed far from crowded life. I arrived late in the afternoon on a frigid December Sunday and, soon after pulling into the farmyard, Dale and son Nigel met me at the gate. This welcoming gesture, extended to all guests no matter the weather conditions, was the start of easily feeling at home with the Tudors.

Weatherbury Farm is a no-frills, kid-friendly, working farm where children are invited to help feed a lamb or calf with a Perrier bottle filled with milk. Or they can accompany Farmer Dale on his rounds of feeding the goats, guineas, ducks, geese, and a small flock of those amazing Araucana chickens that lay blue, green, and pink eggs. In colder weather, they can help feed hay to the sheep and Scottish Highland cattle in the pasture. The Tudors dipped into literature for more than the name of their farm with a sheep named Jacob Marley and goats Billy Goat Gruff and Sleeping Beauty. Even the barn cats are named for storybook characters—Cinderella, Prince Charming, and Thumbelina.

Guests find plenty of books and magazines in their rooms, but no TV or radios. The only television is located in the music room. Unlike accommodations filled with antiques and breakables, you don't have to worry about Johnny climbing on the couch or precious china being knocked off a table in this room.

The Tudors expanded the number of guest rooms by renovating the original summer kitchen, which had stood idle for more than 50 years. They call the room on the lower level Sariah's Kitchen, to honor Sariah Murdock, a member of the family who first owned the farm. The walk-in fireplace used for cooking in the 1880s remains. A Victorian bedstead, decorative tole lamp, and touches of mauve in the quilt and flowered pillows dress up the room. I found a copy of Hardy's novel on the antique chopping block that serves as an end table. For a family stay, the sofa converts to a double bed. On the second floor of the summer kitchen, Mother's Sewing Room has blue-and-white gingham accents, and a genuine Singer sewing machine. The king bed can be converted to twin beds and the daybed sleeps one. Windows from a 1790s brick home in West Middletown were used in the restoration. Jane's Bedroom, the only guest room in the farmhouse, features a flower-stenciled

border with the flower motif repeated on the comforter.

Weatherbury Farm continues to be a work in progress. You might find the Tudors working on a building or involved in a painting project during your stay. The newest accommodation is the Livery Stable, an old barn they found in Washington, Pennsylvania. After being dismantled and moved to the farm, this building now stands as a fine example of adaptive reuse. It will offer three suites with a living room on the first floor and a bedroom and bath upstairs. The spacious new suites can sleep five or six, and a second-story balcony will look out to the meadow. Plans for the Livery include a wheelchair-accessible room and a large room on the lower level of the bank barn where breakfast will be served.

Plan for a hearty country breakfast with kid-pleaser items like Green Eggs, No Ham and banana pancakes. Breakfast at Weatherbury Farm is more than about filling the stomach for the day ahead of work and play on the farm. The Tudor family sit down with their guests at a table set with colorful Fiestaware, as they remember this time of sharing experiences as what they liked most about their European bed and breakfast stays.

Kids who come to stay for two days or more receive their own red packet with Weatherbury Farm's "Official Farm Kid Workbook." It's filled with educationally sound activities and safety advice, which is essential for a stay on a rural spread with animals and farm machinery.

THINGS TO DO:

Marcy Tudor observes that while many guests arrive armed with a list of places to visit, many end up staying on the farm. As one young guest noted in large block letters in the guestbook, "I don't ever want to leave."

Weatherbury also offers on-site events like the Sheep Fest celebrating the heritage of wool and sheep in Washington County. With a resident blacksmith, Nigel Tudor, living on the farm, Weatherbury hosted the first Hammer-In with blacksmith demonstrations in 2002.

Many families stay two or three days and may want an afternoon of exploring nearby attractions. The Meadowcroft Museum of Rural Life, a reconstructed 19th-century village in nearby Avella, offers a full slate of workshops and celebrations. The kids will love the Pennsylvania Trolley Museum in Arden, where you can take a ride on a vintage streetcar. On a return trip to Ohio, stop at the Homer Laughlin China Company and retail outlet for Fiestaware in Newell, West Virginia.

It's only a mile to find lunch or dinner at the Breezy Heights Tavern, a delightful eatery cum miniature golf course. To top it all off, the owner has filled the place with stuffed game animals. Breezy Heights offers ribs, barbecued chicken, and a kid's menu. Another meal option is to pick up the makings for a picnic at the Avella Market.

DIRECTIONS: I-80 to I-79 South to Exit 54 for Bridgeville; west on SR 50 for 22 miles; left on SR 231; right on Sugar Run Rd.

NEARBY ATTRACTIONS: Meadowcroft Museum of Rural Life, Pennsylvania Trolley Museum

Dearborn Inn

Stay in a historic replica home at Henry Ford's inn

In 1930, as Henry Ford watched passengers arriving at the Ford Airport on Oakwood Boulevard, he came to the decision that he needed a hotel to take care of visitors. Ford commissioned the renowned architect Albert Kahn to design the world's first airport hotel, the Dearborn Inn. The red brick Georgian-style inn, situated on a 23-acre site on Oakwood Boulevard, opened for business in 1931. Ford was the first person to sign the guestbook. Other notable guests who have stayed at the Dearborn Inn include Orville Wright, Eleanor Roosevelt, Jack Dempsey, Bette Davis, Jesse Owens, James Doolittle, and Norman Rockwell.

Ford's preference for Early American or colonial-style interiors is reflected by the historic reproduction furnishings found throughout the inn. The lobby, a traditional room with fireplace, towering flower arrangements, and a background of classical music, exudes the elegance of a bygone era. An adjacent sunporch furnished with wicker looks out to the historic replica houses on the green behind the inn.

Accommodations at the Dearborn Inn, now a Marriott Hotel, include the main inn, two colonial lodges—Burbank House and McGuffey House—and five individual colonial homes. Families enjoy the

Dearborn, MI
20301 Oakwood Blvd.
313-271-2700
marriott.com/DTWDI

RATES & RESERVATIONS:
Hours: 24 hours/day
Season: Year round
Rates: $90–$125+
Specials: Children, seniors, singles
Reservations recommended
Visa, MC, Disc, Amex, Diners Club accepted

ACCOMMODATIONS: 222 rooms w/bath; 24 suites w/bath

AMENITIES: Cable TV, pool, phone in room, Internet, air cond.

MEALS: Breakfast, lunch, dinner, brunch; Beer, wine, liquor served

OTHER:
Guest pets allowed
Parking: Lot

inn's parlor rooms, which offer a guest room with king or queen bed, bath, and a parlor with sofa bed.

Families also like to stay in one of five historic replica homes located in a semicircle behind the hotel. Ford got the idea for the colonial homes in the 1930s when he and his son, Edsel, stayed at the Beverly Hills Hotel in Los Angeles. Their accommodation was one of the California bungalows behind the hotel. Ford was enchanted with the bungalows and returned to Dearborn to build five historic homes honoring famous Americans on the hotel property. Architects and crews reproduced the homes of Edgar Allen Poe, Oliver Wolcott, Barbara Fritchie, Patrick Henry, and Walt Whitman. Great care was taken to duplicate the original homes. I stayed in the Edgar Allen Poe cottage, complete with a black raven over the doorway. With a living room, small dining room, kitchen, two baths, and an upstairs bedroom with an attic-like ambience, the Poe cottage is the only individual unit. The remaining four homes have six suites opening from a central foyer. Each suite consists of a parlor with sofa bed, a guest room, and one or two baths. After a recent interior renovation, the Poe cottage is decorated in burgundy and yellow, the Wolcott house in colonial blue and yellow, and the Patrick Henry house, appropriately, in red, white, and blue.

An interesting chapter was added to the Dearborn Inn's history during World War II when pilots from the Detroit Airport a few miles away stayed on the inn's first floor. One wing of the first floor is still referred to today as "Pilots' Row."

After a day of touring Greenfield Village and the Henry Ford Museum, come back to the inn's Ten Eyck Tavern for a meal. This fam-

ily-friendly restaurant has the relaxed ambience of a colonial tavern and an appealing menu with home-style offerings like traditional fish and chips, oven-roasted turkey with stuffing, potpie with a pastry lid, and kid-portion mac and cheese, mini-burgers, and hot dogs. Friday night's special is an Italian pasta buffet, while weekday noons find an all-you-can-eat pasta buffet. Sleep in on the weekends, when breakfast is served until 1:00 p.m. Check out the photographs of the Ford family on the tavern walls.

For steaks, chops, and seafood, plan to dine in the Early American Room. Tall windows with a view of the front lawn and the inn's grand entry make for a pleasant experience. Sunday brunch is a special occasion here. Complimentary champagne is served starting at noon, and brunch proceeds with a choice of carving stations, an omelet bar, hot entrees, and an elegant display of desserts. If Mom and Dad would like to have a quiet meal in the Early American Room, baby-sitting can be arranged during a stay at the inn.

Relax on the grounds of the Dearborn Inn, which offers 23 acres of gardens, a heated outdoor swimming pool, and two tennis courts.

THINGS TO DO:

Dearborn, one of America's most visited cities, offers so many intriguing destination choices that you'll want to allow more than a day to explore. Start your visit at the Henry Ford, the new designation for the list of attractions you'll find down the road from the Dearborn Inn. Included under the Henry Ford's wide umbrella are Greenfield Village, the Henry Ford Museum, an IMAX theater, and, opening in spring 2004, the highly anticipated Ford Rouge Factory tour.

Stroll Greenfield Village, Ford's outdoor museum, for a look at more than 300 years of American history. Stop at the Wright Home & Cycle Shop from Dayton, Ohio, see Edison at work in the Menlo Park complex, and visit the Henry Ford Model T exhibit where you can take a test ride in a restored Tin Lizzie.

Many of America's treasures are on display in the Henry Ford Museum. Everyone seems to have a "must see" exhibit—the rocking chair President Abraham Lincoln sat in the night he was assassinated, the Rosa Parks bus, Buckminster Fuller's futuristic Dymaxion House, the John F. Kennedy presidential limousine.

An exciting new exhibit, "Heroes of the Sky," opened in 2003 with an overview of the first 40 years of flight, 1900-1940. Fifteen airplanes are on display, including a DC-3 with a 95-foot wingspan that hovers over the exhibit. Don't miss the First Flight Gallery with its exact replica of the first Wright Flyer, an experience that takes you back to 1903 as you hear the seagulls and the crashing surf of the Atlantic Ocean.

DIRECTIONS: I-94 East to Exit 206 for Oakwood Blvd. N.; 2 miles on left.

NEARBY ATTRACTIONS: Henry Ford Museum, Greenfield Village, Ford Rouge factory tour

LAKE ERIE STAYS

Any fine summer day is a good time to take off for the Lake Erie islands. There's a holiday air on the ferry as you approach your destination, with each island promising a day of fishing, hiking, swimming, shopping, or visiting wineries. After a summer visit, come back to stay in the "shoulder seasons"—optimum times as the islands are not as crowded and you might find a better accommodation rate. Spring and fall migrations bring birders back to the islands, while special events like the September Butterfly Festival on Kelleys Island offer a great time for a family visit.

I stayed at four island accommodations, hopping from Kelleys Island to South Bass Island and taking a longer ferry trip up to Pelee Island, Ontario. Once the ferries stop running, the only transportation to the Lake Erie islands in the winter is by Griffing Air Service, so I included two Ohio-based inns for year-round stays along Lake Erie

It's worth a longer ferry ride to get to Pelee Island, a relaxing destination with uncrowded roadways, a small summer theater, and the Pelee Island Winery. Take your choice of a bed-and-breakfast room or a suite at the Tin Goose Inn and have the pleasure of dining in the inn restaurant, Gooseberry's Island Cuisine. At Put-in-Bay on South Bass Island, I discovered the Getaway Inn Bed & Breakfast, a rustic log inn located in a quiet residential neighborhood yet within a short three-block walk to downtown Put-in-Bay. Families are welcome during the week at the Getaway Inn. First-time visitors to the island can hop on the Put-in-Bay tour train with stops at significant island venues. On Kelleys Island, I found two distinctively different accommodations to include in this roundup of island stays. The Eagle's Nest B&B, a comfortable European-style cottage and adjacent guesthouse, welcomes families while Sun and Surf B&B, a contemporary inn set on the shores of Lake Erie, is a couple's getaway destination. While on Kelleys Island, explore the Glacial Grooves or spend an afternoon on the sandy beach at Kelleys Island State Park.

East of Cleveland in the resort community of Geneva-on-the-Lake, the sunsets at the Lakehouse Inn are spectacular. Situated at the west end of town, this complex offers a choice of inn rooms, cottages, and a private cottage. It's a short walk to "The Strip," the Lake Road entertainment district. In Port Clinton, SunnySide Tower, an 1879 Victorian with 11 rooms, appeals to a wide range of guests, and hosts weddings and family reunions as well as romantic getaways.

The Lakehouse Inn

Savor the sunsets from this lakeside inn

It's the spectacular sunsets over Lake Erie that bring many to the Lakehouse Inn in Geneva-on-the-Lake. Savor Mother Nature's display from the inn or from lighted decks on the beach. The Lakehouse Inn has lodging choices to please everyone, with eight rooms and suites in the main bed-and-breakfast inn and eight family cottages across from the inn. And then there's the crown jewel of the complex, the Beach House, a newly constructed luxury cottage.

The Fagnilli family, longtime residents of nearby Geneva, Ohio, were looking for a place on Lake Erie's shores when they found the Lakehouse property and purchased it in 2000. Karen and Sam Fagnilli, daughter Andrea, and son Nathan worked together to renovate the existing inn and cottages, and to build the Beach House and winery. Finishing touches were removal of trees to open up the lake view from the inn and extensive landscaping. Andrea became the innkeeper, while Karen plans and prepares meals with help from Nathan.

The inn suites include a sitting room with a gas fireplace, Jacuzzi, bedroom, and bath with shower. I stayed in the second-floor Sunset Suite, aptly named as two sets of double windows and two single win-

Geneva-on-the-Lake, OH
5653 Lake Rd.
440-466-8668
www.thelakehouseinn.com

RATES & RESERVATIONS:
Hours: 7:30 a.m.–10 p.m.
Season: Feb–Dec
Rates: $90–$125 +
Minimum stay 2 nights on weekends Memorial Day to Labor Day
Reservations recommended
Check, Visa, MC, Disc, Amex accepted

ACCOMMODATIONS: 5 rooms w/ bath; 3 suites w/bath; 9 cottages

AMENITIES: Cable TV, phone in room, air cond., Jacuzzis

MEALS: Breakfast (other meals upon advance request); Beer, wine, liquor served

OTHER:
Not fully wheelchair accessible
Parking: Lot

dows provide sunset views. The suite comfortably sleeps five with a daybed, small sofa, and queen bed. A Jacuzzi for two centers the main room, with a gas fireplace in the corner. Welcome extras in the suites include cable television, along with a small microwave and refrigerator. There's a Cape Cod feel to the smallish guest rooms done up in light colors. A full cooked breakfast is served to guests who stay in the inn and the Beach House.

For family stays, the one- and two-bedroom cottages offer a living room, kitchen, and cable television. Kids love the evening bonfires on the beach and a chance to make s'mores. The beach beckons for walks or swims. Other on-site activities include bocce ball, horseshoes, and croquet.

Book a stay at the Beach House and you can view the lake from just about everywhere—the living room, the bedroom, the dining table, even the Jacuzzi tub. Simple white Swedish country-style furnishings set against sun-washed aqua and yellow walls make it a peaceful setting for a getaway. There's a full kitchen, dining area, fireplace, cable TV, queen bed, and spacious bathroom with two-person shower. Step out the glass doors from the bedroom or the living room to your private deck and listen to the waves or catch another of those Lake Erie sunsets.

Take the steps at the side of the Beach House to the Lakehouse Winery tucked under the cottage. Come to the glassed-in tasting room in the fall or winter and stay cozy by the fireplace while sampling wines. In warmer months, move out to the deck right on the water.

The inn's great room with nautical decorative touches encompasses

the dining room with windows to the lake and a comfortable sitting area with sofas and chairs grouped around a gas fireplace. Cable television, games, books, and magazines make it a popular gathering place.

Guests rave about the food that comes from the Fagnilli kitchen. Plan to have a romantic five-course dinner. Some of the entree choices are pork tenderloin, grilled salmon, and stuffed chicken breasts. Innkeeper Andrea has found that while she sets up tables for two for these special dinners, often the couples staying for a weekend end up dining together the second evening. If you want a casual meal, order a Fagnilli homemade pizza.

There's a full complement of inn events and packages at the Lakehouse Inn. With a commercial kitchen, the Fagnilli family can cater special events for 25 to 30 people. Corporate groups, local organizations, and family reunions have found their way to the inn. One of the inn's most interesting gatherings each September is the Spencerian Saga, a group who come to honor Platt R. Spencer, a native of nearby Geneva, who developed the flowing, graceful Spencerian style of penmanship.

Women take over the inn for the Girls' Weekend Out in early December. Cooking classes, pampering sessions, and a chance to make a gingerbread house without children underfoot are the draw for this weekend, along with plenty of time to just hang out and chat. Another popular package is the Murder Mystery dinner, which includes, of course, the chance to play sleuth along with dinner, an overnight stay, and breakfast the following morning.

THINGS TO DO:

Folks are rediscovering Geneva-on-the-Lake with a nostalgic trip back to this resort community, which started as a picnic grounds in 1869. Located at the west end of Geneva-on-the-Lake, the Lakehouse Inn is situated in a quiet area but is within walking distance of "The Strip," the entertainment district along Lake Road. You'll find amusement park rides at Erieview Park like the ones you remember from childhood, and you can enjoy miniature golf at a course that's been in continuous play since 1924. Remember arcades? Spend some time at Woody's World Game Arcade and then stop at Eddy's Grill, reminiscent of a 1950s diner, and order burgers or a foot-long hot dog. Mary's Kitchen is the place for a home-cooked meal.

On the west end of town, the kids will love the bumper boats, go-carts, batting cages, and play area at Adventure Zone. Relax at Geneva State Park's sandy beach or check out the fishing charters at the park's 383-slip marina. Finish the day with a lakefront concert under the stars at Geneva Township Park. Music and ethnic food are on the menu at the Old Firehouse Winery when the Northeastern Ohio Polka Fest comes to the Strip in June, followed by the Celtic Feis in August.

Take time to explore the Wines & Vines Trail along the south shore of Lake Erie. Along the way, you'll come upon some of Ashtabula County's covered bridges. A great place to break for a meal is the Ferrante Winery, with a full-service Italian ristorante.

DIRECTIONS: I-90 to Exit 218; north on SR 534; on left

NEARBY ATTRACTIONS: Geneva-on-the-Lake resort, wineries, covered bridges, historic Ashtabula harbor

Eagle's Nest Bed and Breakfast

A rustic hideaway on Kelleys Island

The Eagle's Nest Bed and Breakfast, a European-style cottage originally built for laborers who came to work in the quarries on Kelleys Island, nestles under the trees on Cameron Road. It's a quiet hideaway.

There's a touch of whimsy in the design of the green board-and-batten cottage and adjoining guesthouse. A third structure on the property, the Eagle's Nest Gift Shop, a sweet Amish-designed building painted cranberry red, is accented with green and white scalloped trim. The shop is stocked with the work of local artists, country crafts, jewelry, gifts for the gardener, special-occasion baskets, and inspirational books.

The guesthouse, stained the same light green as the main house, offers three spacious units. Two have a bedroom, kitchenette, and private bath, while the third offers a living room, kitchen, bedroom, and bath. All the units have sizable sundecks. There's an inviting country feel to the decor. My second-floor unit was furnished with simple white-painted furniture, a few antiques, blue-and-yellow patterned linens, and a soft Grandma's quilt. A compact kitchenette makes meal preparation possible for those on a longer island stay. This comfortable space opens to a deck that

Kelleys Island, OH
216 Cameron Rd.
419-746-2708
www.eaglesnestbnb.com

RATES & RESERVATIONS:
Hours: 8 a.m.–9 p.m.
Season: Spring – Fall
Rates: $105–$125
Specials: Children
Minimum stay 2 nights on weekends in summer
Reservations recommended
Check, Visa, MC, Disc accepted

ACCOMMODATIONS: 4 rooms w/bath

AMENITIES: Pool, air cond.

MEALS: Breakfast

OTHER:
Dog living on premises
Not fully wheelchair accessible
Parking: Lot

looks out on the inn's tree-bordered backyard. The guesthouse decks offer a private spot to sun or to sit in the evening and listen to the night sounds of the island.

Mark and Robin Volz, who have been innkeeping on Kelleys Island since 1992, linger over breakfast and share the history of the island with their guests. Eagle's Nest welcomes children, and the Volzs' dog may become your new pal during your stay. The shady grounds at the front of the property offer outdoor seating; the decks have umbrella tables. You'll find barbecue grills, campfire rings, and a horseshoe pit. One couple who return to stay at Eagle's Nest every year tailor their island visit so that he can fish on Lake Erie while she suns by the B&B's pool. Guests come next door to the Volzs' cottage for a full country breakfast with a view to the yard and pool. Mark prepared a breakfast of fresh fruit, juices, an egg dish, and sausage during my late August visit.

THINGS TO DO:

Take a leisurely drive or hop on a golf cart to enjoy the architecture of Kelleys Island. The entire island has been declared a National Historic District and is listed on the National Register of Historic Places. Along the way, you'll pass the Kelley Mansion, built by Datus Kelley for his son Addison in the 1860s, historic houses with gingerbread trim, snug vacation cottages, and early stone structures like Kelley Hall. The Inscription Rock State Memorial, a large limestone rock with ancient Indian pictographs, stands as a reminder of the time when Erie Indians inhabited the island.

Kelleys Island State Park offers a sandy beach for swimmers, a stone

pier for fishing, a free double boat-launching ramp, picnic areas, and miles of hiking trails. Kelleys Island boasts 30 miles of road for cycling. Known as the "Walleye Capital of the World," the island lures anglers who fish Lake Erie's waters for yellow perch, walleye, smallmouth bass, and white bass. You'll find bait shops and fishing supplies, and you can buy a fishing license on the island.

During your stay, take time to explore the Glacial Grooves, the largest prehistoric glacial grooves remaining in the world. Information plaques help tell the story of the deep grooves and markings sculpted on the soft island limestone by glaciers. While walking the trails or following the Lake Erie shoreline, it's easy to find fossils.

Another fun and informative stop on an island tour is Sweet Valley Trading Post and Butterfly Kingdom on Division Street. Formerly known as the Butterfly Box, the gift shop is stocked with books on nature and butterflies, toys, collectibles, jewelry, and clothing, with many butterfly-theme items. Owner Jean Kuyoth also carries packaged foods, mixes, coffees. and teas. Step into the warmth of the Butterfly Kingdom area and you're in an enclosed flower garden with hanging baskets and fragrant plants—butterfly bush, dahlias, lantana, snapdragons. Children squeal with delight when the butterflies start to light on their colorful summer clothing. Small informational signs can make this short tour a learning experience.

The Kelley Island Historical Museum is located in a stone building that at one time housed the German Reformed Church. Many island events emanate from this location, including the Butterfly Festival in September when folks come to the island to help tag butterflies. Other popular events are Treasure Island Day, an island-wide garage sale, and the July Islandfest.

In downtown Kelleys Island you can stop for ice cream, rent bikes and golf carts, or pick up a pizza or sub at Caddy Shack Square. The kids will want to spend some time at Caddy Shack Square at the Game Shack Arcade or play the 18-hole miniature golf course.

For a casual meal with a lake view, plan to eat at Kelleys Island Brewery located just down the road from the Eagle's Nest. Along with handcrafted beers, you'll find home-style cooking with great hamburgers, homemade brew chips, and beer-battered French fries. There's patio dining and live music at this microbrewery across from the old Neuman's dock. For fine dining, head to West Bay Inn or the Island House Restaurant.

DIRECTIONS: 1 1/2 miles from ferry; west on Lakeshore to Cameron; right on Cameron

NEARBY ATTRACTIONS: Fishing, hiking, swimming, Glacial Grooves

Sun and Surf

*Savor the sunrise
from this lakeside inn*

A contemporary bed and breakfast is a rare find. On my first visit to Sun and Surf Bed & Breakfast on Kelleys Island, I felt I had stumbled onto a stunning private residence. While the view of Lake Erie from the many windows in this lakeside home was compelling, the kaleidoscopic compilation of vivid hues of aqua, purple, and blue pulled me inward to view the cutting-edge rooms.

A colorful mosaic on the home's stone and stucco exterior gives a suggestion of what to expect when you enter. It's all about the lake. Panels with a wave motif in deep blue stained glass side the front door, and iridescent mosaics are set into the wide entrance hallway floor. Straight ahead there's the view of Lake Erie from the living room and dining area. Step up to the second-floor landing and you're treated to soaring two-story vistas of the lake. Sit down for breakfast and you'll find more sparkling mosaics worked into the surface of the dining table. Decorative pieces and whimsical lighting continue the play of colors in Sun and Surf's modern interior. Along with the open space of the living, dining, and kitchen area on the first floor, a room that serves as a den can also be set up for the massage therapist on weekends.

Kelleys Island, OH
102 McGettigan
888-597-3003
419-746-2236
www.sunandsurf.net

RATES & RESERVATIONS:
Hours: 7:30 a.m.–11 p.m.
Season: Year round
Rates: $125 +
Minimum stay on weekends only
Reservations recommended
Check, Visa, MC, Disc, Amex accepted

ACCOMMODATIONS: 4 rooms w/ bath; 1 suite w/bath

AMENITIES: Hot tub, cable TV, phone in room, Internet, air cond., lakefront deck for every room, mini-fridges, separate climate controls

MEALS: Breakfast (other meals avail. upon request)

OTHER:
No children or pets
Not fully wheelchair accessible
Parking: Lot

Innkeepers Beth and Terry Kranyak bring with them a background of living and working on Kelleys Island. Beth is a fourth-generation descendant of the founder of the island, Datus Kelley. Terry serves on the island's planning commission. The Kranyaks relied on experience gained as owners of a previous bed and breakfast on the island in planning and building Sun and Surf. Their list of must-haves included private baths, air-conditioning, Direct TV, and a lakefront deck with seating.

This secluded island accommodation attracts romantics. It's a "same time, next year" destination for honeymooners and anniversary celebrants. Sun and Surf does not accommodate children or pets. The Kranyaks keep a low profile, balancing the fine line of being there if you need them while giving guests the sense that the house is theirs for the duration of their stay. You might find a note on the front door to let you know where to find a cold beer, a snack, directions to your room, and a number to reach the innkeepers if needed. Arrive as I did on a perfect late summer day and enter the house to find music softly playing, a spectacular view of Lake Erie, a welcoming note, and you're ready to call this retreat your own special place.

Each of the four guest rooms on the second floor is a visual treat. One is done in pleasing combinations of blue and green, with a queen bed and leather lounger. In the next room, framed art is brilliant against coral walls, and the contemporary queen wood bed is highlighted with black. A corner room is the dressiest, with a white four-poster and pink-and-white plaid bed and window treatments with touches of lime green. The fourth room, a suite the size of a small apartment, can function as a private meeting space with a full-size kitchen, living room with queen pullout sofa, and a separate bedroom with queen bed and generous sitting area. Three of the guest rooms have Jacuzzis; all offer personal refrigerators and private decks. You catch a different lake view from each room or deck. Sunrises from the Sun and Surf's location on the eastern side of the island are spectacular. Be sure to reserve ahead for this popular Kelleys Island accommodation, as weekends fill quickly in season.

Breakfast at Sun and Surf can turn out to be an event. There's an easy flow of conversation between those cooking and guests in the open kitchen. The Kranyaks have enjoyed having students from Europe as part of their summer staff, and guests appreciate their culinary specialties. A Polish student worked at Sun and Surf during the summer I visited, and pierogi appeared on the breakfast buffet along with made-from-scratch pastries, yogurt, an egg dish, bacon, fresh fruits, and granola. Terry and Beth often invite a neighbor, a longtime resident of Kelleys Island, to come to breakfast, giving visitors a unique insight into the island's history.

THINGS TO DO:

The decks and patio at Sun and Surf provide an extension of the private setting guests love at this bed and breakfast. Some look forward to sunbathing on the dock; others come to observe the migrating birds. The patio is used late in the season, with California heaters extending the time spent near the rocky beach.

An ardent outdoorsman, Terry knows the island like the back of his hand. He can suggest trails like the North Shore Loop Trail, which takes you through thick woodlands along the shoreline, or the East Quarry Trail that follows the edge of an abandoned quarry. Guests are welcome to take one of the Kranyaks' bicycles to explore the island on their own.

The Kelleys Island Audubon Club sponsors several events, including "Nest With the Birds," timed to coincide with the spring bird migration, and bird walks and nature talks in May. The Fall Feathers and

Foliage Festival happens in late September. On weekends you can visit the Charles Herndon Galleries and Sculpture Garden located on 10 acres near Sun and Surf.

I often check with local residents to find the best place for a meal. The Village Pump came out a winner as the favorite watering hole on Kelleys Island. Located downtown on Lakeshore Drive, popular menu items include hand-dipped onion rings, sweet potato and eggplant fries, and Lake Erie perch served up in sandwiches and as a dinner entree. Another spot to enjoy a meal is the Wine Company Bistro at the Kelleys Island Wine Company. Relax in the pavilion and sample some of the wine company's award-winning vintages or dine on pasta dishes or pizza inside the restaurant.

DIRECTIONS: SR 2 West to SR 269 North to SR 163 East to Kelleys Island Ferry Boat Line

NEARBY ATTRACTIONS: Cedar Point, African Lion Safari, Put-in-Bay, fishing, biking

SunnySide Tower Bed and Breakfast Inn

Stay at a restored Victorian farmhouse near Lake Erie

Port Clinton, OH
3612 NW Catawba Rd.
888-831-1263
419-797-9315
www.sunnysidetower.com

It's the tower on the white Victorian farmhouse you notice first as you turn into the lane leading to the SunnySide Tower Bed & Breakfast Inn on Catawba Island. Sandusky businessman Nathaniel Amos Hadden built the original structure on this site in 1879 as a family home. The Hadden family parlor was the setting for meetings of the Catawba Ladies Afternoon Club as well as piano recitals. When Marie Rhodes, current owner John Davenport's great-grandmother, and her husband Almond bought the place, a new chapter was affixed to the home's history. Marie added rooms, which eventually totaled 28 including a tower room. She called the place SunnySide Tower after reading about Washington Irving's home, Sunnyside Manor House, on the banks of the Hudson River in Tarrytown, New York. Irving's home is topped by a three-story tower, and other similarities to Marie Rhodes's home include

RATES & RESERVATIONS:
Hours: 8 a.m.–10 p.m.
Season: Year round
Rates: $90–$125
Specials: Seasonal specials, whole-house bookings
Minimum stay 2 nights in Jun, Jul, Aug
Reservations recommended
Check, Visa, MC, Disc accepted

ACCOMMODATIONS: 10 rooms w/bath

AMENITIES: Hot tub, cable TV, air cond., Jacuzzi, 2 kitchens, great room, grills, children's park, trails, tennis courts, basketball courts, sledding hill, photography services available

MEALS: Breakfast, lunch, dinner, brunch, snacks

OTHER:
Guest pets allowed
Parking: Lot

many additions made to his original two-room Dutch farmhouse.

With 10,000 fruit trees on the acreage, Marie started renting rooms to seasonal orchard workers. The inn was also known at the time for serving family-style chicken dinners. After Marie's death in 1942, the house was converted into apartments used by servicemen from nearby Camp Perry. Subsequently it served as an office and storage space for a lumber company and finally stood unoccupied for years until John Davenport purchased it in 1987. Like many abandoned properties, the interior was left to ruin and John had to gut the structure, saving what he could. The floors in Room 1 and on the inn's second floor are original. All the paints used in the renovation are 1890-1900 reproductions of period milk paints. After three years of hard work, John welcomed the first guests to the inn on Labor Day weekend in 1996.

John likes to reuse things, so "shabby chic" is the style throughout the public rooms and the 10 individually decorated guest rooms. The Spinnaker Room reflects John's interest in sailing, with photos of his first Pacific Swiftsure Race on the deep blue walls. John's brother, Jerry Davenport, carved the bas-relief sculpture above the headboard of the pineapple four-poster. Oars serve as drapery rods in this nautical-theme room, and a sink is set into an antique chest. After retiring from office, President Rutherford B. Hayes stayed at SunnySide Tower when he traveled from his home in Fremont, Ohio, to Mouse Island, his private getaway. The Rutherford B. Hayes Room is a salute to Hayes and the American flag, with red, white, and blue the predominating colors. Accents are patriotic bunting and a folded American flag that flew over the U.S. Capitol, presented to John when he retired after 20 years of

military service. Many guests are intrigued by the Tower Room, with its access to the Widow's Watch. Mind your head as you step up the stairs for a view from the top of the house. You can spot the fences that mark the start of the nature trails and jogging paths that inn guests can use. Popular with honeymooners, a special Tower package consists of a two-night stay, two full breakfasts, a complimentary bottle of wine, and $50 toward dinner at Mon Ami Restaurant and Historic Winery. Another special, the theater package, includes two tickets to Playmakers Civic Theater in Port Clinton, one night's accommodation, and two country-style breakfasts.

Glacial rocks from the grounds surround the fireplace in the great room. John salvaged architectural pieces like the gingerbread attic peaks during the renovation and placed them over the room's doorways. Another of John's collectibles is an 1896 piano that became a piano bar in the great room. Photos of his great-grandmother's early orchards from the 1930s and '40s adorn the beautiful stained walnut walls. The adjoining den is a perfect hangout for kids who come to stay at SunnySide.

John has gone out of his way to make his inn a comfortable place for everyone, including guests who happen to be tall. A tall guy himself, he made sure the showerheads were high enough and used no footboards at the end of the beds. This versatile innkeeper wears many hats. Talk to him about music and he may bring out his guitar to sing and play a while.

In the dining room, a primitive art mural shares the space with one of Great-Grandma Rhodes's plates. Antique pieces include a Hoosier hutch and a sideboard from Mexico. For breakfast, John served an omelet with ham, cheese, and fresh chives and tarragon from his herb garden.

THINGS TO DO:

The welcome sign is out for families at SunnySide Tower. With 10 guest rooms and generous public spaces like the great room, den, sunporch, and dining room, the inn makes a great destination for weddings, reunions, and retreats. Whole-house rentals allow families to visit and have meals together when gathering for these events. And what about the kids? There's ample space to play outdoors. The Sunny-Side Tower property abuts Heigel Park, with tennis courts, a children's playground, basketball courts, and soccer and baseball fields. Winter brings sledding on the 30-foot sledding hill, and inn guests can access 17 acres of wooded nature trails and jogging paths. SunnySide Tower's location on Catawba Island makes it an ideal spot for taking off for other Lake Erie islands, Cedar Point, or Marblehead.

Mon Ami, a historic winery and restaurant constructed in 1872 of locally quarried limestone, is just minutes away from SunnySide Tower. Take a tour of the vaulted wine cellars offered daily at 2:00 and 4:00 p.m. Dine in the formal dining room or the casual chalet. The Saturday-night seafood buffet is popular, and Sunday summer afternoons bring live blues and jazz to the garden at Mon Ami.

Another dining spot to check out is the Garden Restaurant in downtown Port Clinton. Located in the lighthouse-keeper's home built in 1900 after the lighthouse and original home were razed, the restaurant offers a windowed garden room and cozy smaller rooms that remain from the original dwelling.

DIRECTIONS: SR 2 West to SR 53 North; left on Schoolhouse Rd.; right on NW Catawba Rd.

NEARBY ATTRACTIONS: Western Basin Lake Erie Islands, Cedar Point, Marblehead Lighthouse, Hayes Presidential Center, Magee Marsh Wildlife Center, East Harbor State Park, swimming, boating, fishing, antiquing, golfing

Getaway Inn

A quiet stay on a busy island

Guests of the Getaway Inn Bed & Breakfast get a little history lesson when they stay at this South Bass Island accommodation. I learned that the island's first dwellings were log cabins and that the cabin built on this site between 1830 and 1840 was one of the first. In 1998, the cabin was renovated and an addition built. Some of the timbers from the original cabin can be found in an upstairs bedroom and in the cellar. When the site was cleared for the renovation, black walnut milled from felled trees was used for paneling the three-season room; maple wood was utilized as flooring for the second-floor hallway.

The Getaway Inn Bed & Breakfast, located in a quiet neighborhood three blocks from the downtown section of Put-in-Bay, is a true getaway for visitors to South Bass Island.

Put-in-Bay, OH
210 Concord
877-228-1114
419-285-9012
www.getawayinn.com

RATES & RESERVATIONS:
Hours: 8 a.m.–9 p.m.
Season: Year round
Rates: $90–$125 +
Minimum stay 2 nights on weekends
Reservations required
Check, Visa, MC, Disc, Amex accepted

ACCOMMODATIONS: 4 rooms w/ bath; 2 suites w/bath

AMENITIES: Cable TV, air cond.

MEALS: Breakfast

OTHER:
Not fully wheelchair accessible
Parking: Lot

Set back from Concord Avenue, the log exterior is brightened by flower beds and an American flag. Step through the front door into an entryway infused with light from windows in the loft above. Straight ahead is a charming three-season room with a rattan sofa, glass-top table, and chairs. Doors open from this room to the stone patio, with umbrella table, chairs, and a chiminea.

The spacious gathering room surprises first-time visitors. In contrast to the simple rustic exterior, this is a contemporary room with a soaring two-story ceiling and floor-to-ceiling windows that look out to the back lawn and the woods beyond. Breakfast is served in the gathering room; when there's a full house, 14 can be served using both the long dining table and a smaller round table. On my late July visit, a variety of melons and juice set out on the buffet complemented a delicious strata. Other Getaway Inn breakfast favorites are quiche, French toast, and muffins.

The six guest rooms of various sizes have steep European-style ceilings. I stayed in the Captain's Room, with nautical decor in navy and blue, including a ship's border motif in the bathroom. Staying true to the area's history, a painting of a ship from the Battle of Lake Erie high on the bedroom wall provides a reminder of Oliver Hazard Perry's victory. An upstairs room with a train motif featured a quilt-covered queen bed and a loveseat that opens to an extra bed. A favorite room for business stays offers two queen beds. All six rooms have private baths, a good bedside reading light, and a TV. With views to nature and the warmth of black walnut and maple woods, decorative effects are kept simple, with the judicious use of maps of the Great Lakes and prints of local scenes.

While weekends are reserved for adults only at the Getaway Inn, children are welcome from Sunday through Thursday. A suite on the lower level with a TV room and a guest room with one queen bed, two twins, and two vanities and private bath is an ideal space for families. Seniors should check out the special AARP rates available during the shoulder seasons of spring and fall only. Meeting planners find that the Getaway Inn provides a peaceful setting for meetings and special events. Catered meals can be arranged for these functions.

THINGS TO DO:

While the Getaway Inn is located away from the bustle of downtown Put-in-Bay, it's an easy three-block walk to shop or have a meal. For a casual lunch, stop at Mossbacks, located in a historic building, and snag a window-side booth for a view of the bay. Wonder about the name of this restaurant? It seems early in the history of the island, the South Bass islanders were called "mossbacks" for living on a rock. Sample Mossbacks' appetizer menu of Cajun-seasoned walleye nuggets or olivenos (olives stuffed with Asiago cheese), or order a generous-size Mossback burger like the bacon and Roquefort or the black bean burger. For fine dining with a view, I found Ladd's Landing the perfect spot. Take your choice of dining inside or on the east porch or patio. All three settings offer views in one direction of the Perry Monument and two historic homes: Inselruhe, a Steamboat Gothic home built in 1875, and the Hunker Villa, circa 1870. In the other direction, you look out to the busy marina. Menu standouts at Ladd's are crabcakes with a black-bean corn relish and polenta-encrusted fried calamari. Entree choices included Lake Erie perch (a house favorite), grilled rack of lamb with a cabernet rosemary reduction, and several pasta offerings. Specials the night I dined were mahi-mahi with a tropical salsa and roast duck.

To learn more about this island that stretches beyond the familiar downtown, get a golf cart or hop on the Put-in-Bay Tour Train, offering a one-hour tour with stops along the way at Heineman Winery, Perry's Cave, Alaskan Birdhouse Wildlife Museum, and Perry's International Peace Memorial. On your own, stop at the Stonehenge Estates, a stone farmhouse and wine press cottage.

Spend some time at the Lake Erie Islands Historical Society, located behind the Village Hall off Catawba Avenue. The museum has a large collection of written accounts, models, and paintings of the Battle of Lake Erie, along with Ford Tri-motor airplanes, wildlife displays, and ship models. On a Sunday afternoon, find a spot on that lovely green space downtown known as DeRivera Park and watch the weekly parade of vintage cars go by.

DIRECTIONS: SR 2 West to SR 53 North to Miller Boat Line

NEARBY ATTRACTIONS: Perry monument, caves, museums, wineries, live entertainment, golf, shopping, restaurants

Tin Goose Inn

A quiet stay in a Victorian inn on Pelee Island

Pelee Island, Canada's most southerly point and Lake Erie's largest island, appears as a wide swath of green as you approach it from the Sandusky-based ferry. Once ashore, you find a patchwork of pristine beaches, marshes, forest, vineyards, cottages, and a small business area.

I followed the East-West Road past the Pelee Island Winery to find the Tin Goose Inn, a Victorian home built in 1896. Turning into the driveway, I caught a glimpse of the blue of Lake Erie straight ahead. Guests of the Tin Goose have beach access just a stone's throw from the inn. Follow the path from the parking lot to the side entry that leads to a parlor where you check in for your stay. A quiet reading room, the parlor adjoins the game-stocked lounge. At check-in, guests are offered a complimentary glass of local wine.

Take your choice of accommodations at the Tin Goose. If space and amenities like TV and VCR are important, book one of the four

Pelee Island, Canada
1060 East-West Rd.
877-737-5557
519-724-2223
www.goose.on.ca

RATES & RESERVATIONS:
Hours: 24 hours/day
Season: Apr–Nov
Rates: $125 +
Specials: Seniors, singles
Minimum stay 2 nights on weekends in Jul & Aug
Reservations recommended
Visa, MC, Amex accepted

ACCOMMODATIONS: 8 rooms w/ bath; 4 suites w/bath

AMENITIES: Hot tub, air cond.

MEALS: Breakfast, dinner; Beer, wine, liquor served

OTHER:
Not fully wheelchair accessible
Parking: Lot

cottage suites nestled in the woods at the back of the inn. Named for the four points on the island—Sheridan Point, Lighthouse Point, Mill Point, and Fish Point—the suites offer a spacious sitting area, queen bed, private bath, refrigerator, coffeemaker, and electric teakettle. Each is fronted by a lovely screened-in porch complete with hammock. The eight small, cozy inn rooms are true early B&B style and share four full and two half baths. The themed decor is reflected on each door's nameplate: The Music Room, Noah's Ark, Wine Cellar, The Sanctuary, Admiral's Room, Heaven's Gate, The Ruby Room. The Victorian Garden Room, a corner room with views to the side and front yards, offers a sitting area with loveseat and wing chairs. Summer cottage style best describes this room, with green and pink painted furniture, a trellis effect over the bed, and flowers. Inn guests find extras like kayaks, an outdoor screened hot tub, and a deck with umbrella tables.

The inn dining room, a summery enclosed porch, looks out to the lawns and gardens. Striped ticking window treatments and tablecloths in purple, yellow, and deep blue set against yellow walls give the old inn porch a contemporary feel.

In late afternoon, the enticing aromas of dinner greeted arriving guests and those of us in the lounge and parlor. Starters included Pigeon Bay clam chowder, Vintage Goose paté, and Stone Road brie served with an apple and whiskey compote. A memorable Caesar salad served with a basket of inn-made herb flatbreads and pesto butter was followed by a refreshing sorbet. Main course choices included Lake Erie pickerel baked with white wine and lemon, and applejack pork—pork tenderloins with an apple and Jack Daniels compote—served with caramelized onion and smoked cheddar smashed potatoes. Pair one of Pelee Island's wines like their Premium Select Chardonnay or Gamay Noir with the pork entree or Melange Blanc with the pickerel. Dessert offerings include vanilla bean brûlée or cafe au lait parfait along with specialty coffees. Reservations are a must for dinner, as Gooseberry's Island Cuisine is a dining destination for other island visitors as well as those staying at the Tin Goose.

Breakfast is gourmet fare, with a buffet of juices, homemade muffins, a platter of fruit, and coffee set out on the lounge bar. Also offered is a hot dish, which during my stay was a delicious quesadilla. Background classical music with breakfast and soft jazz with dinner added to the ambience.

Package stays include a springtime birding package and an autumn Fall Colors special. A popular fishing package in June features Stewart Simmond, who takes fishing enthusiasts out to the best spots. The Pelee Appreciation package includes an overview of the island's history with complimentary passes for the Pelee Winery tour and the Pelee Island Heritage Center, two nights accommodation with breakfast, a picnic lunch, and bike rental.

During my late August stay, the young staff at the Tin Goose were attuned to guests' needs. Ask for something and it's delivered pronto. Inquire about island events or tours and you're given directions and a map. Service for meals was nicely paced, and the entire inn was spotless.

THINGS TO DO:

Starlight Theatre, opened in 2003, offers a romantic comedy alternating with a cabaret production throughout the summer. Next door to the theater, the Pelee Art Works showcases island art and gifts.

Take time to visit the Pelee Lighthouse, built in 1833. Access to the lighthouse is by a trail through deciduous forest and wetlands to Lighthouse Point on the northeastern spit of Pelee. Uncrowded roadways and flat terrain make the island a delight for bikers of all ages. For a break in your driving or biking tour of the island, stop at Alles Gute Bake Shop and Delicatessen on North Shore Road and pick up a fresh deli lunch or some baked goodies for a lakeside picnic. Find a bench along the shore and enjoy the view of Lake Erie.

You'll find the Pelee Island Heritage Center located in the town hall. Nature walks take off every day from the center at 10:00 a.m. and 2:00 p.m. Birders find that Pelee Island has birding life similar to Point Pelee, and the Heritage Center provides a sightings book.

Stop at the Pelee Island Winery, one of Canada's first and largest estate wineries, for a tour and wine tasting. Pick up a buffalo burger, chicken breast, or sausages at the pavilion's deli and prepare your own

lunch in the pavilion. Parents can sip some wine while the children enjoy a playground.

DIRECTIONS: From ferry dock, follow East-West road past Pelee Island Winery to inn.

NEARBY ATTRACTIONS: Pelee Island Winery, birding, fishing, beaches, cycling

COLLEGE TOWN STAYS

College towns attract seasoned inn-goers with cultural events, collegiate athletics, seminars, and lecture series. Alumni come back for homecoming and commencements. Parents visit with prospective students in tow and find a town so appealing they want to come back to visit on their own. These college hostelries are also becoming destination inns for leisure travelers as well as attractive settings for conferences and retreats.

I found a wide range of architectural styles in the inns visited. The Kenyon Inn is the kind of traditional red brick structure we expect to find on a liberal arts campus like Kenyon College, Ohio's oldest private institution of higher learning. Dine in the Kenyon Inn Restaurant and be sure to stop at the Kenyon College Bookstore, open 365 days a year.

The Allen Memorial Art Museum and the Oberlin College Conservatory of Music draw visitors to the town of Oberlin. Plan to stay at the Oberlin Inn, a contemporary inn constructed in 1954-55, and you'll have a short walk to both the art museum and the conservatory. The view from the Garden Room Restaurant to Tappan Square, the green space that anchors this college town, is pleasant in any season. Allow time to browse Oberlin's interesting mix of shops and eateries.

On my visit to Miami University in Oxford, Ohio, I discovered a charming larger bed and breakfast, White Garden Inn B&B. With spacious gathering spaces, this inn often hosts university-related events. It's also popular with visiting parents of Miami students. Look forward to a gourmet breakfast and time to sit on the porch and enjoy the gardens.

Clevelanders make the trek up to Ann Arbor, Michigan, for a variety of reasons. Some come on fall football Saturdays for UM games; others come to sample the fine theater and music events on this Big Ten campus. Then there are all those intriguing shops in Ann Arbor, including many bookstores. The place to stay in a central location is the Bell Tower Hotel located across from the UM campus. Plan for a leisurely meal at the hotel restaurant, the Earle Uptown

Granville, the final destination in my search for college inns, resulted in a two-for-one visit. I recommend a stay at both the Granville Inn, built in the English Tudor style, and the Buxton Inn, a Federal-style inn built in 1812. Both are full-service inns offering fine dining. It's worth spending a weekend in this college town to take in all the events and shopping options.

Oberlin Inn

Spend a few days in this
quintessential college town

Oberlin Inn's location across from the town's center, Tappan Square, makes it the ideal lodging choice for prospective Oberlin College students and their parents, alumni returning for reunions, and commencement weekends. This college inn's setting also appeals to those who think of the town of Oberlin as a destination. The Oberlin Inn is only a few minutes' walk from the Allen Memorial Art Museum. Shops are clustered nearby on Main and College Streets, and an extensive offering of student recitals and concerts awaits a few blocks away at the Oberlin Conservatory of Music.

Brewster Pelton's log cabin, built in 1833, served as Oberlin's first inn. The college hostelry was variously known throughout the 19th century as Pelton's Cabin, Palmer House, the Park House, the Smith House, and finally the Park Hotel. Oberlin College took possession and management of the Park Hotel in 1895 and after

Oberlin, OH
7 North Main St.
800-376-4173
440-775-1111
www.oberlininn.com

RATES & RESERVATIONS:
Hours: 24 hours/day
Season: Year round
Rates: $125 +
Specials: Seniors
Reservations required
Visa, MC, Disc, Amex accepted

ACCOMMODATIONS: 66 rooms
w/bath

AMENITIES: Cable TV, phone in
room, air cond., Internet, rec center

MEALS: Breakfast, lunch, dinner,
brunch, snacks; Beer, wine, liquor
served

OTHER:
Guest pets allowed
Parking: Lot

extensive remodeling in 1927 changed the name to the Oberlin Inn. The current contemporary-design motel was constructed on the site of the old hotel in 1954–55.

Renovation is an ongoing process in this 66-room property. I stayed in the east wing in a recently renovated room comfortably furnished with classic traditional pieces. There's Oberlin art on the walls, with reproductions of works from Allen Memorial Art Museum exhibitions. In the south wing, a suite that adapts easily for business or family stays is composed of one large room with a fireplace, conference table, wet bar, and Murphy bed with access to an adjoining guest room.

Mondays through Thursdays find business travelers staying at the inn. Guests have privileges at the Philips Recreation Facility on the Oberlin campus, with an Olympic-size pool, Nautilus center, racquetball, squash, tennis, and a jogging track. Meeting planners like the campus location of this full-service inn and utilize the inn's Conference Services Group's personalized approach. Oberlin Inn's multifunction meeting rooms offer full audiovisual capabilities.

Come to dine in the Garden Room when the flower gardens fronting the Oberlin Inn are in full bloom. Across the street, Tappan Square's 13 acres of green space are brightened with 65 flowering baskets. Wintertime is equally lovely; one December Sunday found the grounds covered with fresh snow, evoking a Currier & Ives scene. Sunday brunch at the Oberlin Inn is a leisurely affair and also a good value. It's a chef's choice so you may find a made-to-order omelet bar one Sunday and a waffle bar the following week, along with three hot entrees, sausage gravy and biscuits, corned beef hash, and brunch staples of eggs, breakfast meats, and hash brown potatoes. A full salad bar is offered, and an elegant array of desserts is set up on a round table.

For a casual meal anytime during your stay, stop at Brewster's for salads, sandwich baskets, hearty skillet entrees, and a extensive selection of domestic and foreign beers. The Garden Room menu, featuring

new American cuisine, changes periodically—but a few favorites that remain on the menu include a chicken quesadilla appetizer, warm duck salad served with walnut vinaigrette dressing, and entrees of apple and raisin chicken, and shrimp and scallop tapas drizzled with a light sherry sauce. Holidays bring special meals and events to the Oberlin Inn. The New Year's Eve Gala features a four-course candlelight dinner, dancing, entertainment, and a midnight champagne toast. The overnight stay includes a sumptuous New Year's Day brunch. Murder Mystery Weekends are fall and winter events.

THINGS TO DO:

Oberlin has earned its share of accolades, and is considered by some to be the most cosmopolitan small town in America. Arts enthusiasts can take a walk on Main Street and find three art venues. Start with a visit to the Allen Memorial Art Museum, a splendid building designed by Cass Gilbert at the corner of Main and Lorain Streets (Route 511). Next, stop at Ginko Gallery on Main Street, a shop housing six working fiber studios and a contemporary craft gallery. Continue on Main to Firelands Association for the Visual Arts (FAVA), located at the New Union Center for the Arts. Check out the current exhibition and browse FAVA's gallery shop, Uncommon Objects.

Step inside the Ben Franklin Store and along with the fabrics, notions, toys, and paper supplies you expect to find in a five-and-dime, you'll encounter Mindfair Books. Bookstore owner Krista Long stocks a large selection of remainders, as well as new and used books, along with classic wooden toys such as Lincoln Logs, Tinker Toys, and puzzles. Make your own jewelry at Bead Paradise II at the Studio on the Park. The shop carries an extensive collection of beads from around the world, as well as ethnic, retro, and vintage clothing. Gifts from Mexico, fabrics from Africa, and musical instruments from around the world are showcased on the second floor of Bead Paradise II.

On Tuesdays, Thursdays, and Saturdays, the Oberlin Heritage Center offers tours of three historic houses: the 1866 James Monroe House, the 1884 Jewett House, and the 1836 Little Red Schoolhouse. You can visit one of Frank Lloyd Wright's Usonian houses, Oberlin College's Welzheimer/Johnson House, on the first and third Sunday of every month from 12:00 to 4:00 p.m.

DIRECTIONS: I-90 to SR 58; on right

NEARBY ATTRACTIONS: Oberlin College & Conservatory, Frank Lloyd Wright house, Underground Railroad Quilt & Monument, Splash Zone

Kenyon Inn

A classic inn on the Kenyon College campus

The Kenyon Inn, a Williamsburg-style hostelry, is located on the grounds of Kenyon College, Ohio's oldest private institution of higher learning. Today's inn, with 32 rooms (including a wheelchair-accessible room), replaced the original white clapboard inn, the Alumni House, in 1985.

The red brick, white pillared exterior of the Kenyon Inn belies the interior, which was completely updated in 2002. The look is fresh and bright, with an eclectic mix of colors and furnishings. Returning alumni find the Kenyon colors in several first-floor rooms, where purple duvets cover the beds and purple-and-green plaid accents are used for window treatments and pillows. A refreshing color palette of lemon, lime, and mango highlights what general manager Ernie Linger refers to as the "sherbet rooms." On the inn's second floor, the style is a bit more formal, with strong colors used in French country-style ceiling treatments and furnishings. On my December visit, I stayed in a spacious corner room named for the Right Reverend Philander Chase, founder of the village of Gambier and Kenyon College. The Philander Chase

Gambier, OH
100 W. Wiggin St.
800-258-5391
740-427-2202
www.kenyoninn.com

RATES & RESERVATIONS:
Hours: 24 hours/day
Season: Year round
Rates: $90–$125
Specials: Children, seniors, AAA, Kenyon visitor discount, corporate guest discount
Reservations recommended
Check, Visa, MC, Disc, Amex, Diners Club accepted

ACCOMMODATIONS: 32 rooms w/bath

AMENITIES: Cable TV, pool, phone in room, Internet, air cond., use of Kenyon College fitness facility, golf at Mt. Vernon Country Club, sweetheart room

MEALS: Breakfast (Continental), lunch, dinner, brunch (Sunday); Beer, wine, liquor served

OTHER:
Parking: Lot and on-street

Room, with its deep aqua ceiling and coordinating colors of coral and gold, overlooks the campus. An example of the stylistic mix used in the renovation can be seen in the bathrooms, which pair contemporary polished chrome sconces and fixtures with a porcelain sink reminiscent of earlier times. All rooms have writing tables, good lighting, plump pillows, and puffy duvets. A popular room for weekend getaways is the Sweetheart/Anniversary Room. With an extra-large bath featuring a Jacuzzi tub, the room overlooks the valley and the Kokosing River.

A stroll down the inn's halls provides a short trip through the history of Kenyon College. I was drawn to early photographs of the college's 1924 centennial celebration and the 1894 football team.

Reservations are a must for this busy college accommodation. There's a waiting list for many dates, including homecoming, alumni week, and graduation; prospective students and their parents come to stay throughout the year. Business travelers find amenities like high-speed Internet access and comfortable writing desks in the guest rooms. Corporate groups can expand their meeting space to the Eaton Center on campus.

"While the inn caters first to the needs of the college," says Ernie Linger, "it is also becoming a destination inn." The Kenyon Inn Restaurant brings folks back for special occasions such as anniversaries and birthdays. Alumni who return to Kenyon for their weddings often book the inn and arrange a bridal luncheon or rehearsal dinner. A compact and intimate dining space, the restaurant seats 34 and in warmer months can expand to the patio to seat 50. Chef Mark Cheffins came to the Kenyon Inn from the Worthington Inn's Seven Stars Restaurant, which garnered a four-star Mobil rating under his tutelage. His prior experience includes stints at New York City's Four Seasons and Helmsley Palace, as well as top spots in Dallas. For a celebratory meal, you can look forward to being served at a leisurely pace, which invites lingering over four courses. The a la carte menu changes seasonally. A winter menu sampling during my visit included seared ahi tuna or carpaccio mezzaluna appetizers, followed by an arugula or Mediterranean salad, and entrees of roast rack of New Zealand lamb or bourride setoise, Atlantic grouper poached in a Mediterranean fish soup. Dessert selections include a dense chocolate caramel pecan torte, wildberry Charlotte, and crème brûlée. Reservations are suggested. I stopped for lunch before noon on a Monday and found the dining room buzzing, with most tables taken by 12:30. Breakfast for inn guests only is an expanded continental.

THINGS TO DO:

Everyone stops at the Kenyon College Bookstore—students, faculty, and visitors who come to Gambier for just that purpose. This bookstore, open 365 days a year, started in 1828 in a log cabin and is the oldest college bookstore in the United States. According to manager Jack Finefrock, who also teaches Classical Chinese Language and Literature at Kenyon, "nothing about the place is slick—it's real." A first visit gives the impression of a friendly country store with a little bit of everything on the shelves, from books to gifts to toiletries. Stocked with academic and scholarly books geared to those 18 to 25, the bookstore is also a gathering place for students and residents of this village of 600. You can

pick up a cup of coffee and a muffin or croissant and settle down on a comfortable couch to read. Students find study tables in a quiet area of the store. *New Yorker* editor Paul Goldberger (whose son attended Kenyon College) described the bookstore as "the least Disneyland-looking place" he'd ever seen. The only other retail store I found in Gambier was the Weather Vane, a tiny shop tucked into the alley by the post office, offering unique women's clothing.

Guests of the Kenyon Inn can play golf at the Mount Vernon Country Club. Hikers and bikers can take off on the 14-mile paved Kokosing Gap Trail. Stop at the Village Market and pick up lunch from the sandwich deli. Follow the Middle Path, a gravel walkway through campus that has been there since the college's founding, to find a bench or an Adirondack chair for an impromptu picnic.

I visited the first week of December, when two special events attract visitors: the Gambier Craft Show and the Advent Festival of Lessons and Carols at the Church of the Holy Spirit. A half hour before the advent concert, carillon bells rang out over the snow-covered campus, calling us to the celebration. Trees strung with tiny white lights and the candlelit chapel made it a perfect Christmas card scene.

DIRECTIONS: I-71 South to exit for SR 13 (Mansfield); south on SR 13

NEARBY ATTRACTIONS: Amish country, cycling, canoeing, museums, antiquing, crafting, festivals

The Buxton Inn

Look for the sign of the cat

Step into the foyer of the Buxton Inn and you immediately feel a sense of history. The inn's original registration desk remains, and old guest registers carry the signatures of notable guests—including President William McKinley, John Philip Sousa, Harriet Beecher Stowe, and Henry Ford. Built as a tavern in 1812, the inn served as Granville's first post office and as a stagecoach stop on the line between Columbus and Newark. Listed on the National Register of Historic Places, the Buxton Inn is the oldest continuous operating Ohio inn still using the original building.

With its peach exterior and white spindle railing, it's easy to spot this two-story Federal-style inn on East Broadway. The sign of the cat, an early welcoming sign to 19th-century travelers, provides further identification on the front tree lawn. On the Fourth of July,

Granville, OH
313 E. Broadway
740-587-0001
www.buxtoninn.com

RATES & RESERVATIONS:
Hours: 24 hours/day
Season: Year round
Rates: $90–$125
Reservations required
Check, Visa, MC, Disc, Amex accepted

ACCOMMODATIONS: 25 rooms w/ bath; 5 suites w/bath

AMENITIES: Cable TV, phone in room, air cond.

MEALS: Breakfast, lunch, dinner, brunch, snacks; Beer, wine, liquor served

OTHER:
Not fully wheelchair accessible
Parking: On-street

American flags hang from the second-story portico, which is draped with red, white, and blue bunting.

Orville and Audrey Orr bought the inn in 1972 and spent two years painstakingly restoring the 160-year-old building and researching its history. They welcomed their first guests in 1974 with five guest rooms in the original building. Since that time they have methodically worked their way around the block, purchasing houses as they became available, and now offer a total of 25 overnight guest rooms and suites. The Warner House, circa 1815, was added to the Buxton Inn complex in 1983. Built around 1880, the Victorian House was the next restoration project, adding six more rooms in 1986, and Founders' Hall opened in 1994 with another six guest rooms. Both the Victorian House and Founders' Hall at one time offered overnight guest rooms and later boarding rooms for students at the Granville Female Academy across the street. The Ty Fy Main House, a Sears catalogue house built in 1900, was opened to guests in 1992 with two guest rooms and two guest suites. Named by the builder, Ty Fy Main means "my mother's house."

The Orrs have carefully furnished the rooms with fine antiques appropriate to each house's style. Their collection includes items from the Early Empire, Victorian, and Arts and Crafts eras. It's good to know the stewardship of this traditional inn will continue with the Orrs' daughter, Melanie, as general manager. Guests find a small refrigerator and coffee and tea service in their rooms.

Walk to the back of any of the historic houses in the Buxton Inn complex and find a formal garden with fountains and masses of flowers. Orville Orr uses 600 container pots and 200 hanging baskets of flowers for the garden area. A row of ornamental pear trees lines the brick paths, and a pergola overlooking a sunken garden is a setting for weddings.

Select one of the Buxton Inn's dining rooms and sit down to the pleasures of the table. The main dining room, located in the old part of the inn, is a formal white-tablecloth dining option, while the Victorian dining room offers a cozy setting with a bar. I met Audrey and Melanie

Orr for lunch in the greenhouse. With exposed brick walls, a tile floor, and a profusion of green plants within the glass expanse, it's the most pleasant of dining settings.

Favorites on the American/French menu include coquille of seafood (shrimp, scallops, and crab baked on the shell in a rich Mornay sauce), roast duckling served with a cranberry-orange sauce, and Louisiana chicken (breaded breast of chicken served with a mushroom-pimento cream sauce). Vegetarians find sun-dried tomato pasta and Mediterranean vegetable ragout. Topping the dessert list is triple chocolate mousse cake prepared by Orville's mother, known to most who come to the inn as "Grandma." Old-timey desserts include peach melba and gingerbread served with warm lemon sauce. For lighter fare, head downstairs to the old Tavern featuring a menu of appetizers, sandwiches, salads, and burgers. During the stagecoach era, the Tavern—with original rough-hewn beams, an open hearth, and stone walls—provided sleeping quarters for the coach drivers.

THINGS TO DO:

Granville, home to Denison University, presents a perfect destination for an architectural walking tour. First settled in 1805 by families from Granville, Massachusetts, and five nearby towns, Granville was laid out as a typical New England village. Today on the tree-lined streets, you'll find fine homes representative of this early American settlement, including many structures listed on the National Register of Historic Places. Take time to tour the Robbins-Hunter Museum located just steps from the Buxton Inn in the Avery Downer House on East Broadway. Built in 1842, it is an outstanding example of a Greek Revival building. Robbins Hunter Jr. bequeathed his house, filled with fine 18th- and 19th-century furniture and decorative arts, to the Licking County Historical Society. Another museum to visit is the Granville Lifestyle Museum, an Italianate house with 19th- and 20th-century furnishings and family items. If you remember post-WWII America, check out the state-of-the-art 1949 kitchen.

There's a small group of shops worth exploring on East Elm. I stopped at Home Pleasures, Ltd., and found French country linens, candles, Caspari papers, and works by local artists. Enticing aromas of freshly baked bread from the Village Baker pulled me into the shop. If you're ready for a coffee break, select from the pastries and muffins and find a table on the patio.

DIRECTIONS: I-71 South to I-70 to SR 37 North to downtown Granville

NEARBY ATTRACTIONS: Denison University, Dawes Arboretum, Octagon Indian Mounds, golfing, cycling, hiking

Granville Inn

An inn that looks like an English country house

The Granville Inn, an English Tudor-style manor house designed by Frank Packard, was built in 1924 by John Sutphin Jones, president of the Sunday Creek Coal Company. Jones used native sandstone quarried from his nearby country estate, Bryn du Farm, and employed Welsh stonemasons who had settled in Granville to build the structure on the grounds once occupied by the old Granville Female Academy. Based on the model of an English country house, the inn is set back from East Broadway under a canopy of mature maples. The interior reflects the popularity of 1920s Tudor design, with leaded glass, tapestries, and carved oak paneling. Jones hosted a grand party when the inn opened, sending engraved invitations to everyone in the community.

Initially the inn thrived as an upscale full-service hostelry, but later went through a period of decline until the current owners, the Robert Kent family, took over in 1976. During a five-year restoration, new oak paneling, painstakingly stained to match the original woodwork, was installed on the inn's lower level. Oak paneling is repeated in the library, an informal meeting room with bookcases and fireplace. Photographs of earlier days at Denison University line the walls of the Denison Room. The Granville Inn, a popular setting for weddings and

Granville, OH
314 E. Broadway
888-472-6855
740-587-3333
www.granvilleinn.com

RATES & RESERVATIONS:
Hours: 24 hours/day
Season: Year round
Rates: $90–$125
Reservations recommended
Check, Visa, MC, Disc, Amex accepted

ACCOMMODATIONS: 27 rooms w/ bath; 3 suites w/bath

AMENITIES: Cable TV, phone in room, air cond., Internet access

MEALS: Breakfast (Continental), lunch, dinner, snacks; Beer, wine, liquor served

OTHER:
Not fully wheelchair accessible
Parking: Lot

receptions, displays wedding photographs in the gallery on the main floor of the inn.

With 27 rooms and three suites in the uniquely configured building, no two rooms are exactly alike. The Squire's Loft, a charming room under the eaves, is long and narrow with sloping ceilings due to the roofline. The expansive Marquis Suite features a grouping of sofa and chairs, fireplace, wet bar, dining table, desk, and spacious sleeping area. The wallpaper in this suite sports a fruit motif, and a bay window looks out over the landscaped lawns. Most rooms have a queen or twin beds and are done up in traditional reproduction furniture and flowered wallpaper. Public spaces include the Club Room. Popular with groups who stay at the inn, this is the place to gather for a game of pool or cards, or a comfortable chat. Amenities for corporate guests include data ports, voice mail, and a national newspaper each morning.

Like most accommodations in college towns, the Granville Inn is quickly booked for special college weekends. The inn handles this by offering a lottery for rooms for Fall Parents Weekend and graduation.

The inn's main dining room, with its copper-hooded fireplace and tall leaded-glass windows, provides an elegant setting for lunch and dinner. Settle back in the camel leather chairs at tables set with maroon-rimmed china and small gaslights. House specialties include spice crusted ahi tuna, roast quail, and chicken ravioli. With an inhouse bakery, the inn is known for its trademark loaf of homemade raisin bread, thickly frosted and served with honey butter, and dessert favorites like English walnut pie. Reservations are suggested for the inn's popular Easter and Thanksgiving buffets.

For lighter meals or to relax over a cocktail, stop in the Granville Inn's pub. In warm weather, the pub opens to a flagstone terrace. Inn guests find a continental breakfast set up in the hallway at 6:30 A.M. Stop in the Granville Pub on Sunday evening for jazz.

A popular package at the Granville Inn is the Dinner Theatre Weekend offered in March and November. The Licking County Players bring in a production with performances in the Great Hall. This overnight package includes a buffet dinner and breakfast. The inn hosts an annual craft show in early November with juried crafts for sale. If you'd like to have time to see all the holiday decorations, the Granville Inn gives you that chance after Christmas, as the inn's decorations are not taken down until January 11.

Summertime brings patio cookouts every Friday night, weather permitting. Golf packages are available through the inn at the historic Granville Golf Course designed by golf architect Donald Ross in 1924.

THINGS TO DO:

Denison University's hillside campus beckons with a full calendar of events. Before your visit, check to learn about upcoming lecture series, theater offerings, and musical performances.

You'll find a variety of browsable shops a few blocks from the inn. Pick up new and used books at Readers' Garden, a cozy corner bookstore. East Broadway shops include the James Store with classic clothing for women and children. Kussmaul Gallery carries contemporary American crafts, jewelry, and fine art, and you'll find fresh-cut flowers daily in the back room. Take a lunch break or have an ice cream treat at Victoria's Olde Tyme Deli & Cafe, an old-fashioned ice cream parlor that spills out to the sidewalk in warm weather. A short drive from the inn, at the Shoppes at Seven Pines complex on River Road, the Andrew Lidgus Galleries showcase the work of 60 national and international artists. Neighboring shops include the Toy Station with a selection of vintage toys and unique toys from around the world, and the Scrapbookery with a large inventory of scrapbooking supplies.

DIRECTIONS: I-77 South to I-70 East to SR 37 North

NEARBY ATTRACTIONS: Denison University, Dawes Arboretum, Longaberger Baskets, the Homestead

White Garden Inn

Superb hospitality combined with charm

Many who come to stay at a bed and breakfast dream of someday owning one of their own. Such was the case for Linda and John Alexander, who followed their dream of becoming innkeepers after John retired. They traveled from their home in Florida to the Midwest, with stops in Alabama and North Carolina, in their quest to find a college-town setting. A friend suggested they take a look at Miami University in Oxford, Ohio, and on their initial visit they fell in love with the campus and the city. "It felt right," John says. "I said to Linda, 'This is it.'" When they weren't able to find an older house that met their specifications, the Alexanders purchased five acres two miles outside Oxford on which to build. Linda was the general contractor for the 9,000-square-foot, three-story slate gray house. The inn's spaciousness is apparent from the generous entryway to the common areas with 10-foot ceilings on the first floor and second-floor guest rooms with nine-foot ceilings. A stroll through the back lawns and gardens planted with peonies, butterfly bush, daylilies, roses, and hydrangea—all in white—explains the name, White Garden Inn B&B.

Based on their own bed-and-breakfast stays, the Alexanders place

Oxford, OH
6194 Brown Rd.
800-324-4925
513-524-5827
www.whitegardeninn.com

RATES & RESERVATIONS:
Hours: 24 hours/day
Season: Year round
Rates: $90–$125
Minimum stay on some weekends (call for details)
Reservations required
Check, Visa, MC, Disc, Amex accepted

ACCOMMODATIONS: 4 rooms w/ bath; 1 suite w/bath

AMENITIES: Cable TV, phone in room, air cond.

MEALS: Breakfast

OTHER:
Not fully wheelchair accessible
Parking: Lot

a high priority on public gathering spaces. Guests can find quiet spots in the sunroom, parlor, veranda, and the foyer at the top of the stairs. The sunroom, with windows to the garden and woods, welcomes with groupings of flower-splashed wicker and a vibrant mural painted by Sarah Alexander, the Alexanders' daughter-in-law. A wet bar with refrigerator is stocked with sodas and wine. The parlor, a formal space with antique-mantled pine fireplace and oak player piano, is often the setting for receptions. The Alexanders enjoy opening their home to outside groups and frequently host university-related events. Autographed photographs of guest artists who have stayed at the White Garden Inn grace an upstairs hallway. Pianist Andre Watts, the Canadian Brass, classical guitarist Robert Bluestone, and National Public Radio's Diane Rehm have been guests.

Linda made all the duvet covers, window treatments, and shower curtains for the garden-themed guest rooms. In the Autumn Rose Room, the four-poster mahogany bed with a rose and gold duvet is set against goldenrod walls. Linda pays tribute to her grandmother in Iva's Garden Room, with some of Iva's gardening implements displayed atop the armoire. An old brass bed with a blue-and-white checked duvet sprinkled with roses and two twig chairs fill the cozy space, which overlooks the garden and gazebo. I stayed in the Butterfly Room, with sunshine yellow walls, a simple pine wardrobe, white iron bed, and wicker chaise longue. At the end of the hall, the Periwinkle Room is highlighted by a quilt in the blue-and-white periwinkle pattern. A burnished brass bed, antique caned lounge chair, and maritime prints complete the room. John Alexander says that when guests first see the

Queen Anne Suite, they gasp in surprise. Nearly 700 square feet, the cathedral-ceilinged suite is furnished with a massive walnut wardrobe, heavily carved bed, and Victorian settee and chairs. The room opens to a luxurious bath with a soaking garden tub, twin sinks, and a separate shower area.

Breakfast is served in the dining room at a table made of a cypress tree trunk the innkeepers brought from Florida, topped with a six-foot circle of glass. Antique maple chairs, refinished by the Alexanders, and a magnificent chandelier of dull brass and frosted glass provide a nice contrast to the modern table. Photography by their son, Aaron, is displayed on the gray-green walls. During my stay, breakfast starters included a fruit cup, freshly squeezed juice, and pumpkin bread, followed by scrumptious orange-pecan French toast. The Alexanders offer a special brunch on Sundays for guests who are parents of Miami University students. Extra tables are set up so families can enjoy a meal together.

The Alexanders say that as innkeepers they value the wonderful friends they have made. One guest who loved the Queen Anne Suite returned for a stay and brought some Victorian prints she thought Linda would like for what has become that guest's favorite room. At times their house is filled with sports-related groups like the parents of field hockey teams. The White Garden Inn also provides a beautiful setting for weddings, using the formal parlor and the gardens.

THINGS TO DO:
A full range of cultural offerings and athletic events take place on the nearby Miami University campus. Check out the university's per-

forming arts series and current exhibits at the art museum. Hikers find 13 miles of hiking tails in the Miami University natural areas, which border the campus. I also found a brochure for a walking tour of the uptown Oxford Historic District.

While many of the shops and restaurants lined up chockablock on High Street cater to the college kids, there are some unique gift and specialty stores. You'll find handcrafted jewelry and crafts from around the world at Collected Works. Apple Tree stocks gifts for the home along with clothing and baby items. Pick up a specialty sandwich at La Bodega Delicatessen—muffalata subs, Bodega clubs, or build-your-own sandwiches. Kona Bistro & Coffee Bar offers gourmet fare in a casual setting. This busy eatery tempts with vegetarian cuisine. Favorites on the menu include Moroccan vegetable stew and Indian stuffed burritos, but Kona also has items for carnivores. A great starter on the October evening we dined there was a Southwestern crab and corn chowder. For elegant dining, reserve at the Alexander House, a grand Federalist home built in 1869 on College Avenue. Antiquers will find a collection of shops in College Corners and West College Corners. Golfers can head out to Indian Ridge Golf Course or the Hueston Woods State Park Golf Course.

DIRECTIONS: I-71 South to !-70 West to I-275 to Exit 33 for SR 27; right on College Ave.; becomes Brown Rd., on right

NEARBY ATTRACTIONS: Miami University, Hueston Woods, Kings Island

Bell Tower Hotel

A quietly elegant hotel on a university campus

When you visit a college for student orientation, a sports event, concert, or commencement, you generally want to stay as close as possible to the campus. Book a room at the Bell Tower Hotel, a European boutique-style hotel on South Thayer in Ann Arbor and you're right across the street from the University of Michigan. The Bell Tower takes its name from its proximity to the Burton Memorial Tower. Built in 1935-36, this carillon tower has announced the hour to generations of UM students. If you're near campus at noon or on a Saturday morning, you'll be treated to a carillon concert. Cross the street from the hotel to the recently renovated Hill Auditorium at the corner of Thayer and North University Streets for orchestra and jazz performances. A two-block walk takes you to the University of Michigan Museum of Art, with a permanent collection that includes works by Dürer, Guercino, Whistler, Monet, and Picasso, photography by Ansel Adams, and world-class holdings in Asian art and antiquities. Head down South State Street to the Michigan Union and along the way pass the university's castle-like Kelsey Museum of Archaeology.

Ann Arbor, MI
300 S. Thayer St.
800-562-3559
734-769-3010
www.belltowerhotel.com

RATES & RESERVATIONS:
Hours: 24 hours/day
Season: Closed between Christmas and New Year's Day
Rates: $125 +
Specials: Seniors
Minimum stay for special event dates
Reservations recommended
Check, Visa, MC, Disc, Amex accepted

ACCOMMODATIONS: 55 rooms w/ bath; 10 suites w/bath

AMENITIES: Cable TV, phone in room, Internet, use of University of Michigan fitness facility

MEALS: Breakfast (expanded Continental), lunch, dinner; Beer, wine, liquor served

OTHER:
Parking: Complimentary valet parking

Recipient of Ann Arbor's coveted Award for Outstanding Historic Preservation, the Bell Tower exudes old-world charm—from the formally furnished lobby, to gold-leaf framed art in the public spaces and guest rooms, to the efficient desk staff. An addition built in 1966 that staff refer to as the "new side" provided a quiet night's stay on my January visit. Built in 1947, the hotel was renovated in 1985 and updated in 2003-04.

Traditional English decor is the style of the hotel's 66 rooms and suites. Mahogany furnishings with acorn-style headboards, brass lamps, and window treatments and comforters in pale florals are set against green carpeting. Amenities include two speakerphones with voice mail and data ports, an expanded continental breakfast, a morning newspaper at the door, and free valet parking. Guests have use of the university fitness facilities. Chocolate mints and a card with the local weather forecast for the next morning are left at evening turndown.

The Bell Tower offers a choice of 10 suites. The parlor suites at the front of the hotel are spacious L-shaped rooms with a king bed. The one-bedroom atrium and corner suites feature a living room, bedroom with queen bed, small dining table or bar area, and desk. All the suites have a self-service mini-bar, in-room safe, double sofa-sleeper, and an extra you may need during your stay on this Midwestern campus: a set of umbrellas. The hotel also offers two-bedroom atrium suites.

Every college and university has its own system for dealing with requests for stays during commencement week. The Bell Tower opens the phones the Monday after commencement for reservations for students who are planning to graduate in two years. Often the rooms are filled in 30 minutes.

Plan to have dinner right in the Bell Tower at the Earle Uptown, a fine French restaurant located on the hotel's main floor. It's a sophisticated dining room with elegant furnishings and crystal chandeliers. A sampling from the menu includes first courses of foie gras with green grapes and sauternes, a selection of house patés, and fish terrine with horseradish crème fraiche. Some of the beautifully presented entrees include duck breast with poached pears and raspberries, beef tenderloin with cognac and cracked pepper, sweetbreads in puff pastry with sorrel sauce, and bouillabaisse. A basket of eight-grain bread and baguettes comes to the table with herb butter. All breads, puff pastry, and desserts are made in house. A warm apple tart is served with clove ice cream and caramel sauce, the frozen hazelnut soufflé with hazelnut praline. A wine list that spans the globe and attentive servers invite lingering over a dinner at the Earle Uptown.

THINGS TO DO:

In 2002, Ann Arbor's Main Street was voted the "Best Main Street in the State" by the readers of AAA's *Michigan Living* magazine. This shopping district is home to clothing boutiques, galleries, fine restaurants, and cafes. In the State Street area just around the corner from the Bell Tower Hotel, you'll find Ann Arbor's rich offerings of independent bookstores and the flagship Borders Books & Music.

You can catch a festival or fair throughout the year in this Midwestern city. Bibliophiles come in April for the Ann Arbor Book Festival, a three-day celebration with literary symposiums, author readings, book signings, and an antiquarian bookfair. In June, it's the Taste of Ann Arbor and the Rest of the World when restaurants in the greater Ann Arbor area offer tastings of their cuisine in the Main Street area. The award-winning Ann Arbor Art Fairs literally take over downtown in July. Folks come to the fairs to browse and buy the work of juried artists from across the United States and Canada. It's an easygoing and colorful celebration with ethnic foods, street performers, and fun activities for children. A shuttle keeps the crowds moving from outlying parking areas. In September, the Ann Arbor Blues and Jazz Festival takes center stage for a weekend celebration.

There's an eclectic menu at Grizzly Peak Brewing Company, a microbrewery known for its hearth-baked pizzas and handcrafted beer. Vegetarians love Seva, a full-scale vegetarian restaurant with a wide selection of salads, soups, Mexican specialties, stir-fry dishes, and pastas. Conor O'Neill's, an authentic Irish pub, was designed and built in Dublin, then shipped to Ann Arbor. The menu features Irish lamb, stew, corned beef and cabbage, and shepherd's pie, and traditional Irish music adds to the fun on Sunday evenings.

Come to Ann Arbor from early to mid-June to view the peonies in bloom at the Nichols Arboretum, known as the "Arb" to locals. This 123-acre "living museum" on the University of Michigan campus is famous for its 27-bed peony garden with 260 varieties.

Ann Arbor is the destination for many on fall football Saturdays when the Wolverines play in Michigan Stadium. Several hundred thousand fans come to "The Big House," the nation's largest college-owned football facility.

DIRECTIONS: I-23 North to Exit 37 B for Ann Arbor; follow Washtenaw Ave.; left on N. University; right on S. Thayer

NEARBY ATTRACTIONS: Hill Auditorium, University of Michigan, shopping, restaurants

CITY INNS

Arrive in a city on business or for a weekend getaway and you'll find a new mix of accommodation choices—boutique hotels, European-style inns, and traditional hotels.

There are no cookie-cutter rooms in the three boutique hotels—the Mansion on Delaware Avenue, the Lofts, and Glidden House—included in this chapter. Each of these inns boasts individual character due to architectural features. These chic newcomers can sometimes fool the arriving guest. That was my experience upon pulling into the parking lot at the Mansion on Delaware Avenue in Buffalo, New York. The decidedly Victorian facade of this Second Empire home belies the interior done up in European Modern decor. It's a fresh approach combining the existing home's bay windows, high ceilings, and original black walnut and white oak woodwork with contemporary art and furnishings. In Columbus, a warehouse built in 1882 has been transformed into the Lofts. The 12-foot ceilings, exposed ductwork, tall loft windows, and minimalist decor give this city boutique hotel a Soho-like feel. Glidden House, located on University Circle in Cleveland, represents the best of classic urban inns. The exquisite craftsmanship of this French Gothic eclectic-style mansion retained during extensive renovation serves as a backdrop for traditional furnishings, antiques, and contemporary art.

Two European-style inns have incorporated bed-and-breakfast dwellings into larger facilities. Detroit's Inn on Ferry Street—four grand old homes and two carriage house—offers 42 rooms. In Pittsburgh's historic Shadyside neighborhood, an 1884 Italianate home and a 1904 Colonial Revival across the street, make up the Inns On Negley, with 14 rooms and suites.

Pampering is a way of life at each of these six urban inns. Count on finding luxurious high-count linens, European expanded-style breakfasts, and outstanding personal service. There are butlers at the Mansion on Delaware Avenue, chef innkeepers at the Inns on Negley, a concierge at the Lofts, and dedicated staff at the Inn on Ferry Street and Glidden House. Road warriors enjoy high-speed Internet access, business desks, and dual-line phones, while corporate meeting planners find flexible meeting space.

For business travelers with extended in-town assignments or in the midst of corporate relocation, Cincinnati's Vernon Manor Hotel, built as a residential hotel in 1924, answers their needs with spacious one- or two-bedroom suites and junior suites. Situated on one of Cincinnati's seven hills, the it also offers a great view of the city below.

Glidden House

A jewel of a small luxury hotel

Cleveland, OH
1901 Ford Dr.
800-759-8358
216-231-8900
www.gliddenhouse.com

RATES & RESERVATIONS:
Hours: 24 hours/day
Season: Year round
Rates: $125 +
Specials: Seniors, AAA
Reservations recommended
Check, Visa, MC, Disc, Amex accepted

ACCOMMODATIONS: 52 rooms w/
bath; 8 suites w/bath

AMENITIES: Cable TV, phone in
room, Internet, air cond.

MEALS: Breakfast; Beer, wine, liquor
served

OTHER:
Parking: Lot

Visitors who come to the Case Western Reserve University campus, University Hospitals, or the museums and cultural institutions of University Circle have discovered Cleveland's boutique hotel, the Glidden House.

This French Gothic eclectic-style mansion built in 1920 for Francis (Frank) Kavanaugh Glidden, Mary Grasselli Glidden, and their daughter, Ida, is on the CWRU campus. Son of the founder of the Glidden Varnish Company, Frank was vice president of the company, which eventually became Glidden Paint. Ida lived in the family home until 1953, when CWRU purchased the property. The mansion housed the university's Department of Psychology and later saw use as the Law School Annex. Purchased by a group of local investors in 1987, the Glidden House underwent extensive renovation and opened in 1989 as an inn.

Care was taken during the renovation to retain the mansion's original structural integrity. You can appreciate the exquisite craftsmanship of the ornate ceilings in the original dining room, library, and foyer. Look closely at the beamed ceilings in the parlor, and you can spot the letter "G" in the hand-painted filigree on the beams. A story from the renovation period relates that a workman accidentally put a hammer through the drywall in the parlor and discovered hand-carved English walnut paneling. Morning guests are treated to a European continental breakfast in the library and can settle in the dining room by the fireplace for breakfast or move out to the loggia. I found this vintage sunroom to be a pleasant spot on a sunny winter morning.

Eight two-room suites are located in the original mansion, with preserved architectural features like dormer windows. The Glidden House was placed on the National Register of Historic Places in 1987.

Enter the grand foyer and you get an immediate sense of the Glidden House's subtle elegance. The inn underwent the first phase of a renovation in 2002, starting with the public rooms. Traditional furniture with nontraditional coverings in ruby, cobalt, and gold make up comfortable seating areas accented with antiques. Art adds a contemporary edge to the rooms, and it all fits the mansion's architecture. At breakfast, our group of midweek travelers enjoyed listening to jazz, which seems the right musical choice for this inn from the 1920s.

The style of the 52 guest rooms is gradually being changed to business professional with furnishings in warm cherry and walnut. One wheelchair-accessible room is available.

The Glidden Inn's expansive main-floor rooms and lawn provide a pleasant atmosphere for both formal and informal gatherings. Meeting planners find that the Glidden House staff pay attention to details when helping to plan events. Meeting rooms include the Magnolia and Bellflower rooms. The loggia and dining room are also utilized for meetings, banquets, and small conferences. The staff will help with onsite catering requests and audiovisual support. Business travelers find

comfortable rooms with data ports and voice mail, coffeemakers, room service, and a daily newspaper.

Like many urban inns, the Glidden House is busy from Sunday through Thursday with business guests. Leisure travelers come in on the weekend, with many headed to the museums or Severance Hall for Cleveland Orchestra concerts. Extras I appreciated during my stay included parking just once behind the inn and hopping aboard the Circle Link bus that comes around every 20 minutes to take you to the various venues. Ask about the special rate for museum stays at the inn.

The Glidden House has become one of the most popular settings in Cleveland for weddings. A tent is set up on the lawn for the ceremony and wedding luncheon or dinner. The charming gazebo is the site for wedding photos. You can move inside and have use of the dining room, library, and loggia for cocktails.

The Glidden House is one of the best lodge-and-dine destinations I've found in my travels, with easily 25 restaurants within walking distance. The wonderful aromas from Sergio's, located in the coach house next to the inn, pulled us into this compact dining spot. From a Brazilian-inspired menu, you can order starters or small meals, salads, and entrees like Brazilian-style beef or seafood, or prato misto, a savory mix of black beans, Brazilian rice, vegetables, farofa, fried spinach, and carioca relish. Finish with Sergio's own freshly made fruit sorbet or a Brazilian caramel custard topped off with a pot of sweetened Brazilian coffee. When warm weather allows, folks move out to Sergio's tropical garden patio. A real plus for the busy traveler is room service provided by Sergio's to the Glidden House. Another fun dining spot is the Silver Spartan Diner located on Bellflower Road behind the inn. Order omelets all day or have some pie and ice cream with a bottomless cup of coffee in this diner done up in red vinyl and chrome. Photos of classic cars like Ford Thunderbirds and Chevy Impalas line the walls, along with musical greats from the era.

THINGS TO DO:

The Glidden House is within walking distance of the cultural riches of the square mile that encompasses the University Circle area. Walk across the street to the Cleveland Botanical Garden, showcasing 10 acres of beautifully landscaped gardens and the stunning Eleanor Armstrong Smith Glasshouse with two diverse and contrasting environments—the spiny desert of Madagascar and the cloud forest of Costa Rica. Plan to attend a concert at Severance Hall, home of the renowned Cleveland Orchestra, located in the heart of University Circle. The orchestra is in residence from September to May at this beautiful hall. Stop at the Shafran Planetarium & Astronomy Exhibit Hall at the Cleveland Museum of Natural History where you can catch a live show by astronomy experts. Visit the Cleveland Museum of Art's fine permanent collection and, while you're there, check out the special exhibitions, the scheduled concerts, and browse the Museum Shop. A final destination close to the Glidden House is Little Italy, a compact neighborhood of galleries and restaurants.

DIRECTIONS: I-90 to exit for Chester Ave.; right on Chester; left on Euclid Ave.; left on Ford Dr.; on right

NEARBY ATTRACTIONS: Cleveland Museum of Art, Cleveland Museum of Natural History, Western Reserve Historical Society, Crawford Auto/Aviation Museum, Cleveland Botanical Garden, downtown Cleveland attractions, shopping

The Lofts

*An 1882 warehouse transformed
into a boutique hotel*

Touted as "New York-style lodging for the sophisticated traveler," the Lofts has garnered rave reviews from the architectural, historic preservation, and hospitality communities. A group of local visionary leaders transformed the Carr Building, one of the last remaining original warehouse buildings from the 1800s in Columbus's transportation district, into the Lofts, a chic boutique hotel. Located at Nationwide Boulevard and High Street, the Carr Building, listed on the National Register of Historic Places, was home to the Columbus Transfer Company from 1882 to 1932 and next served as headquarters for the Carr Plumbing Supply Company from 1936 to 1979.

Wood and steel beams, original ductwork, and 12-foot ceilings retained from the 19th-century warehouse contribute to the Soho-like feel of the 44 guest rooms and suites. No two are alike. French doors connect the living and sleeping areas in the spacious suites. Take your choice of 20 king suites and double-bed suites or 24 loft-style guest rooms. Entrance to my third-floor king loft room was via a long interior hallway, indicative of the hotel's variety of unique room configurations. It's a sophisticated yet calming space with dominant colors of gray and white highlighted by a sleek red headboard, a color repeated in the armoire doors. And the Loft's armoires are worth a mention.

Columbus, OH
55 E. Nationwide Blvd.
800-735-6387
614-461-2663
www.55lofts.com

RATES & RESERVATIONS:
Hours: 7 a.m.–11 p.m.
Season: Year round
Rates: $125 +
Specials: Seniors, AAA
Reservations recommended
Check, Visa, MC, Disc, Amex accepted

ACCOMMODATIONS: 24 rooms w/
bath; 20 suites w/bath

AMENITIES: Sauna, cable TV, pool,
phone in room, Internet, air cond.

MEALS: Breakfast; Beer, wine, liquor
served

OTHER:
Parking: Lot ($10/day)

Fitted out with terry robe, iron, ironing board, and safe, each armoire also has a shoe storage system thanks to Aretha Franklin. When Franklin was a guest of the Lofts, she wondered where she could park her pumps. Management listened and hanging shoe units were installed. Another feature of the custom-designed armoires are fabric sides that allow clothes to breathe.

Talk about luxury! In my Lofts room, six pillows lined up on a king bed encased in Italian Frette linens and covered with a burnished gold Silkara duvet. Floor-to-ceiling windows infuse the room with natural light and provide your own lookout to the city. On the morning of my September stay, I gazed down from my third-floor perch and watched the city come to life below as workers and convention attendees streamed into the Convention Center across the street.

National Geographic Traveler took note of the Lofts' sharp black-and-white bathrooms with authentic New York subway tile in listing stellar hotel baths around the globe. The all-natural Aveda toiletries, bath sheets instead of towels, and garden tubs add to the baths' appeal.

Business travelers discover that the Lofts was planned with their needs in mind. Focus groups helped decide how room space and accessories were designed and implemented. Amenities include oversize desks, high-speed Internet access, Touhy executive chairs, and dual-line phones. The in-room coffee is Seattle's Best, with luxurious Italian leather sofas and chairs inviting relaxation. Guests can select a complimentary newspaper—*USA Today, New York Times*, or *Wall Street Journal*—to be left at the door. A knowledgeable concierge and personal

butler staff stand ready to answer questions or help plan your stay in the capitol city.

There's a cardio workout center and Scandinavian sauna on the hotel's lower level. A pool and a 24-hour business center are easily accessed by a walkway to the adjacent Crown Plaza. The Loft's Wine Cellar Rooms—the Merlot and the Chardonnay, with stone walls and exposed beams—offer a rustic setting for meetings, conferences, and special events. Future plans call for using the Merlot Room for European breakfast service for hotel guests.

Historic black-and-white photographs throughout the building help celebrate the history of Columbus. In my room, I found a Columbus High Street scene from 1889 and a photograph of Scott Kraus News from 1903. You come upon more of these framed photographs mounted on the exposed brick walls in the hotel hallways. Another piece of Columbus history on display is a cell door from the Ohio Penitentiary, which once stood across the street from the Carr Building.

Looking for a romantic getaway in the city? Check out the Italian Escape package at the Lofts, including an overnight stay, champagne, a gift of Acqua Di Parma toiletries, dinner for two at Martini Italian Bistro, breakfast for two, and valet parking. Hockey fans love the Columbus Blue Jacket "Ignite the Night" package with an overnight stay, two adult tickets to a Blue Jackets home game at Nationwide Arena, valet parking, and breakfast for two. Management works closely with the Columbus arts community in planning other packages centered around special exhibits and events.

THINGS TO DO:

An on-site restaurant, Max & Erma's on the Boulevard, a Columbus favorite best known for its gourmet hamburgers, tortilla soup, and build-your-own sundae bar, also offers a great breakfast. Try the signature breakfast scrabble sandwich or eggs Benedict served with Max's cheddar potatoes and fresh fruit cup. A few blocks from the Lofts, the Red Star Tavern, today's version of the classic American tavern with a retro feel, offers upscale comfort food. Look for homey favorites like pot roast with mashed potatoes, and skillet mac and cheese, along with contemporary favorites like blackened salmon and hazelnut-crusted trout. Sample a German lager brewed on the premises at Gordon Biersch, a sporty Arena District brew-pub/restaurant.

Located in the heart of downtown Columbus, the Arena District is home to the Columbus Blue Jackets NHL team, Nationwide Arena, the Arena Grand Theatre, and PromoWest Pavilion, an indoor/outdoor concert facility. A block north of High Street, you can spend an hour or an afternoon at the North Market, a historic public market in business since 1876. In warm weather, plan to pick up lunch and dine outside at a picnic table. Name your cuisine and you're likely to find it at the North Market, where you can select from Indian, Mediterranean, German, and Italian fare. Pick up a deli sandwich or sample European pastries. Just beyond the Arena District, the Short North, a lively neighborhood of art galleries, boutiques, and trendy restaurants, awaits exploration.

DIRECTIONS: I-77 South to Columbus to I-670 to 3rd St. exit; right on Chestnut St.; right on High St.; right on Nationwide Blvd.; on right

NEARBY ATTRACTIONS: Arena District, Short North Arts District, Convention Center, COSI Science Center, Columbus Museum of Art, Ohio State University, Ohio Expo Center

Vernon Manor Hotel

*Savor the view from
an English-style hotel atop
one of Cincinnati's seven hills.*

Perched atop one of Cincinnati's seven hills, the Vernon Manor Hotel has been a Cincinnati landmark since 1924. Built by a group of wealthy businessmen as a residential hotel in the English Renaissance Revival style, it was modeled after the Hatfield House, circa 1611, in Hertfordshire, England. Located in the historic Uptown District, the hotel commands a stunning view of the downtown area, the Ohio River, and northern Kentucky. The Vernon Manor is a member of the Historic Hotels of America.

Occupying a prominent spot in the Vernon Manor lobby is Armoured Hammer, one of 300 fiberglass pigs displayed in Cincinnati in the year 2000. At the conclusion of the event, the hotel took part in a benefit auction of the porkers and brought Armoured Hammer home to reside in the lobby. The pig's name is a multilevel pun on the name of art collector Armand Hammer, the baking soda, and the collection of antique armor in the Hatfield House in England.

Decorative interior accents reflecting the English style include heraldic crests, English prints, and rich wood paneling in the public rooms. You'll find an English-style pub, and one of the large recep-

Cincinnati, OH
400 Oak St.
800-543-3999
513-281-3300
www.vernonmanorhotel.com

RATES & RESERVATIONS:
Hours: 24 hours/day
Season: Year round
Rates: $65–$90
Specials: AAA
Reservations required
Check, Visa, MC, Disc, Amex accepted

ACCOMMODATIONS: 177 rooms w/bath; 60 suites w/bath

AMENITIES: Cable TV, phone in room, Internet, air cond.

MEALS: Breakfast, lunch, dinner, brunch, snacks; Beer, wine, liquor served

OTHER:
Guest pets allowed
Parking: Lot & valet (both free)

tion rooms is named Kensington Garden. The hotel's 177 guest rooms, including 60 suites, underwent extensive renovation in 1999. Traditional rooms are furnished with cherry and oak reproductions. Florals are used in drapes and bedcoverings set against pale striped walls and green carpet. Some of the hotel's original black walnut woodwork remains along with furnishings that have outlasted the hotel's reincarnations—Murphy beds and bowed-out, double-panel valet doors that allowed guests to place items for laundry or dry cleaning between the door panels. Hotel staff would unlock only the valet portion of the door to remove the items, then return the cleaned garments in the same manner. In the office area, I found an old PBX used by the last hotel switchboard operator.

Located in the heart of the hospital and university district locals refer to as Pill Hill, the Vernon Manor appeals to those seeking longer-term stays, including relocation. The hotel is also popular with Monday through Thursday road warriors who've discovered its home-like atmosphere. Junior suites (600 to 700 square feet) feature an expanded living area, dining area, and galley kitchen. On my stay in a junior suite, I found everything needed for quick meal preparation, including a small dishwasher (think European style) tucked into a bottom cabinet. The most spacious suites range in size from 900 to 1,600 square feet, with a separate bedroom, parlor, dining room, and kitchen. The rooms and suites have a generous work area with two phones—one with computer data port—and guest room voice mail. Two 24-hour business centers and a 24-hour fitness room are on the main floor. Executive breakfasts are part of a business stay, as is complimentary on-site parking. The

hotel appeals to conference planners, with meeting facilities for groups up to 250, audiovisual equipment, and satellite videoconferencing. The Vernon Manor has two outdoor venues—the Rooftop Garden, with fine views of the city skyline, and Kensington Garden, a tented patio setting. Shops on the hotel's lower level include a barbershop, floral shop, and beauty salon.

Through the years the Vernon Manor has counted among its guests U.S. presidents John F. Kennedy, Lyndon Johnson, and George W. Bush. Other VIP guests include Loretta Young, Mikhail Baryshnikov, Judy Garland, and the Beatles. To mark the Liverpool group's 1966 stay in the hotel, the Vernon Manor dedicated a suite to the Fab Four marked with a star on the door. Beatles memorabilia and local photographer Gordon Baer's images of the group's Cincinnati visit are found throughout the suite. With accents of lime green and purple, it's a large space with kitchen, living room, separate bedroom, two full baths, and a den.

Weekend Escapes include the Reds package with a deluxe room, tickets to the ballgame, shuttle service to the stadium, topped off with a breakfast buffet the next morning. Ask for a Beatles package and you'll be treated to champagne, chocolates, a Beatles CD, and breakfast in bed in that fun and funky Beatles suite.

The Vernon Manor was one of the first hotels in the city to institute a Sunday brunch. This popular tradition continues with brunch offered in the Forum Grill from 10:00 a.m. to 2:00 p.m. on Sundays. On weekend evenings, jazz drifts out of the hotel's English-style pub, Club 400, named for the hotel's address at 400 Oak Street. The library, an intimate space with fireplace, is the place for quiet conversation or

a business lunch. A Saturday-night special in the Forum Grill is prime rib carved tableside. Other dinner selections include jerked salmon filet, porterhouse pork chop with apple apricot sauce, and filet mignon with portabella and brie cream sauce.

THINGS TO DO:

If you're heading off to a Cincinnati Reds game in the Great American Ball Park or down to the Main Street Entertainment District, you can forget about the hassle of driving and finding a place to park. The Vernon Manor offers its guests complimentary shuttle service within the area from 7:00 a.m. to 10:30 p.m.

Check the calendar for Cincinnati's festivals. The May Festival, the oldest continuing festival of choral and orchestral music in the Western Hemisphere, brings the Cincinnati Symphony Orchestra and a 200-member chorus to the Music Hall each May. Riverfest happens at the end of August. Oktoberfest-Zinzinnati celebrates Cincinnati's rich heritage in September, and every four years in October folks gather down by the riverfront for the Tall Stacks Music, Arts & Heritage Festival. It's minutes to the Cincinnati Zoo & Botanical Gardens and downtown shopping from the Vernon Manor.

DIRECTIONS: I-71 to Exit for Taft Rd.; right on Reading Rd.; left on Oak St.

NEARBY ATTRACTIONS: Downtown Cincinnati, Kings Island

Inns on Negley

A charming set of historic homes in Pittsburgh's Shadyside neighborhood

Two restored period houses make up the Inns on Negley in Pittsburgh's historic Shadyside neighborhood. The Inn at 714 Negley, a brick Colonial Revival built in 1904, stands across the street from the Appletree Inn, a circa 1884 Italianate structure.

In taking on the restoration of the house at 714 Negley, Liz Sullivan, proprietor of the Inns on Negley, respected the integrity of this house built by Robert A. McKean for his family at the turn of the century. In symmetrical form with hipped roof, and details like keystone lintels and rounded dormer pediments, the house had been cut up into six apartments. Although it had to be completely gutted, Liz was able to save the mantle in the living room, as well as some of the hardwood floors and stained-glass windows. She found that it was hard to anticipate problems during the seven-month conversion of this family home into a commercial property.

There's an easy elegance to the English and French country decor of the inn's 16 guest rooms, suites, and public spaces, custom designed by Richard Lawrence Interiors and furnished with handcrafted American reproductions. I found the Bellefonte Suite, the largest at the 714 address, appointed with a king four-poster in a light distressed wood, a generous sitting area with two chairs done up in plaids, a fireplace,

Pittsburgh, PA
703 and 714 S. Negley Ave.
412-661-0631
www.theinnsonnegley.com

RATES & RESERVATIONS:
Hours: 8 a.m.–9 p.m.
Season: Year round
Rates: $125 +
Specials: AAA
Reservations recommended
Check, Visa, MC, Disc accepted

ACCOMMODATIONS: 16 rooms w/ bath; 8 suites w/bath

AMENITIES: Cable TV, Internet, air cond., phone in room

MEALS: Breakfast, brunch, snacks

OTHER:
Parking: Lot

and little touches like an antique cashier's box from London. The bath features an oversize soaking/Jacuzzi tub, a jetted shower system, and a beautiful stained-glass window—a reminder of the home's earlier times. Liz insisted on first-floor guest rooms in both houses and finds that these rooms are often requested not only by those with disabilities but also by guests who simply aren't able to take the stairs. At 714 Negley, the Ivy Suite is a fully wheelchair-accessible room with fireplace, full-size bed, and large built-for-two walk-in shower with two showerheads and a jetted shower system.

Across the street, the Victorian Appletree features bay windows, original hardwood floors, and exquisite decorative plasterwork on ceilings and skirtings. As a frequent midweek traveler, I could easily settle into the Granny Smith Apple Suite, with a wing chair in the private sitting room, desk, queen sleigh bed, fireplace, and bay windows. Another standout is the Cortland Apple Suite with an 18th-century reproduction king four-poster, armoire, and a desk in a small alcove. This room has more of those bay windows, a fireplace, and Jacuzzi tub. The Appletree's main-floor wheelchair-accessible room, the Braeburn Apple Room, is a luxurious space with a sitting area, king canopy bed, fireplace, and bath with shower.

Those who frequently stay at inns tell me that they often gauge an accommodation by the comfort of the mattress. Management at the Inns on Negley seem to have found some of the best mattresses, as evidenced by guests' comments. Down comforters and 300-thread-count linens cover the beds. Extra luxuries are suede-like robes lined in terry, thirsty Egyptian cotton towels, and Lady Primrose toiletries.

Turndown service brings a small box of chocolates and bottled water to bedside.

A first in my many stays at inns was finding two live-in chef innkeepers at the Inns on Negley, Albert Cappuccio and Jackie Karkowsky. A welcoming tray of homemade cookies on the dining room table with a pitcher of iced tea gave a hint of what to expect at breakfast the next morning.

A sunny breakfast room adjoins the dining room and looks out to the garden area. At tables for four, business travelers can find a place to chat with a colleague or read the morning paper. During my September visit, a corporate group staying at the inn found the dining room table a good spot for a breakfast meeting. Chefs Albert and Jackie vary the breakfast offerings from sweet to savory and are happy to honor requests from returning guests. Their imaginative cuisine includes frittatas, lemon soufflé pancakes, smoked salmon, baked apples, and potato pancakes. A plate of scones, tiny apricot muffins, and a fruit cup accompanied my veggie frittata. You can always request Irish oatmeal or homemade granola. Book an event at the inn for 50 to 100 and the chefs will prepare a special menu for your group. Check out their menus for weddings, bridal and baby showers, afternoon teas, luncheons, and cocktail parties.

Business travelers find all the comforts of home, along with essentials for a business stay: private phones with voice mail, high-speed Internet access ports in every room, cable television, and videocassette players. Ask about the corporate rates from Sunday to Thursday. The inn offers meeting space for 30, providing easels, overhead projectors, and other

audiovisual equipment. Want a massage or need some information about the area? Contact the innkeepers.

I found the back garden to be a work in progress during the inn's initial year of operation. A sculptured stone bench and plantings will shield those sitting in the garden from the parking lot. A local gardener provides gorgeous bouquets found throughout the public spaces of this city inn.

THINGS TO DO:

Located one block from Walnut Street and Ellsworth Avenue, guests staying at the Inns on Negley find they are just around the corner from Shadyside's art galleries, gift stores, boutiques, and familiar stores like J. Crew, Ann Taylor, Talbots, and Williams-Sonoma. There's award-winning Pan-Asian cuisine at Soba, Italian fare at Girasole's, burgers, salads, and steaks at Walnut Grill's upstairs location, and brick-oven pizzas and salads downstairs at Walnut Grill's sister restaurant, Shady Grove.

The inn is five minutes from downtown. Carnegie Mellon University, the University of Pittsburgh, Chatham College, Carlow College, and Pittsburgh's major hospitals are nearby.

DIRECTIONS: I-80 to I-76 to SR 376; west on 376; left on Braddock Ave.; right on Forbes Ave.; left on Beechwood Blvd.; right on Fifth Ave.; left on Negley

NEARBY ATTRACTIONS: Pittsburgh attractions, Carnegie museums, University of Pittsburgh

Mansion on Delaware Avenue

Old World elegance infused with contemporary style

Buffalo, NY
414 Delaware Ave.
716-886-3300
www.mansionondelaware.com

RATES & RESERVATIONS:
Hours: Butler on duty 24 hours/day
Season: Year round
Rates: $125 +
Specials: AAA, packages, preferred rate for businesses mid-week
Reservations required
Check, Visa, MC, Disc, Amex, Diners Club, Carte Blanche accepted

ACCOMMODATIONS: 25 rooms w/ bath; 3 suites w/bath

AMENITIES: Cable TV, phone in room, Internet, air cond., whirlpool jet tub, complimentary evening cocktails, downtown transport.

MEALS: Breakfast; Beer, wine, liquor served

OTHER:
Parking: Lot

If walls could talk, those at the Mansion on Delaware Avenue would have many stories to tell from its colorful past. Designed by George Allison as a private residence in 1869, it became a luxurious Buffalo hotel at the turn of the 20th century. Next the old hotel served as a rooming house and later is rumored to have been a bordello. From 1947 until the mid-1970s, it housed one of Buffalo's finer restaurants, Victor Hugo's Wine Cellar, and its final use was as an apartment building for a few years. The building stood vacant for 25 years until purchased in 1998 by Geno and Diana Principe along with principal owner Dennis Murphy. This intrepid trio of preservationists spent 18 months planning and 14 months restoring the property, which had suffered heavy vandalism. The Mansion on Delaware Avenue owners received the Buffalo Preservation Award in 2002 for their efforts in saving the structure.

Twin griffins guard the entrance to the Mansion, a Second Empire red brick and stone structure with bay windows, mansard roof, and pedimented dormers. First glance at the decidedly Victorian facade would suggest a Victorian interior. Instead, once you step inside, you find sophisticated European Modern decor. And it's a style that works. In the Fireside Salon, glass tabletops and contemporary art juxtapose with beautiful hand-honed black walnut woodwork and a heavy mirrored mantle. Two white 1920s chairs stand out on the navy and cream carpeting in the wide hallway. The original white oak woodwork has been retained in the billiard lounge, where guests gather from 5:00 to 7:00 p.m. for a complimentary cocktail reception. The next morning this room is the setting for a European expanded breakfast, an elegantly presented spread of yogurt in parfait glasses, blintzes, croissants, coffeecakes, granola, and a generous platter of fresh fruits. With jazz playing softly in the background, folks tended to linger and chat the morning of my June stay. I met a traveler from Poland and talked with road warriors who discovered this boutique hotel and return to stay when they have business in the area.

With its 175 windows, including 14 bay windows, it was no surprise to learn that when the Mansion was built in 1869, it was referred to as "The House of Light." Today the tall windows infuse the 28 guest rooms and suites with light. General manager Geno Principe likes to tell the story of the one suite with a king bed. Singer Faith Hill came to stay and, upon learning that there were only queen beds, bought a king-size bed for the Mansion. Unlike the cookie-cutter rooms found in many hotels, architectural features like fireplaces, window placement, and ceiling height give the Mansion's rooms individual character. My room was done up in greens and golds with an arched fireplace, bay windows to one side, and another window looking out to the street. Dark wood

wainscoting contrasted with the cream walls. And the creature comforts at the Mansion are deluxe—duvet-covered beds, Italian linens, one perfect strawberry dipped in chocolate, and chilled water left at turndown service in the evening. The contemporary look extended to my bathroom, with sleek fixtures, granite counters, and more of those magnificent windows. A multihead shower massage and whirlpool-jet tub are encased in a clear circular shower door. Wheelchair-friendly guest rooms are available. The Mansion was the featured hotel in *Architectural Digest*'s February 2003 issue.

Business travelers find two phones—one wireless phone, one multiline desk phone with speakerphone—and voice mail message system. On the desk in my room I found personalized stationery and calling cards with the imprint of a griffin, the Mansion's trademark. The fitness studio on the lower level has treadmill, stair climber, and multistation workout unit.

Planners of corporate meetings. seminars, and social events find flexible meeting space, award-winning on-site catering, and a boardroom with ergonomic seating. Perhaps the best testimonial for the Mansion came from a business guest who said as he was leaving, "I love this place."

Don't expect a doorman or a concierge to greet you when you arrive at the Mansion. Instead, butlers are at your service. They're not Jeeves, but the three butlers on duty during my stay anticipated guests' needs and were ready with answers to every question. Their 24-hour service extends to driving you to dinner or the theater. They'll arrange in-room dining or massage, and pick up your dry cleaning and your shoes for

the complimentary overnight shoeshine. The butlers know their city well and are ready with directions and suggestions for seeing Buffalo. The Travel Channel recognized their expertise in acknowledging that the Mansion is a place "where butler service really exists."

THINGS TO DO:

While the Mansion seems perfectly suited to business travelers during the week, on weekends it gets high marks as a romantic getaway. This historic hostelry offers a sophisticated interior and welcoming common rooms with lavish fresh flower arrangements. If you choose to dine in your room, the butlers will bring a favorite meal from an area restaurant, served on Mansion china. Located between the Theatre District and the Allentown Art & Antique District, the Mansion is also within easy walking distance of shops and art galleries.

Just a few of the venues that art and architecture enthusiasts will find in Buffalo are the Albright-Knox Art Gallery, one of the world's top international collections of modern art, and the Burchfield-Penney Art Center, with the world's largest collection of work by celebrated watercolorist Charles Burchfield. Enlist the aid of the butlers to plan a Buffalo architecture tour. Visit two of Frank Lloyd Wright's houses--the Darwin D. Martin House, Wright's greatest "Prairie House," and Graycliff, Darwin and Isabelle Martin's summer estate, in the nearby towm of Derby.

If you feel like going out for a meal and don't want to venture far from the Mansion, try Chris's Sandwich Shop located right across the street from the inn. The sandwiches and salads come in one size—large—and Chris's mother makes the pies. For a special dinner, be it with business associates or on a romantic weekend getaway, stroll to Rue Franklin, located right around the corner from the inn. The cuisine is French, the interior cozy.

DIRECTIONS: I-90 to Rt. 33 West to Goodell St.; Goodell becomes Edward St.; on corner of Edward and Delaware Ave.

NEARBY ATTRACTIONS: Albright-Knox Art Gallery, Buffalo & Erie County Historical Museum, Buffalo & Erie County Botanical Gardens, Shea's Performing Arts Center, Studio Arena, Studio Arena Theater, Kleinhan's Music Hall, HSBC Arena, Frank Lloyd Wright's Darwin D. Martin Complex, Graycliff, Niagara Falls area and attractions

Inn on Ferry Street

An urban inn in a historic neighborhood

The Inn on Ferry Street, comprising four restored Victorian homes and two carriage houses, served as an anchor for the renaissance of this street named for the Ferry Seed Company. Detroit's fine museums, Wayne State University, and the Detroit Medical Center are easily accessible from the inn, located in the city's midtown Historic District. The restoration, an $8.5 million project that took 18 months to complete, was a joint effort between the Detroit Institute of Arts (DIA) and the University Cultural Center Association (UCCA). Susan Mosey and Jennifer McNulty, UCCA's president and community development manager, respectively, directed the restoration. "We decided not to use an overly dripping Victoriana in the decor," says Mosey, "but rather a sophisticated classic look that appeals to both the corporate and leisure traveler." Mosey and McNulty were delighted that most of the home's architectural features

Detroit, MI
84 E. Ferry St.
313-871-6000
www.theinnonferrystreet.com

RATES & RESERVATIONS:
Hours: 24 hours/day
Season: Year round
Rates: $125 +
Specials: Children, seniors, singles, AAA, weddings, parties, special events
Reservations recommended
Check, Visa, MC, Disc, Amex, Diners Club accepted

ACCOMMODATIONS: 42 rooms w/bath; 11 suites w/bath; 1 carriage house

AMENITIES: Cable TV, phone in room, air cond., Internet, shuttle service, coffee makers

MEALS: Breakfast (deluxe Continental), snacks; Beer, wine served

OTHER:
Not fully wheelchair accessible
Parking: Lot

remained intact, which allowed the integrity of the original structures (built between 1886 and 1892) to be retained. Everything was custom designed for the 42 guest rooms and suites, with a different color palette—including coordinating fabrics, carpets, and paints—used for each historic dwelling. Furniture throughout the homes is from Drexel Heritage and Lexington.

The Garden Club of Michigan underwrote the landscaping planning for the grounds, utilizing period plantings from the Victorian era. Devotees of earlier architecture will be delighted to find that the inn faces the Shingle-style Charles Lang Freer House, built in 1887 by Philadelphia architect Wilson Eyre.

All guests stop at the Scott House to check into their accommodations. Built as a family residence in 1886 by John Scott, a prominent Detroit architect, the house's high wainscoting in the breakfast room, well-proportioned furniture in the parlor, and furnishings and colors—sage, burnt orange, and gold—used in the four upstairs guest rooms reflect the Arts and Crafts era. All inn guests return to the Scott House for a self-service breakfast buffet. It's a substantial spread of juices, pastries, make-your-own waffles, hot and cold cereals, homemade granola, and a tray of fresh fruit—pineapple, blueberries, and raspberries.

Spacious public rooms can be found in each historic house. The library in the Roehm House, built in 1888 by Herman Roehm, president of the Detroit Carriage Company, offers floor-to-ceiling shelves filled with books and CDs . Photographs of the Roehm family line the walls, and a leather sofa paired with an oversize ottoman and traditional chairs invites lingering. On the second floor, a four-poster canopy bed set against terra-cotta walls is the centerpiece of a suite where in pleasant weather guests enjoy a balcony filled with wicker furniture and hanging flower baskets. Another favorite room in the Roehm House features an

oversize bath with the original cast iron tub. Two wheelchair-accessible rooms are located on the first floor.

The most Victorian decor can be found in the Pungs House, built in 1891 for William Pungs, vice president of the Michigan Railroad Supply Company and founder of the Anderson Carriage Company. A pleasing color scheme of blues and golds flows throughout the house, which is furnished with traditional pieces. The parlor of the Owen House, built in 1887 for George A. Owen, owner of a dry goods firm, often serves as the setting for weddings and meetings. A magnificent staircase dominates the entrance, and rooms are decorated in jewel tones.

The carriage houses have proved popular for meetings and seminars. There's a cottage feel to the Raymond C. Smith Carriage House, located behind the Pungs House, and Arts and Crafts furnishings and decorative items fill the John R. Carriage House.

Corporate guests find a desk or writing table, two-line phones with data ports and voice mail, an in-room coffeemaker with Starbucks coffee, and complimentary newspapers. The Inn on Ferry Street exemplifies the best of urban inns with extras like triple sheeting on the beds, same-day valet service, and a responsive staff. There's a complimentary shuttle service within a five-mile radius of the inn, which I utilized on a snowy day. Returning after dinner, I thought I caught the aroma of cookies baking and learned that freshly baked chocolate-chip cookies and decadent chocolate truffles are part of the turndown service. If you decide to work in your room for the evening, room service is available through the Union Street Restaurant.

THINGS TO DO:

The Detroit Institute of Arts, one of the country's top 10 fine arts museums, is within walking distance of the Ferry Street Inn. While at the DIA, don't miss Diego Rivera's "Detroit Industry" fresco cycle. Check out the museum's series of documentaries and classic and foreign films offered in the Detroit Film Theatre on Friday through Monday. You can stop for a quick bite at the nearby Traffic Jam, a small cafe offering sandwiches, salads, soups, and desserts. Other museums located in the Detroit Cultural Center are the Charles H. Wright Museum of African American History, the Detroit Historical Museum, and the Detroit Science Center.

Union Street, with its classic Art Deco interior, is a popular dining spot for lunch or dinner. The original neon lighting remains from the late 1940s, along with a streamlined bar backed by rose-tinted mirrors. The Union Street menu features Cajun specialties like jambalaya and tenderloin New Orleans. Another good lunch stop is Twingos. Located in a former bookstore, the restaurant's exposed-brick interior is eclectic with a French touch. Famous for its French onion soup, other stars of the menu include chicken champagnois and wild mushroom ravioli. For fine dining before or after a Detroit Symphony Orchestra concert at Orchestra Hall, head to Maria's for great Italian cuisine.

DIRECTIONS: I-94 to exit for Woodward, John R.; right on John R.; right on Ferry St.; on left

NEARBY ATTRACTIONS: Detroit Institute of Art, Museum of African History, Detroit Historical Museum, Wayne State University, College for Creative Studies, Max M. Fisher Music Center

Index by Name of Inn

Index by State & City

Idea Index

Historic Inns

Lake Nearby

Museums

Pets Allowed

Wineries